VIZ GRAPHIC NOVEL

EL-HAZARD

THE MAGNIFICENT WORLD

volume 2

Story and Art by Hidetomo Tsubura

Based on El-Hazard
Created by Hiroki Hayashi and Ryoe Tsukimura

This volume contains the monthly comics *El-Hazard*
Volume 2 Number 1 through Number 5 in their
entirety.

Story & Art by
Hidetomo Tsubura

English Adaptation by
Gary Leach

Translation/Lillian Olsen
Touch-up & Lettering/Dan Nakrosis
Cover & Graphics Design/Sean Lee
Editor/Andy Nakatani

Managing Editor/Annette Roman
Vice President of Sales and Marketing/Rick Bauer
Editor-in-Chief/Hyoe Narita
Publisher/Seiji Horibuchi

Published by Viz Comics
P.O. Box 77010
San Francisco, CA 94107

10 9 8 7 6 5 4 3 2 1
First Printing, September 2002

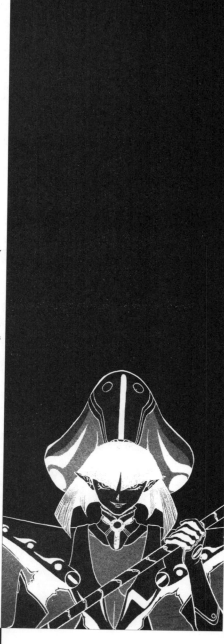

PULP
www.pulp-mag.com

ANIMERICA
anime & manga monthly
www.animerica-mag.com

store.viz.com

VIZ
www.viz.com

- get your own vizmail.net email account
- register for the weekly email newsletter
- sign up for VIZ INternet
- voice 1-800-394-3042 fax 415-384-8936

VIZ GRAPHIC NOVEL

EL-HAZARD

THE MAGNIFICENT WORLD

volume 2

Story and Art by Hidetomo Tsubura
Based on El-Hazard
Created by Hiroki Hayashi and Ryoe Tsukimura

THE STORY THUS FAR

A mysterious and beautiful woman transports Makoto Mizuhara to an alternate world called El-Hazard. Makoto soon discovers that his teacher, Mr. Fujisawa has also been sent to El-Hazard. In this magical world they discover that a war is going on between the Allied Kingdoms and the Bugrom – a race of giant bug-like creatures.

Makoto has aligned himself with the beautiful princess of Roshtaria, Rune Venus, and the three elemental priestesses who defend the Allied Kingdoms. They debate amongst themselves whether or not they should use a devastatingly powerful superweapon called The Eye of God.

Meanwhile, Makoto's classmate and self-proclaimed arch-nemesis, Katsuhiko Jinnai, has also been transported to El-Hazard and has established himself as generalissimo of the Bugrom. Jinnai has discovered the existence of another superweapon called the Demon God Ifurita that lies deep beneath the castle of Roshtaria. He sets out after it intending to use it to usurp full control over all of El-Hazard.

Racing to get to the Demon God before Jinnai does, Makoto and the others run into a member of the Phantom Tribe, a race of malevolent beings. They are also somehow involved in the power struggle between the Bugrom and the Allied Kingdoms.

Jinnai gets to the Demon God first and Makoto is dumbfounded to discover that the Demon God is the very woman who sent him to El-Hazard in the first place.

Will Jinnai succeed in taking control of El-Hazard utilizing the power of the Demon God? Will the Allied Kingdom resort to using the Eye of God to stop him, despite the devastating consequences? How is the Phantom Tribe involved in all of this? Will Makoto ever make it back to homeroom? There's no place like home, there's no place like home, there's no place like home…

CONTENTS

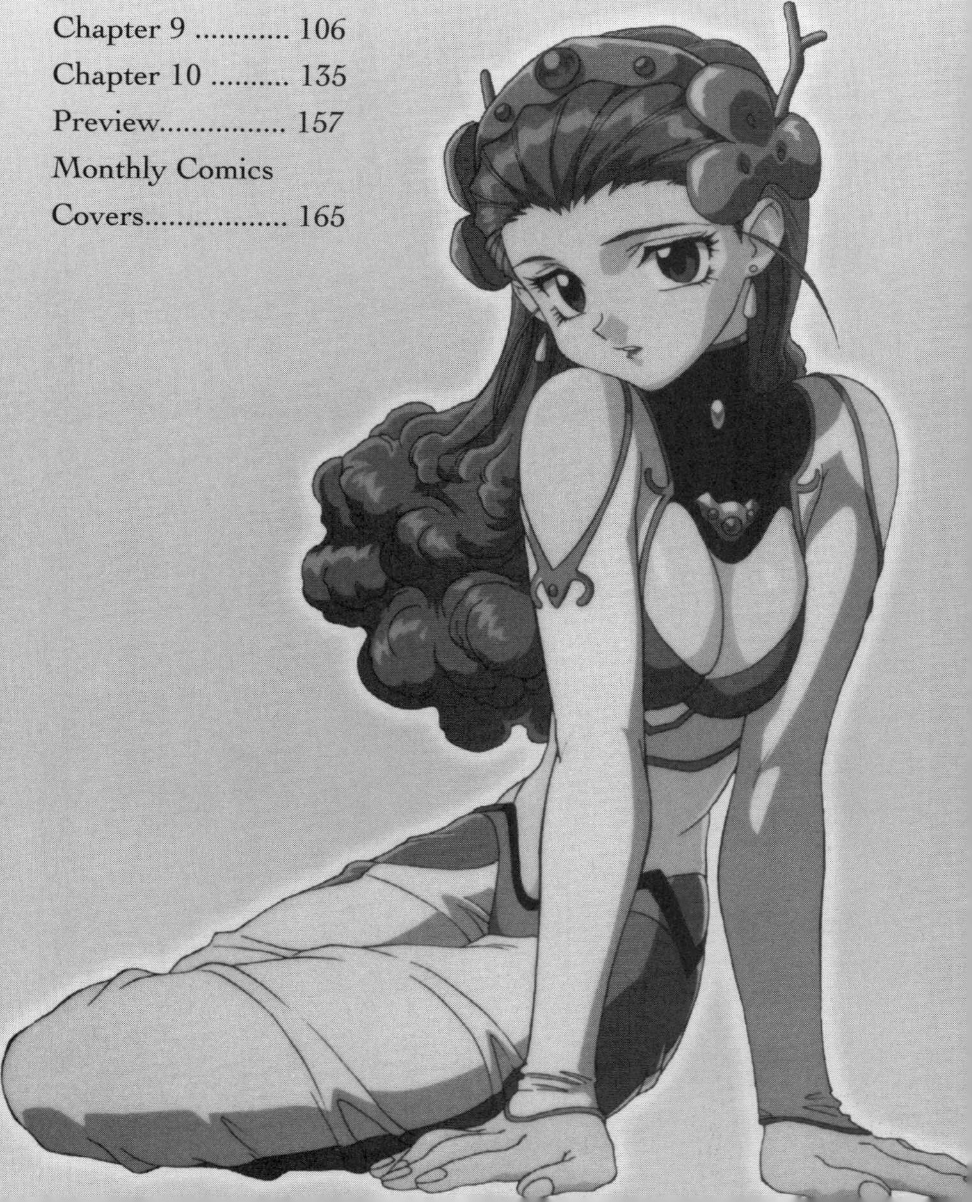

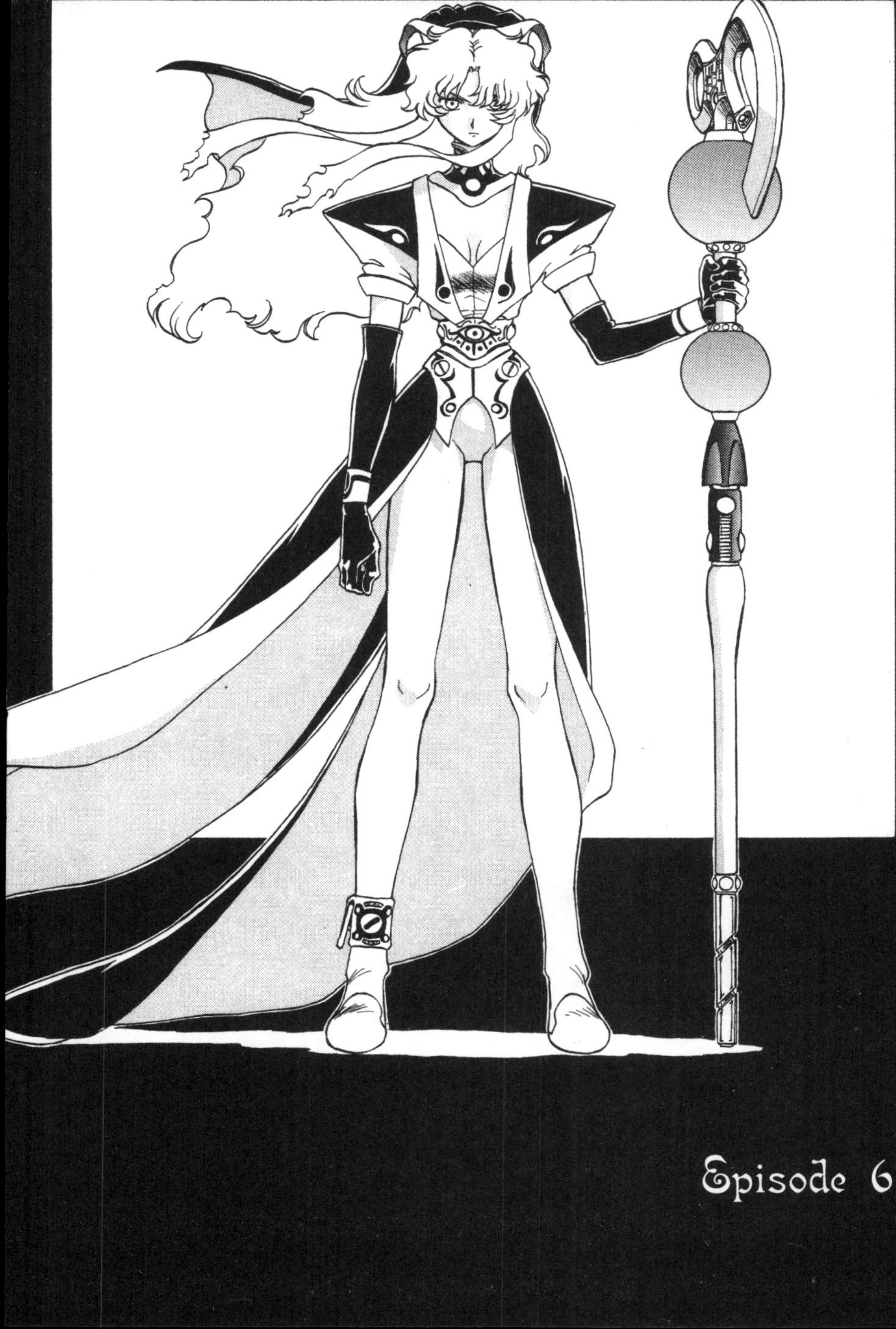

Episode 6

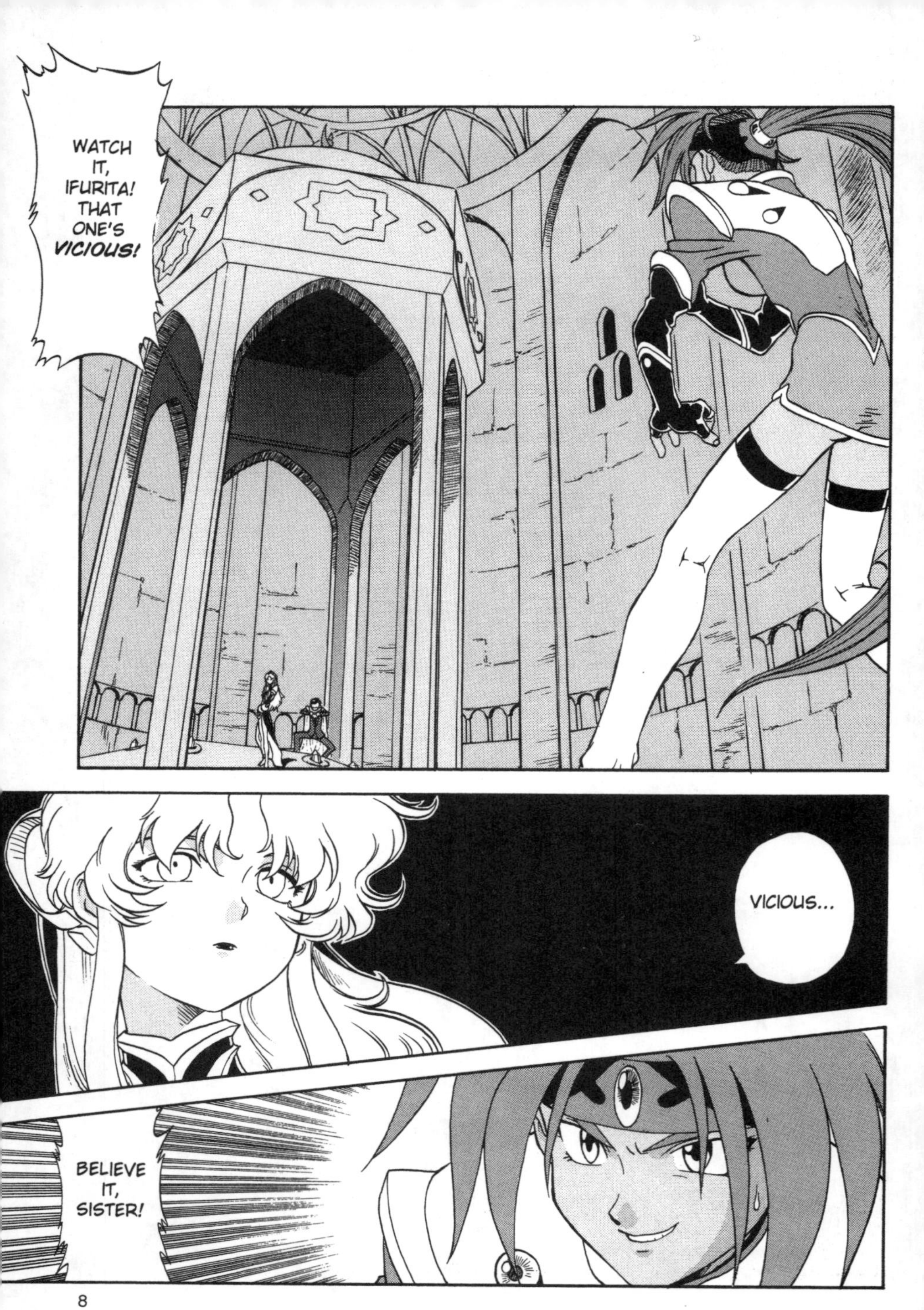

WATCH IT, IFURITA! THAT ONE'S ***VICIOUS!***
VICIOUS...
BELIEVE IT, SISTER!

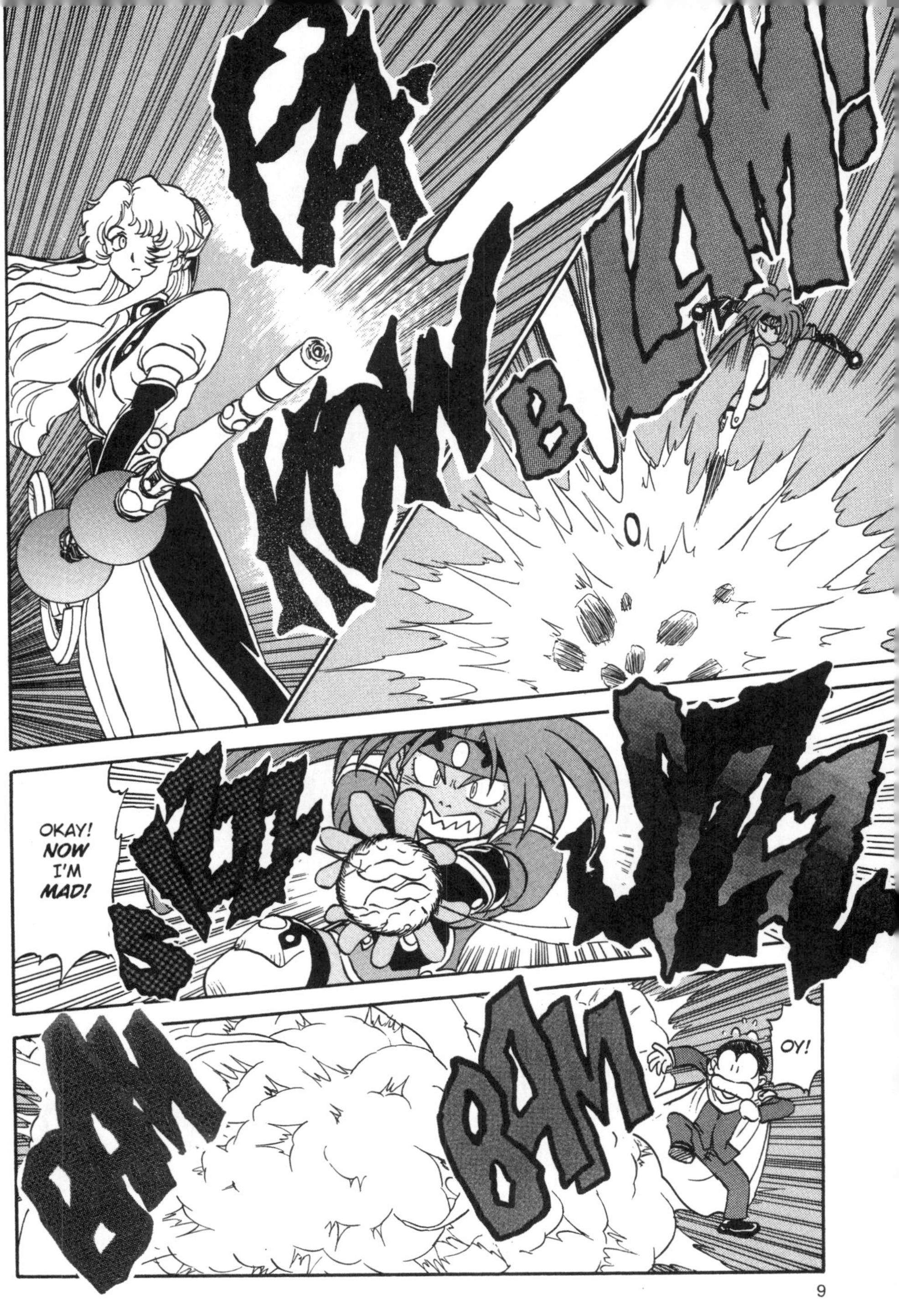
BLAM!
OKAY! NOW I'M MAD!
BAM
BAM
OY!

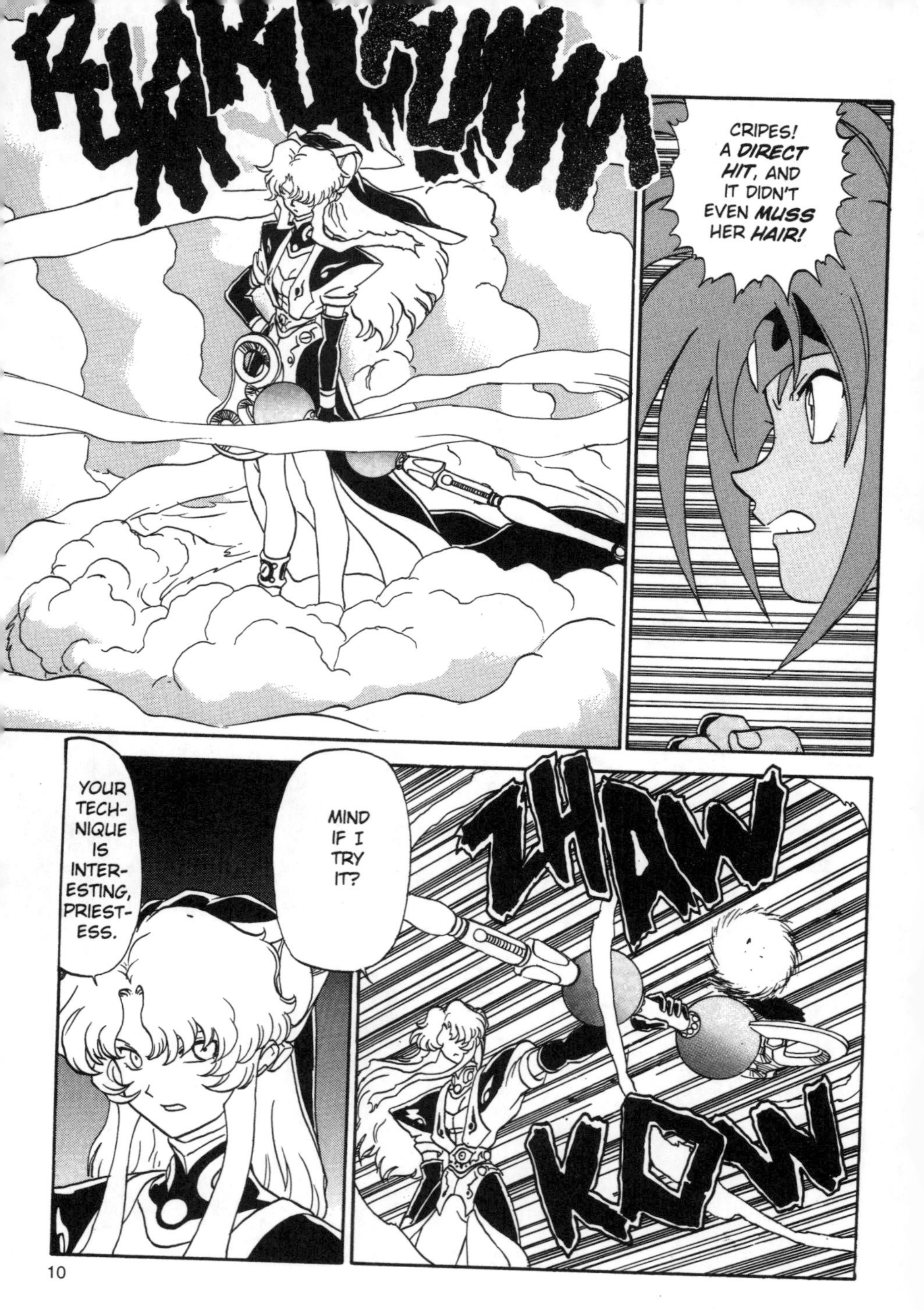
CRIPES! A DIRECT HIT, AND IT DIDN'T EVEN MUSS HER HAIR!
YOUR TECH-NIQUE IS INTER-ESTING, PRIEST-ESS.
MIND IF I TRY IT?
ZHAW KOW

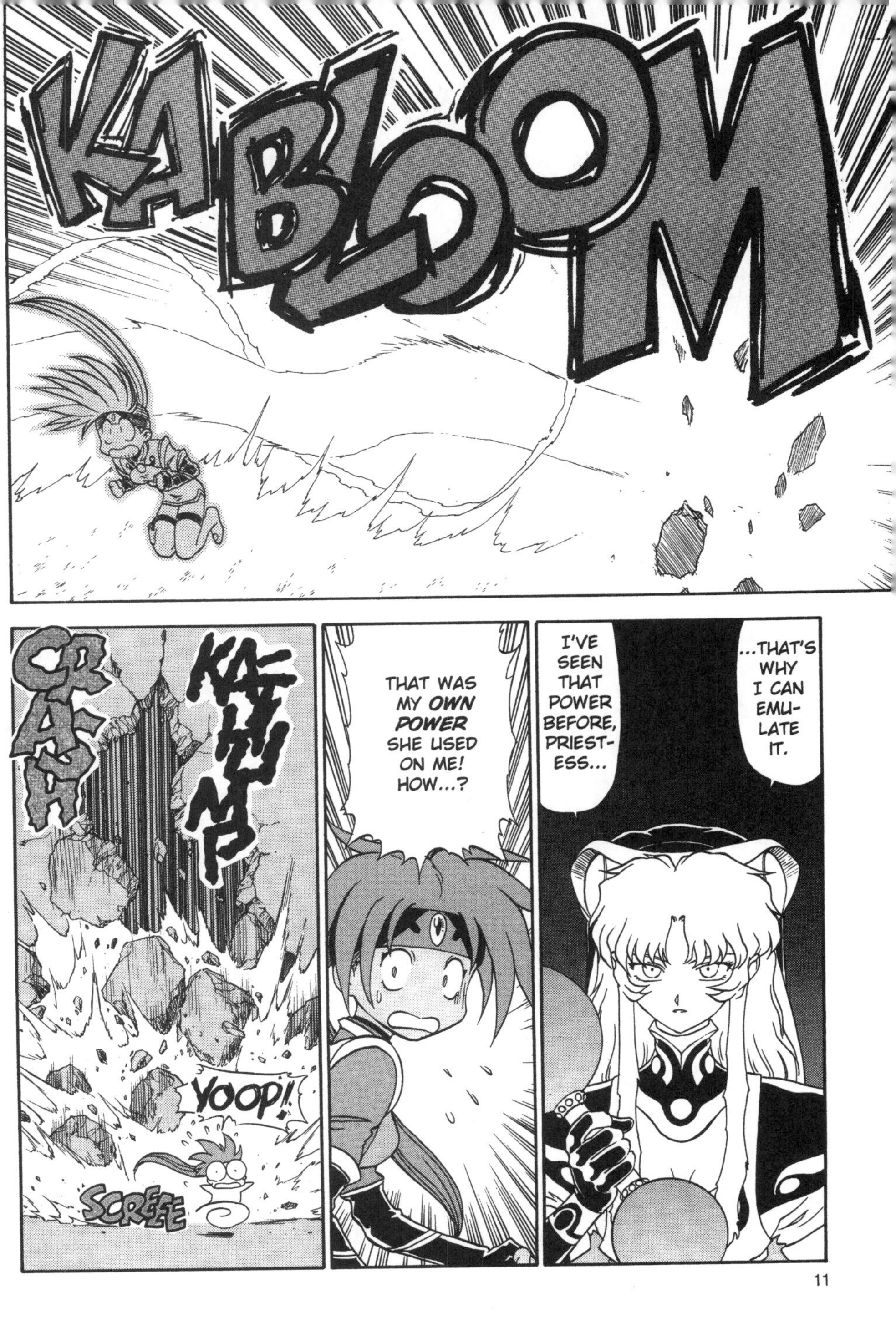
KABLOOM
CRASH
KATHUMP
YOOP!!
SCREEE
THAT WAS MY *OWN POWER* SHE USED ON ME! HOW...?
I'VE SEEN THAT POWER BEFORE, PRIEST-ESS...
...THAT'S WHY I CAN EMU-LATE IT.

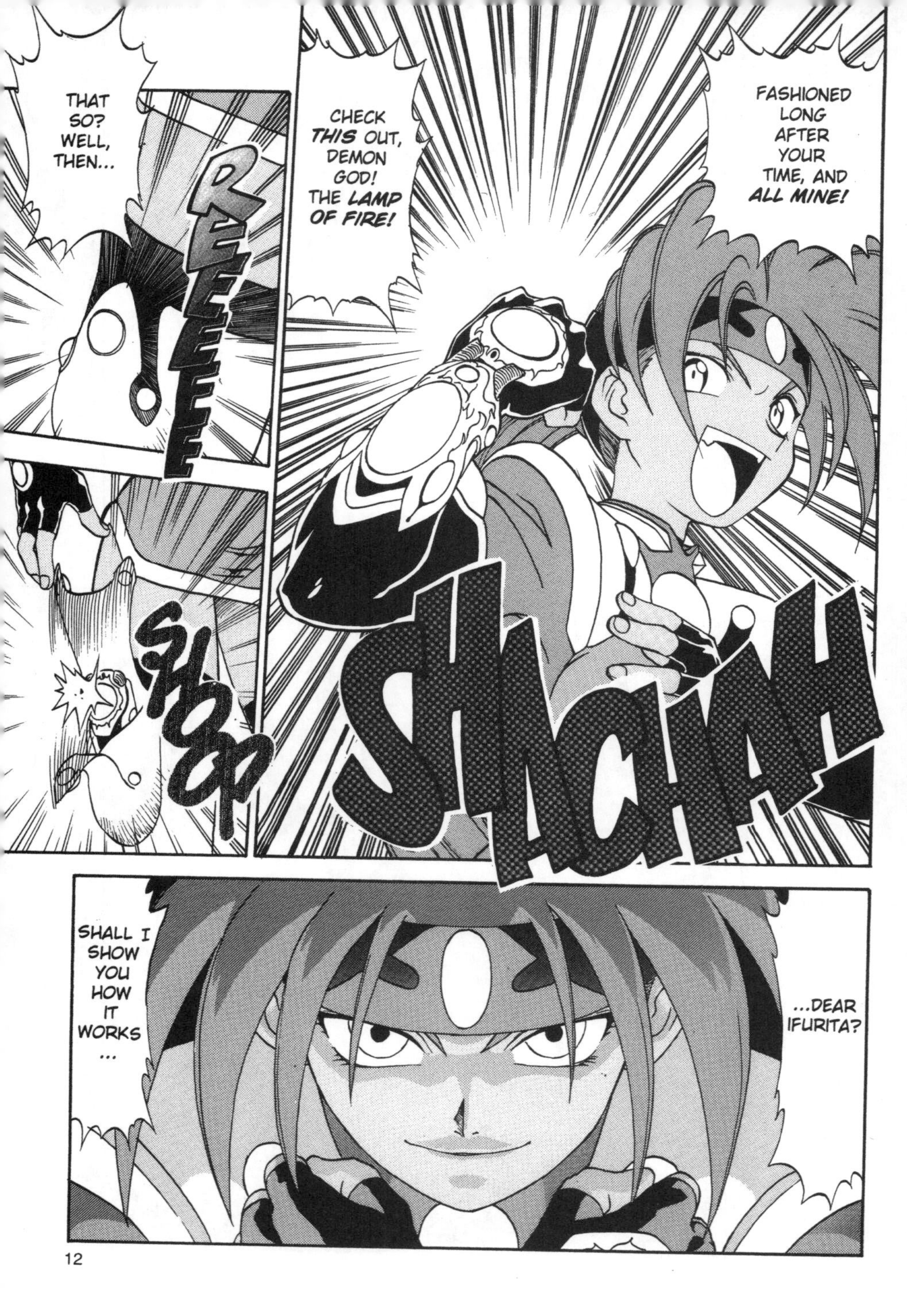
THAT SO? WELL, THEN...
REEEEEEE
SHOOP
CHECK **THIS** OUT, DEMON GOD! THE ***LAMP OF FIRE!***
FASHIONED LONG AFTER YOUR TIME, AND ***ALL MINE!***
SHACHAH
SHALL I SHOW YOU HOW IT WORKS ...
...DEAR IFURITA?

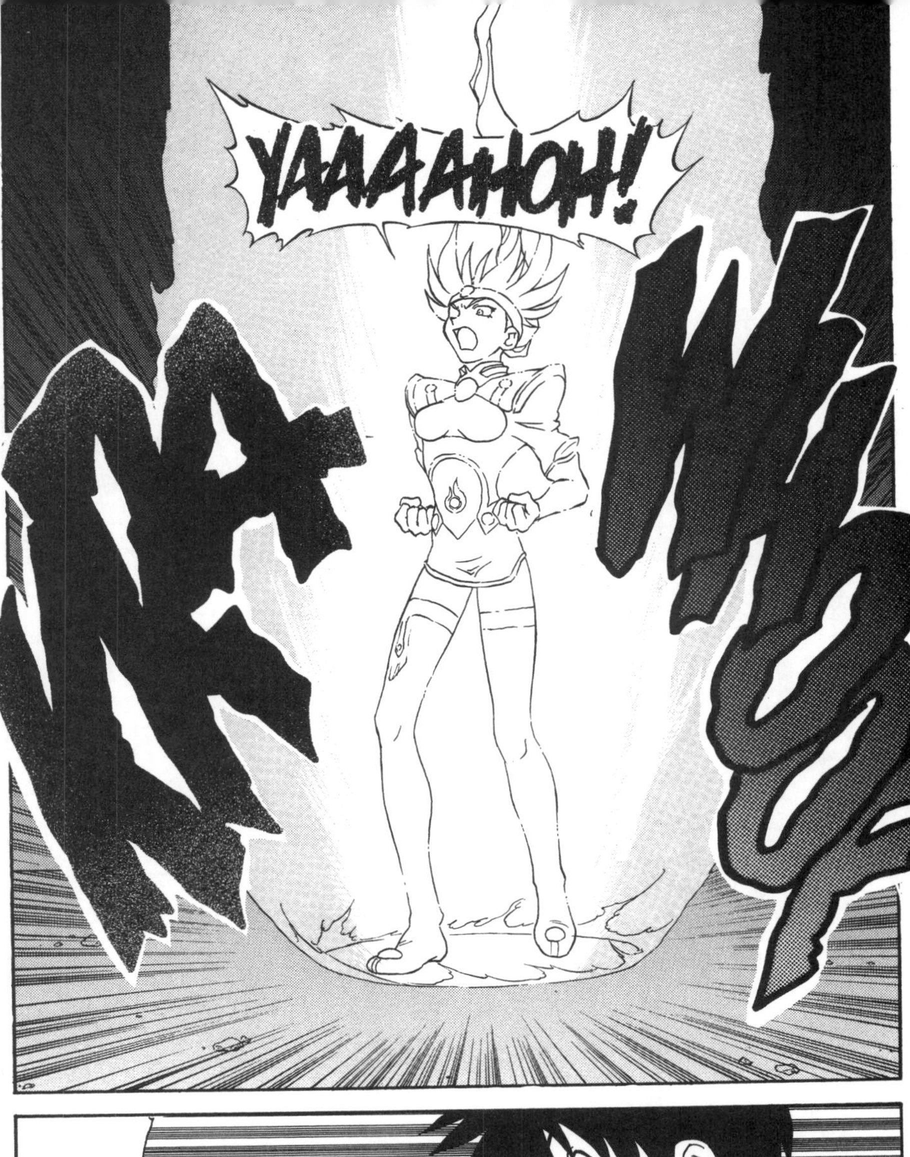
YAAAAHOH!

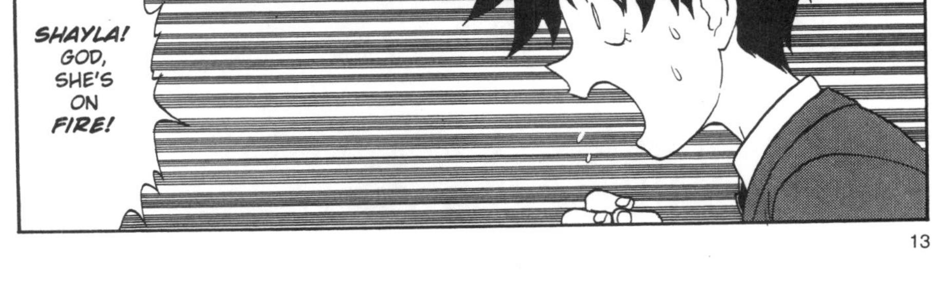
SHAYLA! GOD, SHE'S ON FIRE!

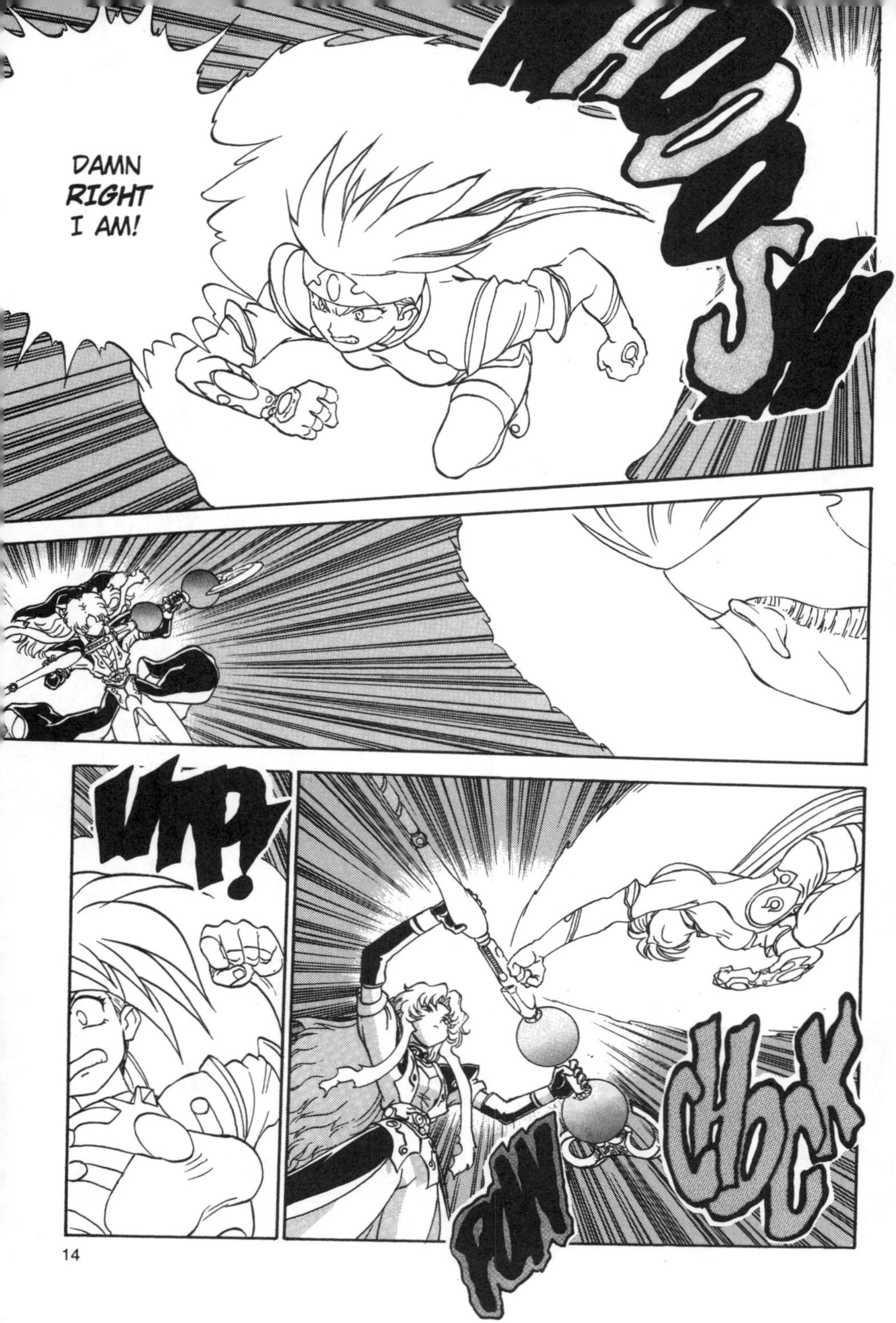
DAMN RIGHT I AM!
WHOOSH
WIP!
CHOCK
POW

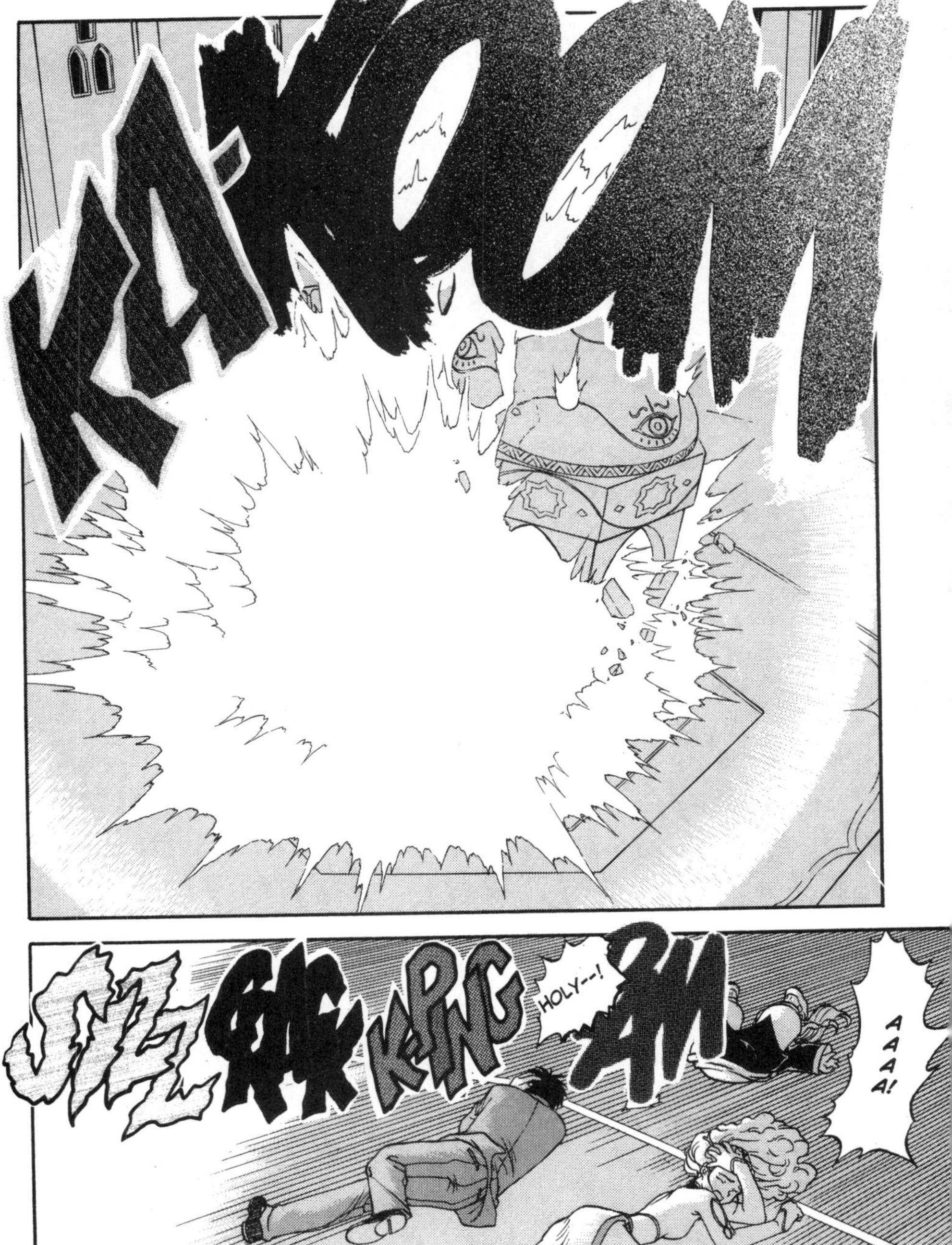
KA-KOOM
SIZZ
CRACK
K-PING
HOLY--!
BAM
AAAA!

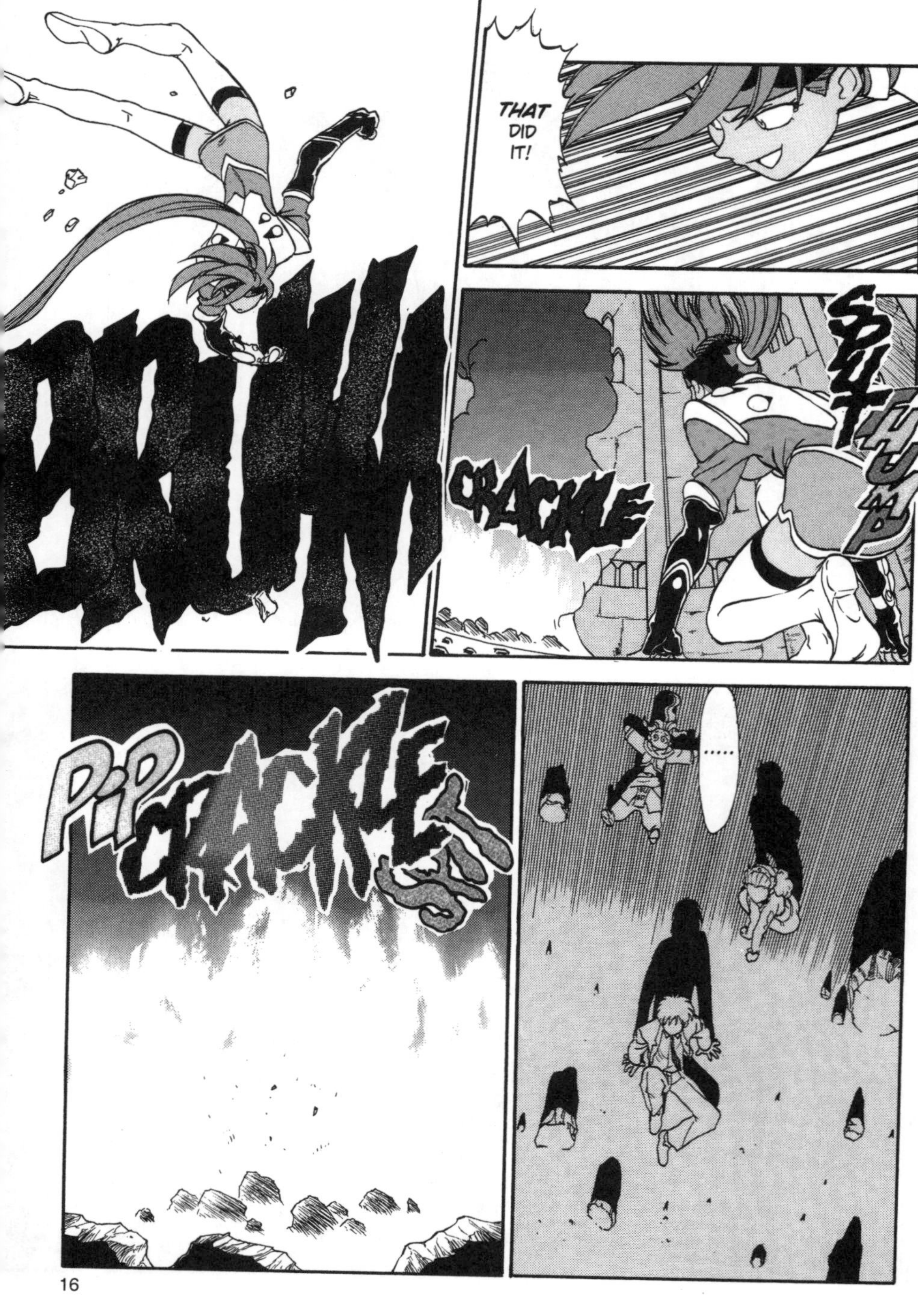
THAT DID IT!
CRACKLE
PIP CRACKLE
......

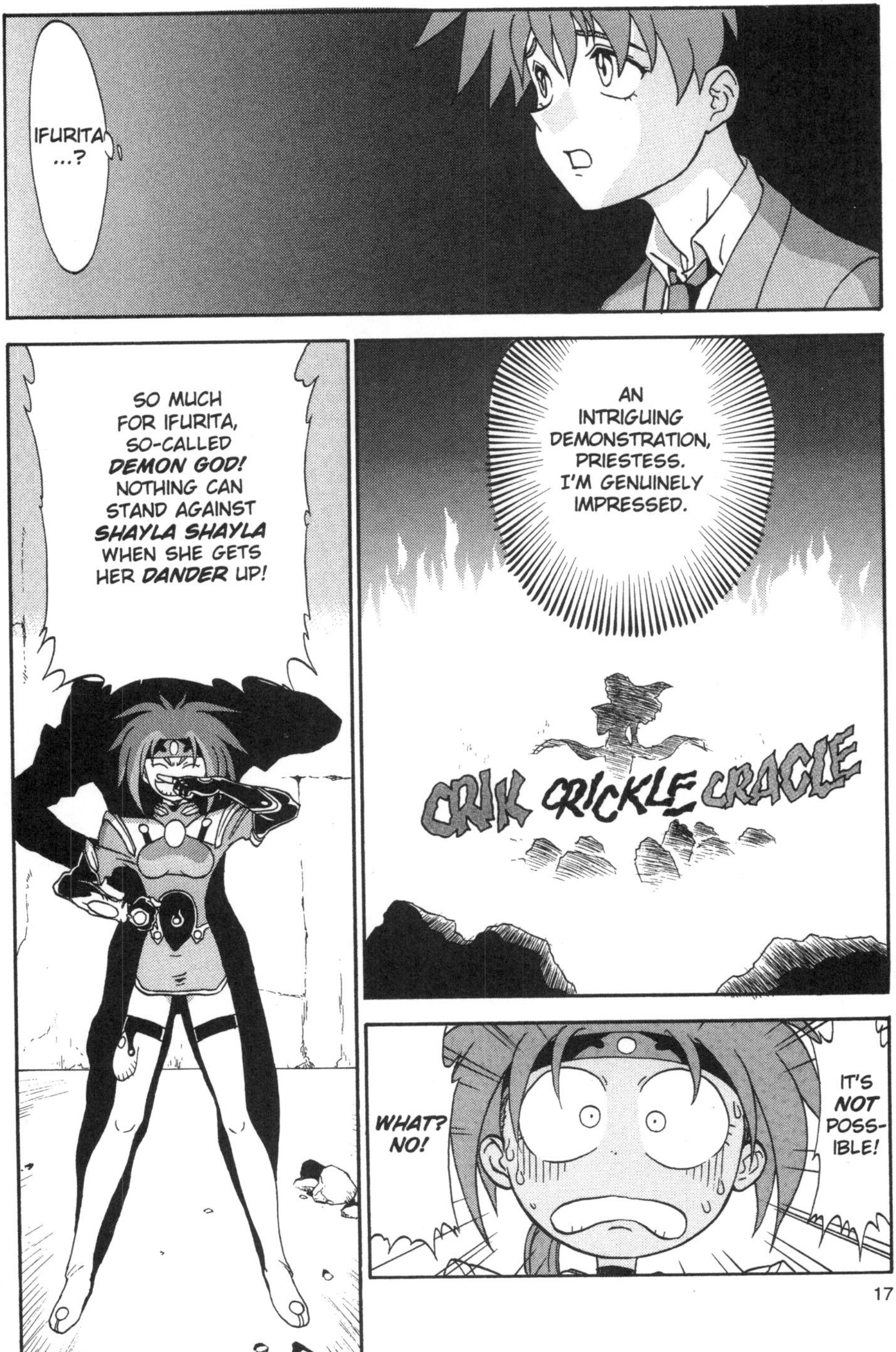
IFURITA ...?
SO MUCH FOR IFURITA, SO-CALLED **DEMON GOD!** NOTHING CAN STAND AGAINST **SHAYLA SHAYLA** WHEN SHE GETS HER **DANDER** UP!
AN INTRIGUING DEMONSTRATION, PRIESTESS. I'M GENUINELY IMPRESSED.
CRIK CRICKLE CRACLE
WHAT? NO!
IT'S **NOT** POSS-IBLE!

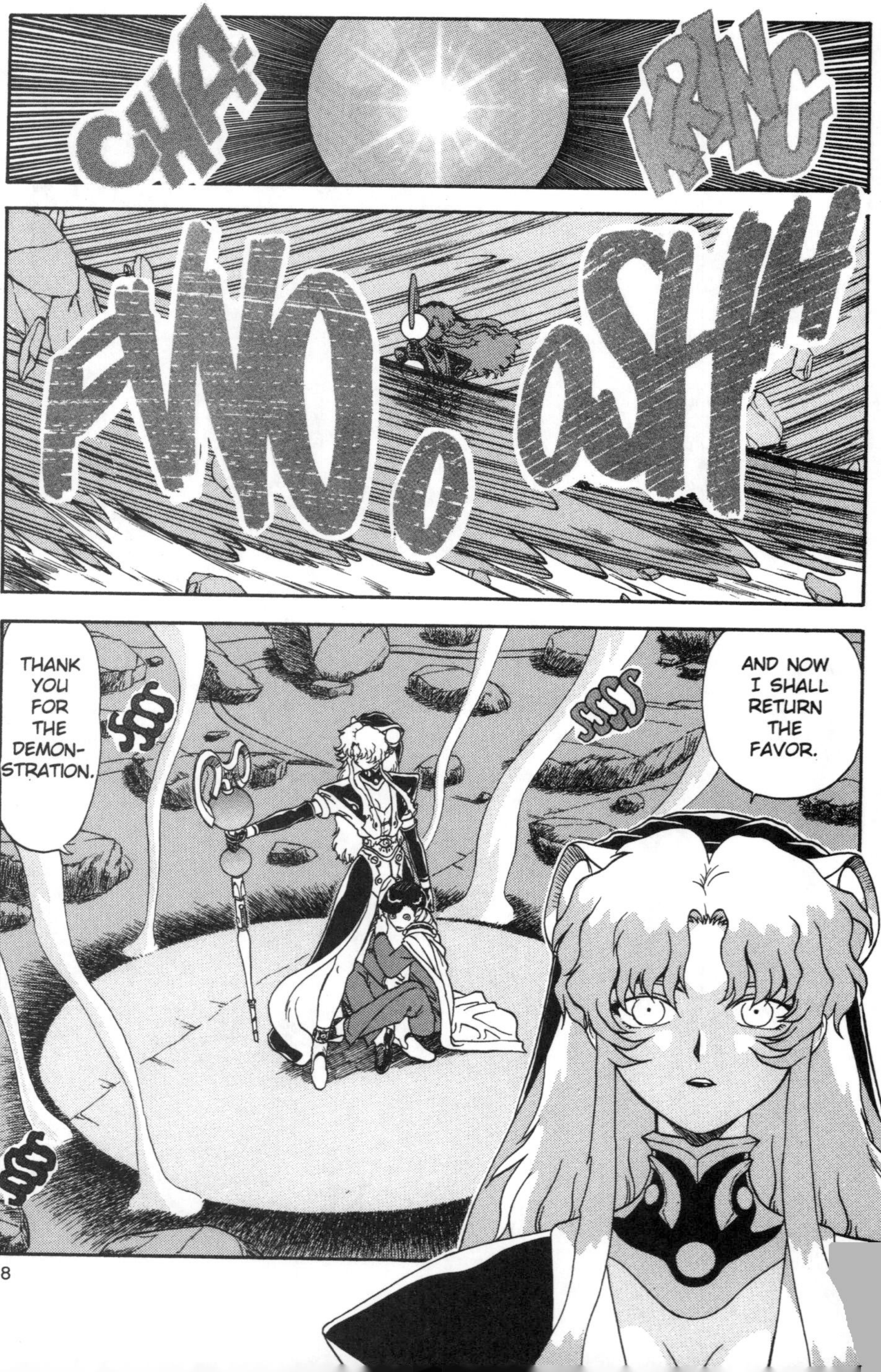
THANK YOU FOR THE DEMON-STRATION.
AND NOW I SHALL RETURN THE FAVOR.

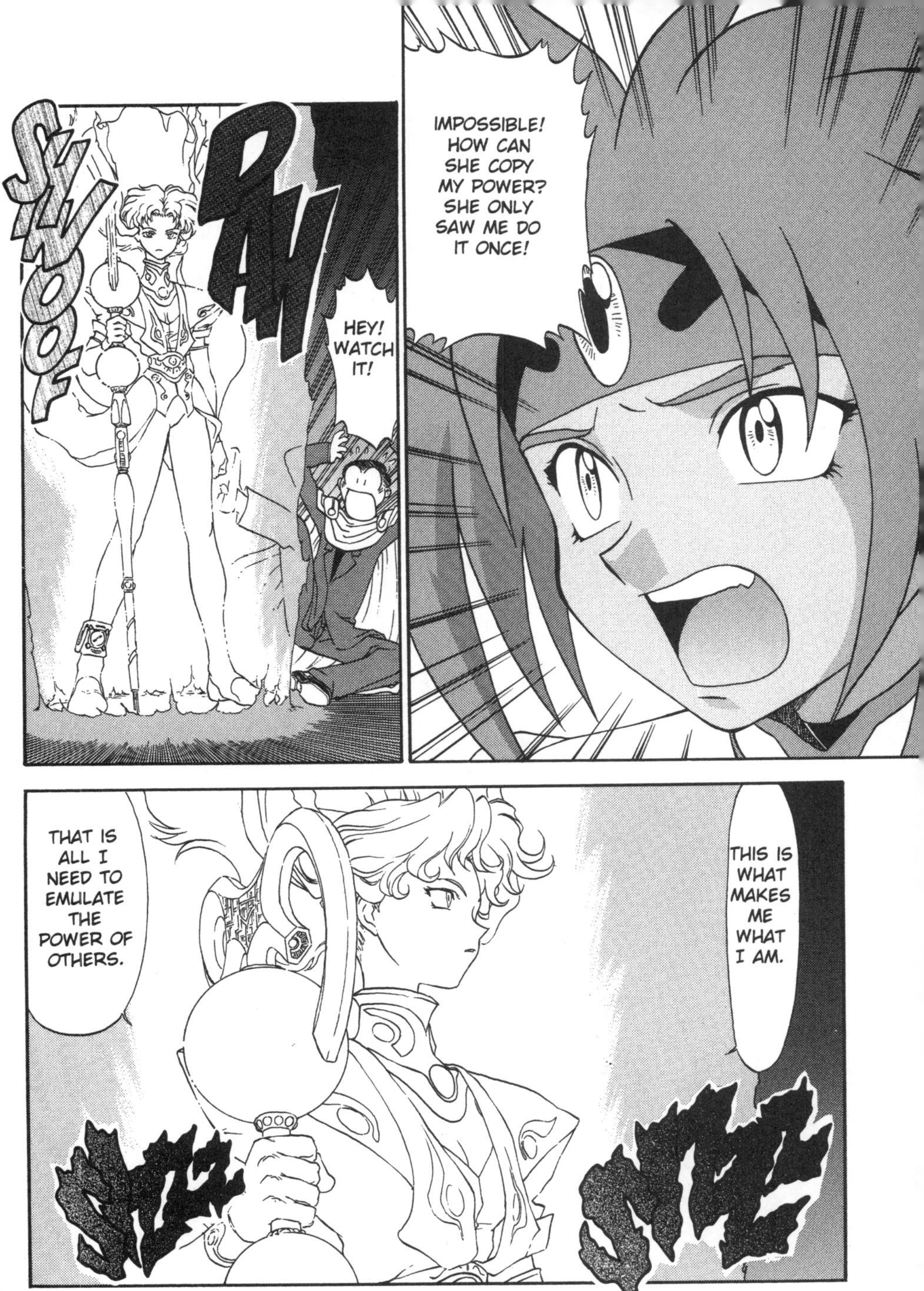
SHWOOF
PAH
HEY! WATCH IT!
IMPOSSIBLE! HOW CAN SHE COPY MY POWER? SHE ONLY SAW ME DO IT ONCE!
THAT IS ALL I NEED TO EMULATE THE POWER OF OTHERS.
THIS IS WHAT MAKES ME WHAT I AM.
SIZZ
SIZZ

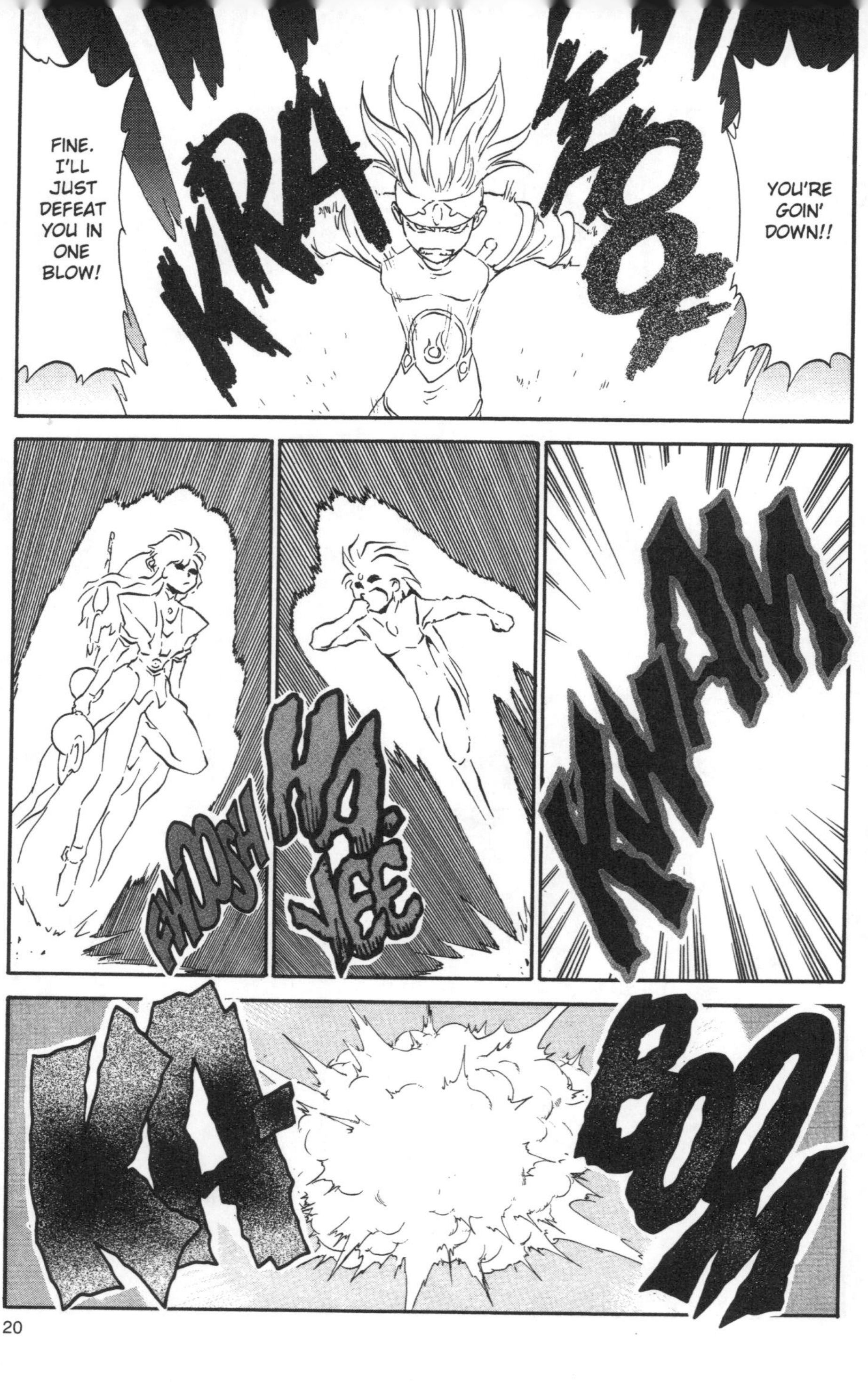
FINE. I'LL JUST DEFEAT YOU IN ONE BLOW!
KRA
YOU'RE GOIN' DOWN!!
WHOOSH
HA-YEE
KWAM
KA-BOOM

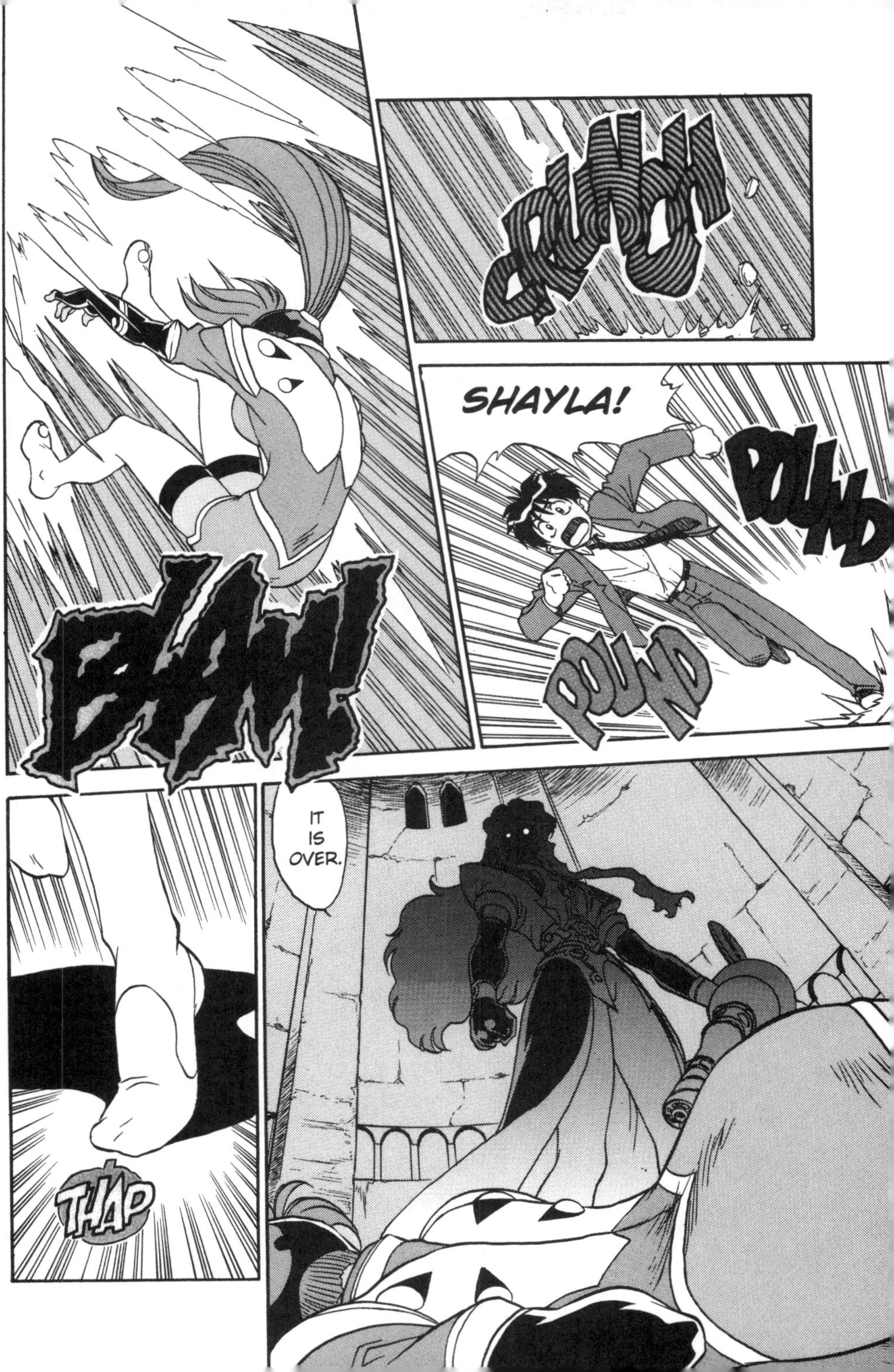
BLAM!
CRUNCH
SHAYLA!
POUND
POUND
THAP
IT IS OVER.

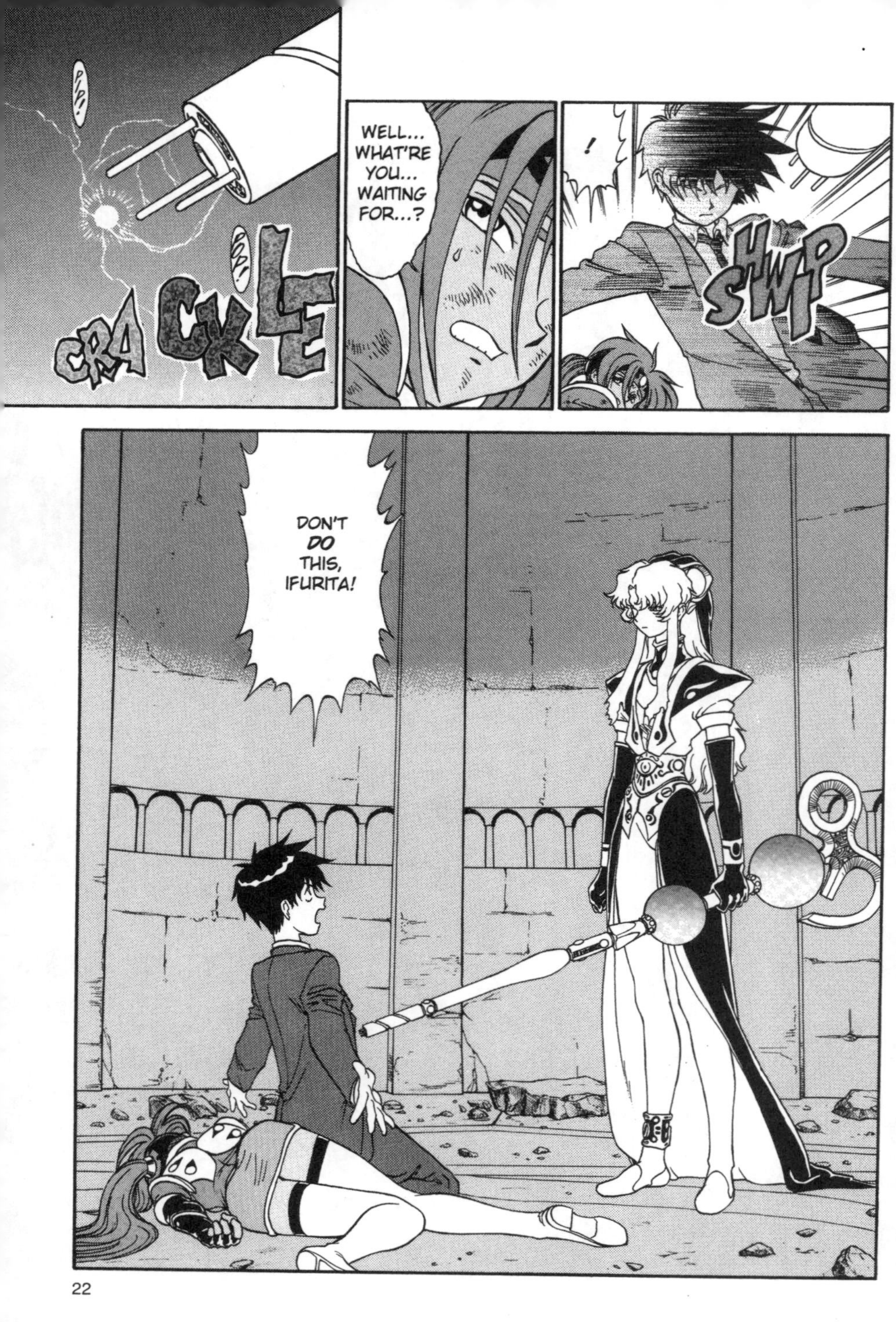
PIP!
POP!
CRACKLE
WELL... WHAT'RE YOU... WAITING FOR...?
!
SHWIP
DON'T *DO* THIS, IFURITA!

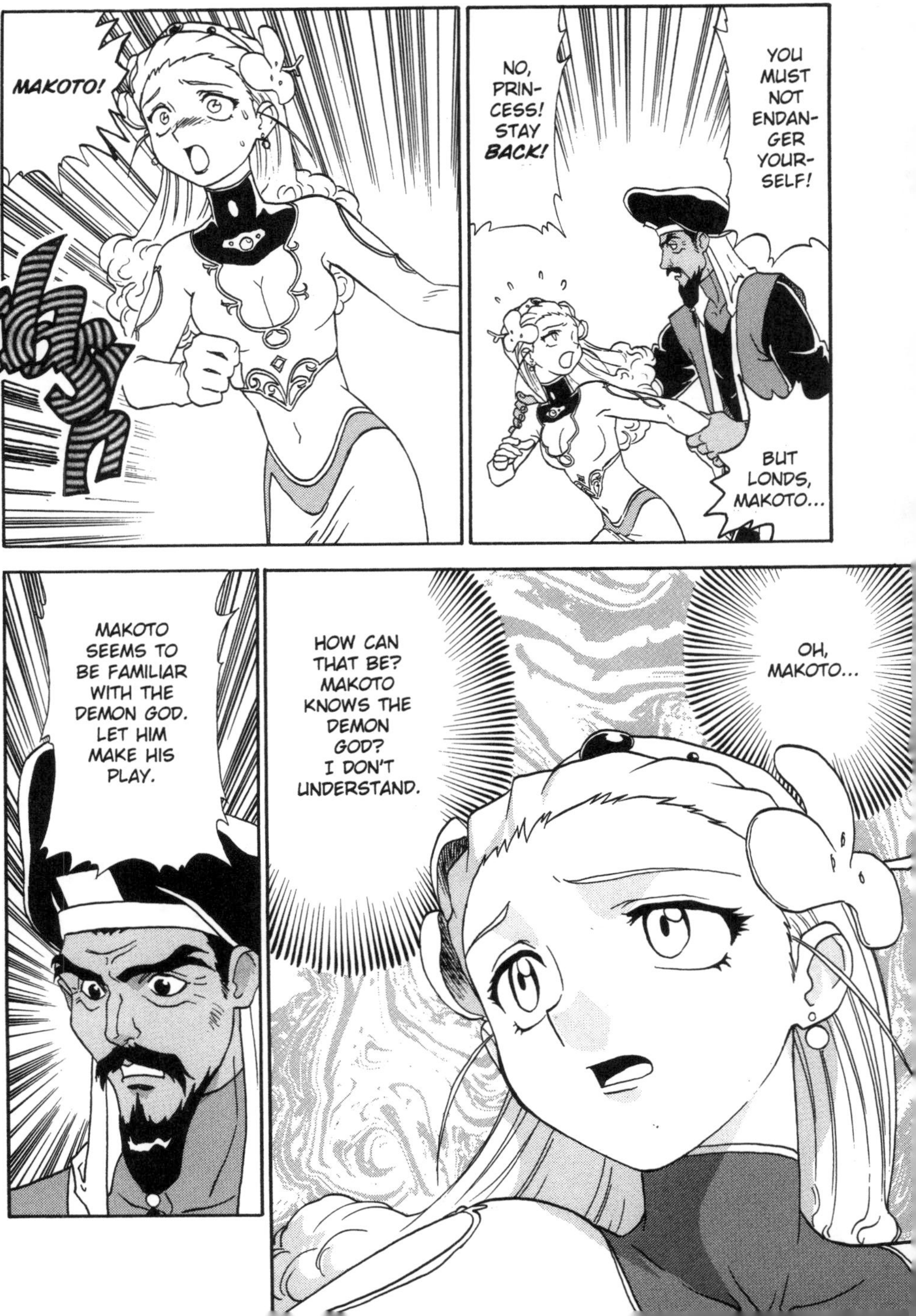
MAKOTO!
NO, PRINCESS! STAY BACK!
YOU MUST NOT ENDANGER YOURSELF!
BUT LONDS, MAKOTO...
MAKOTO SEEMS TO BE FAMILIAR WITH THE DEMON GOD. LET HIM MAKE HIS PLAY.
HOW CAN THAT BE? MAKOTO KNOWS THE DEMON GOD? I DON'T UNDERSTAND.
OH, MAKOTO...

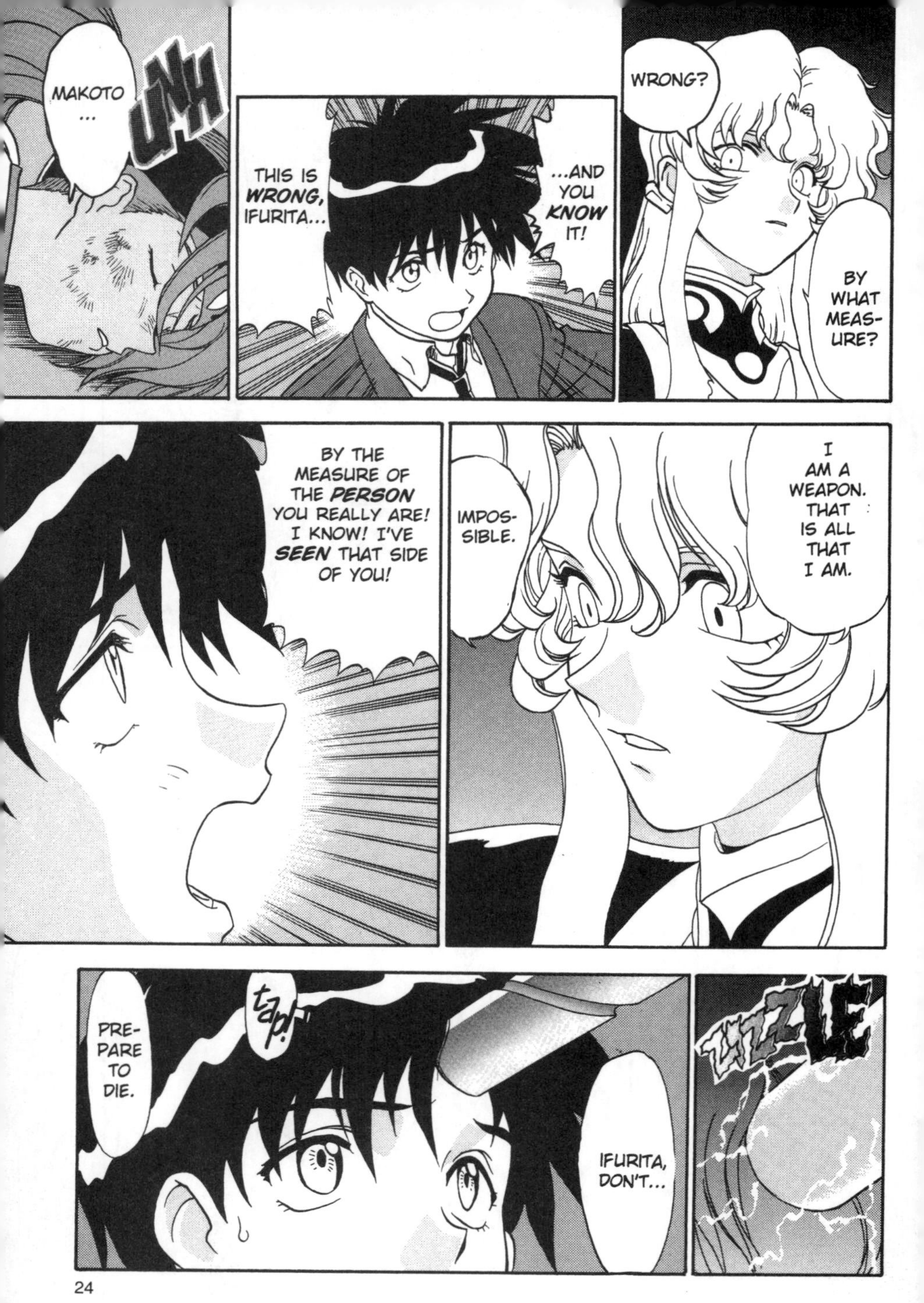
MAKOTO ...
UNH
THIS IS WRONG, IFURITA...
...AND YOU KNOW IT!
WRONG?
BY WHAT MEAS-URE?
BY THE MEASURE OF THE PERSON YOU REALLY ARE! I KNOW! I'VE SEEN THAT SIDE OF YOU!
IMPOS-SIBLE.
I AM A WEAPON. THAT IS ALL THAT I AM.
PRE-PARE TO DIE.
tap!
IFURITA, DON'T...
TZZZLE

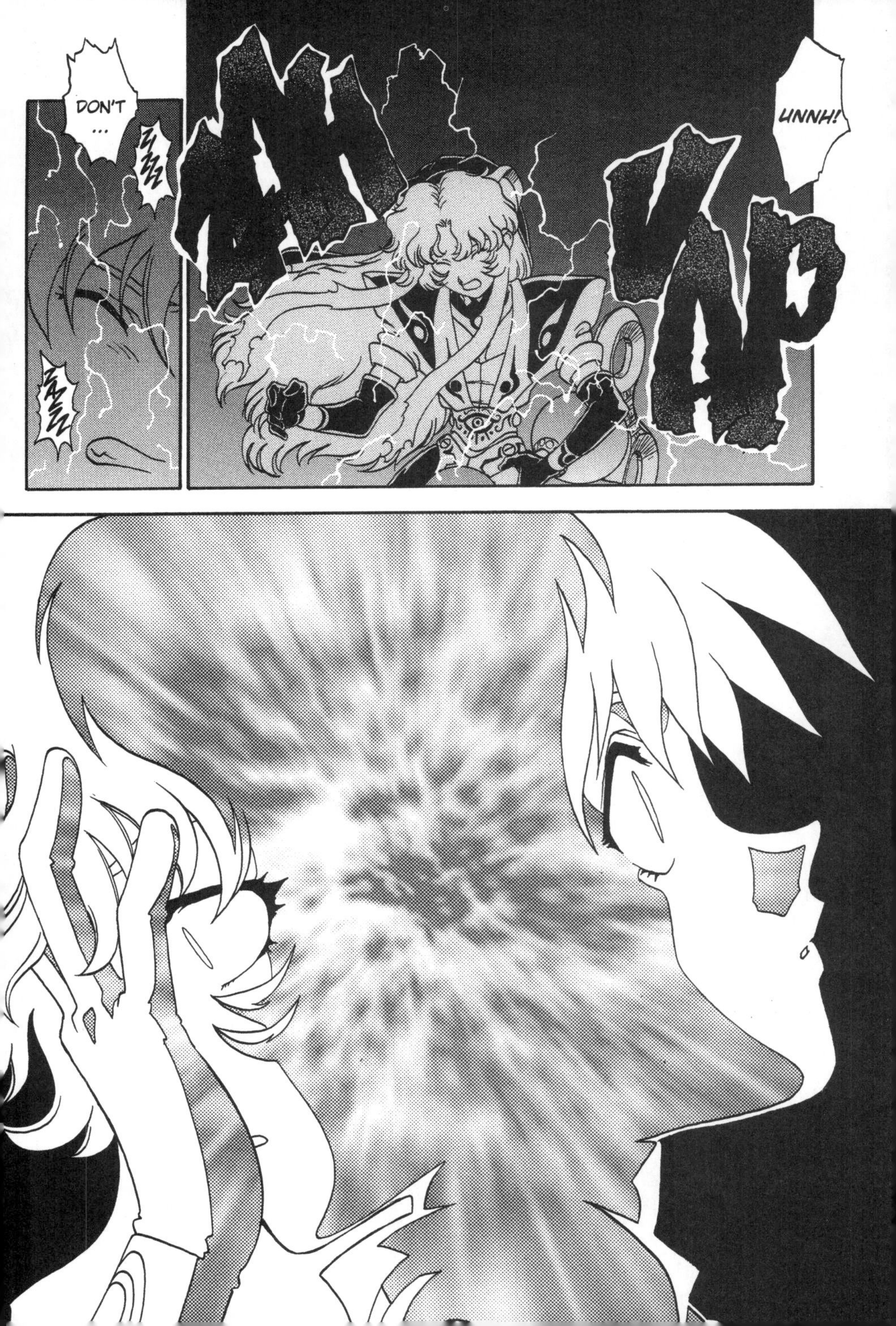
DON'T ...
UNNH!

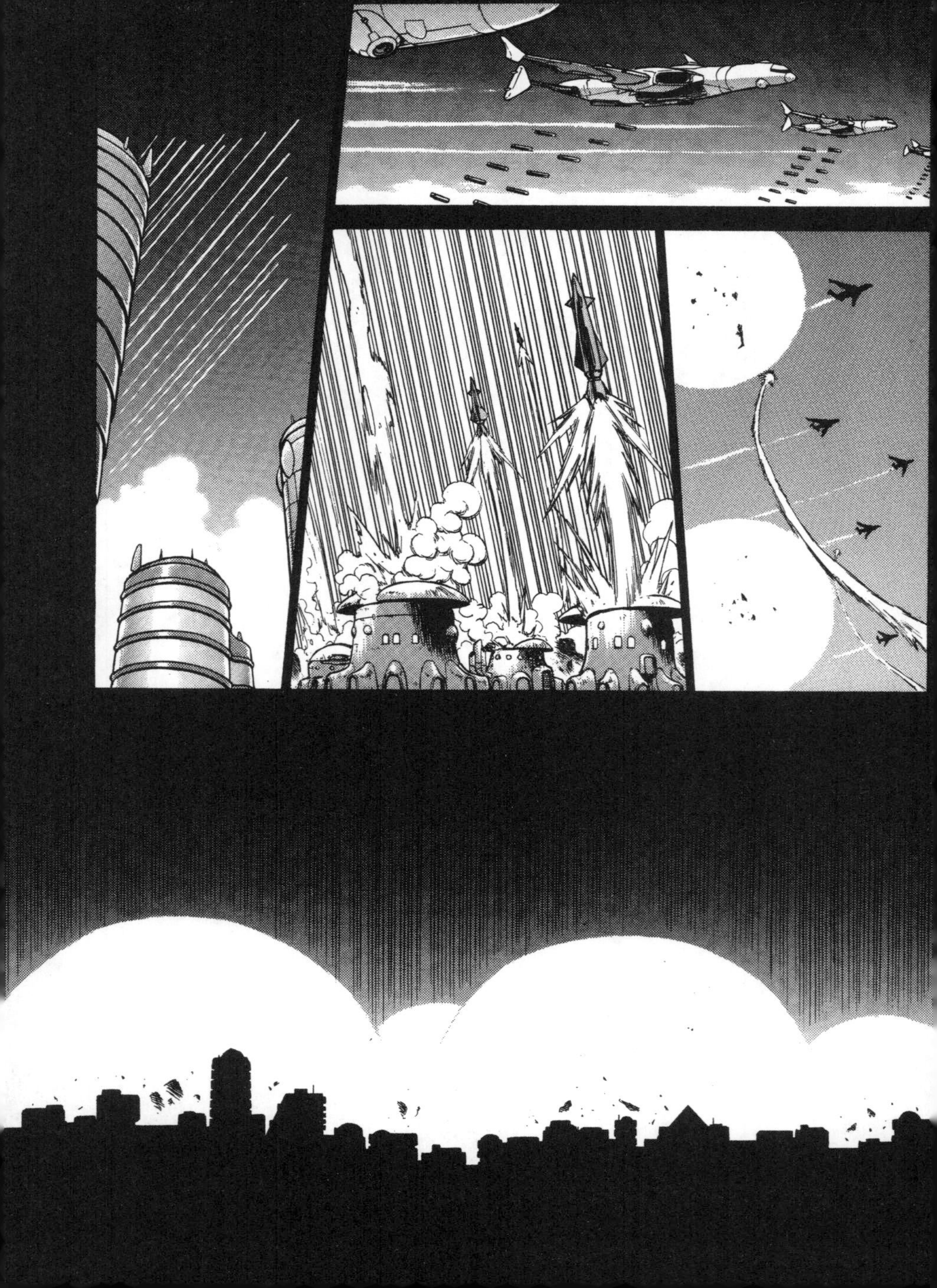

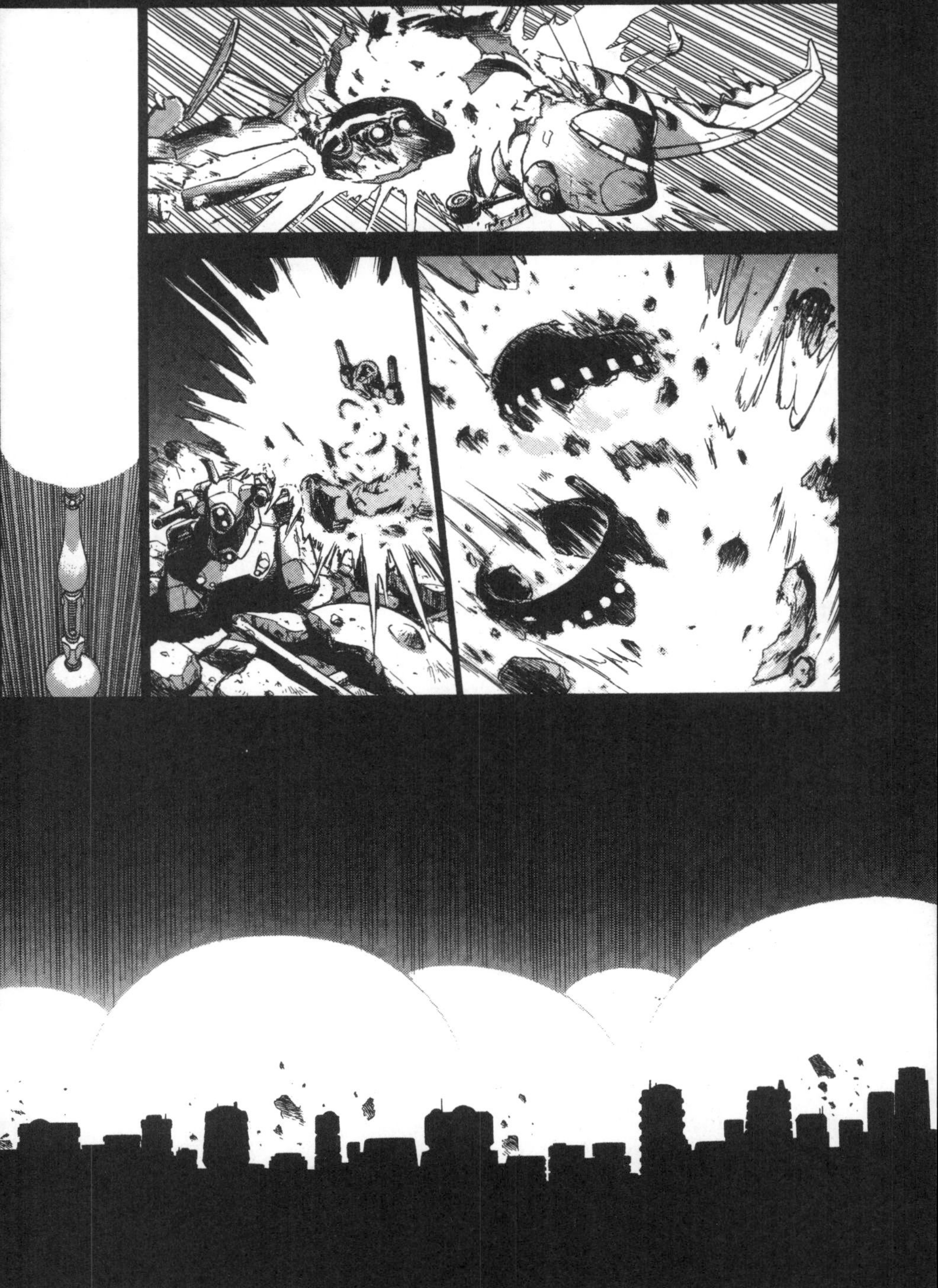

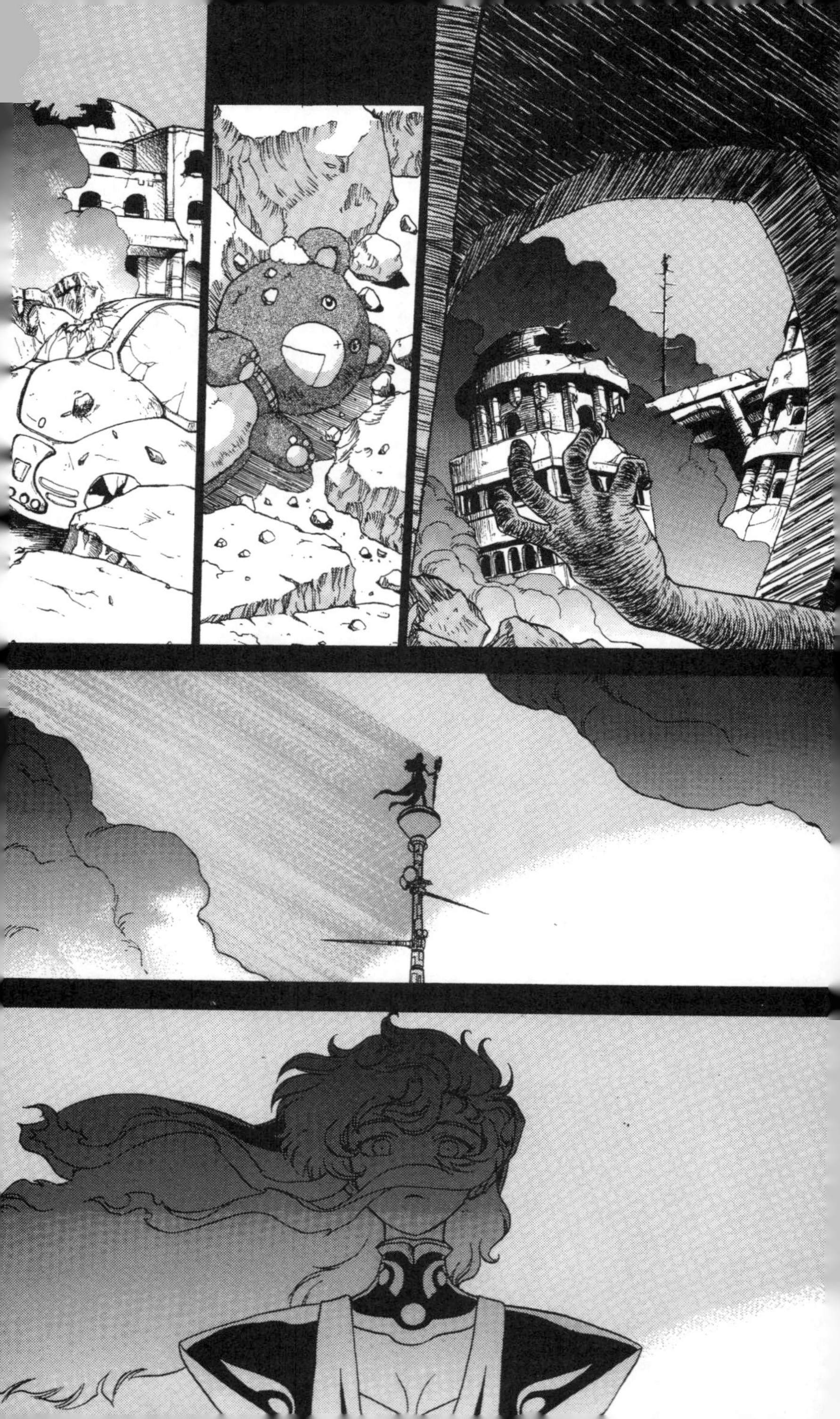

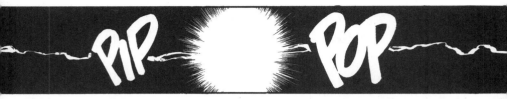

MY...

...MY GOD, SUCH *HORROR*...

HOW...

HOW DID YOU *DO* THAT?

WHAT DID YOU DO !?

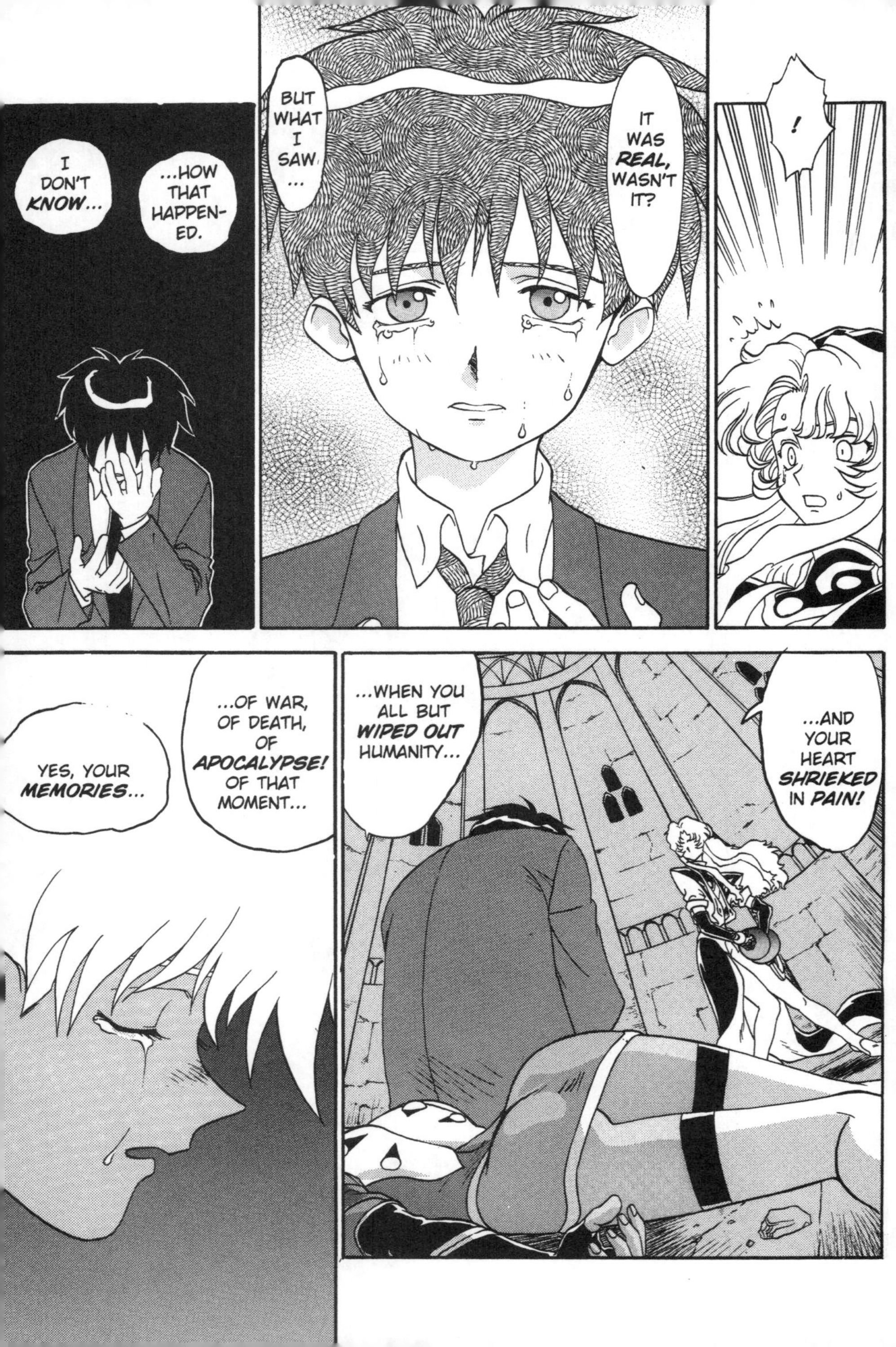
I DON'T KNOW...
...HOW THAT HAPPEN-ED.
BUT WHAT I SAW...
IT WAS REAL, WASN'T IT?
!
YES, YOUR MEMORIES...
...OF WAR, OF DEATH, OF APOCALYPSE! OF THAT MOMENT...
...WHEN YOU ALL BUT WIPED OUT HUMANITY...
...AND YOUR HEART SHRIEKED IN PAIN!

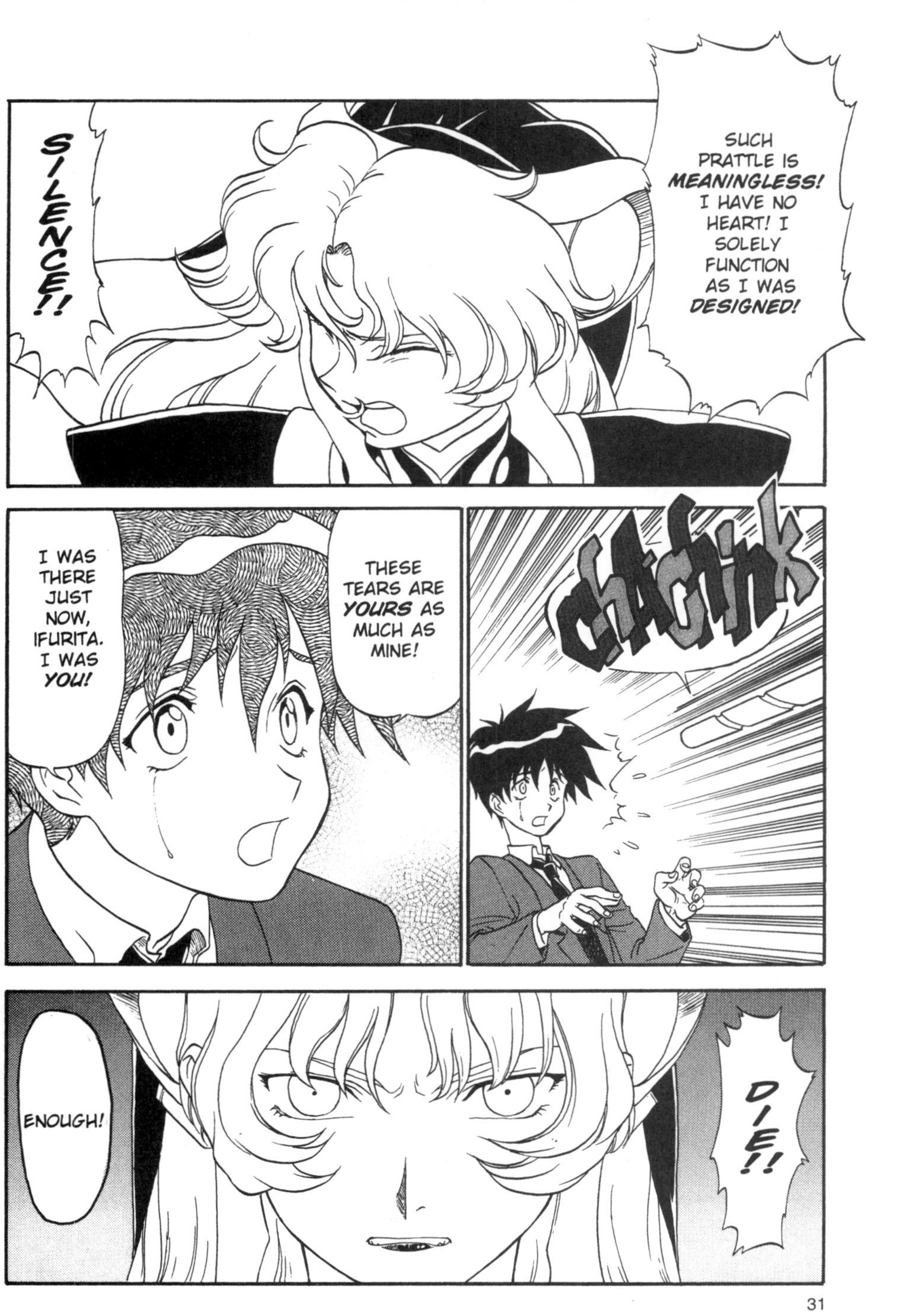
SILENCE!!
SUCH PRATTLE IS MEANINGLESS! I HAVE NO HEART! I SOLELY FUNCTION AS I WAS DESIGNED!
I WAS THERE JUST NOW, IFURITA. I WAS YOU!
THESE TEARS ARE YOURS AS MUCH AS MINE!
chAchink
ENOUGH!
DIE!!

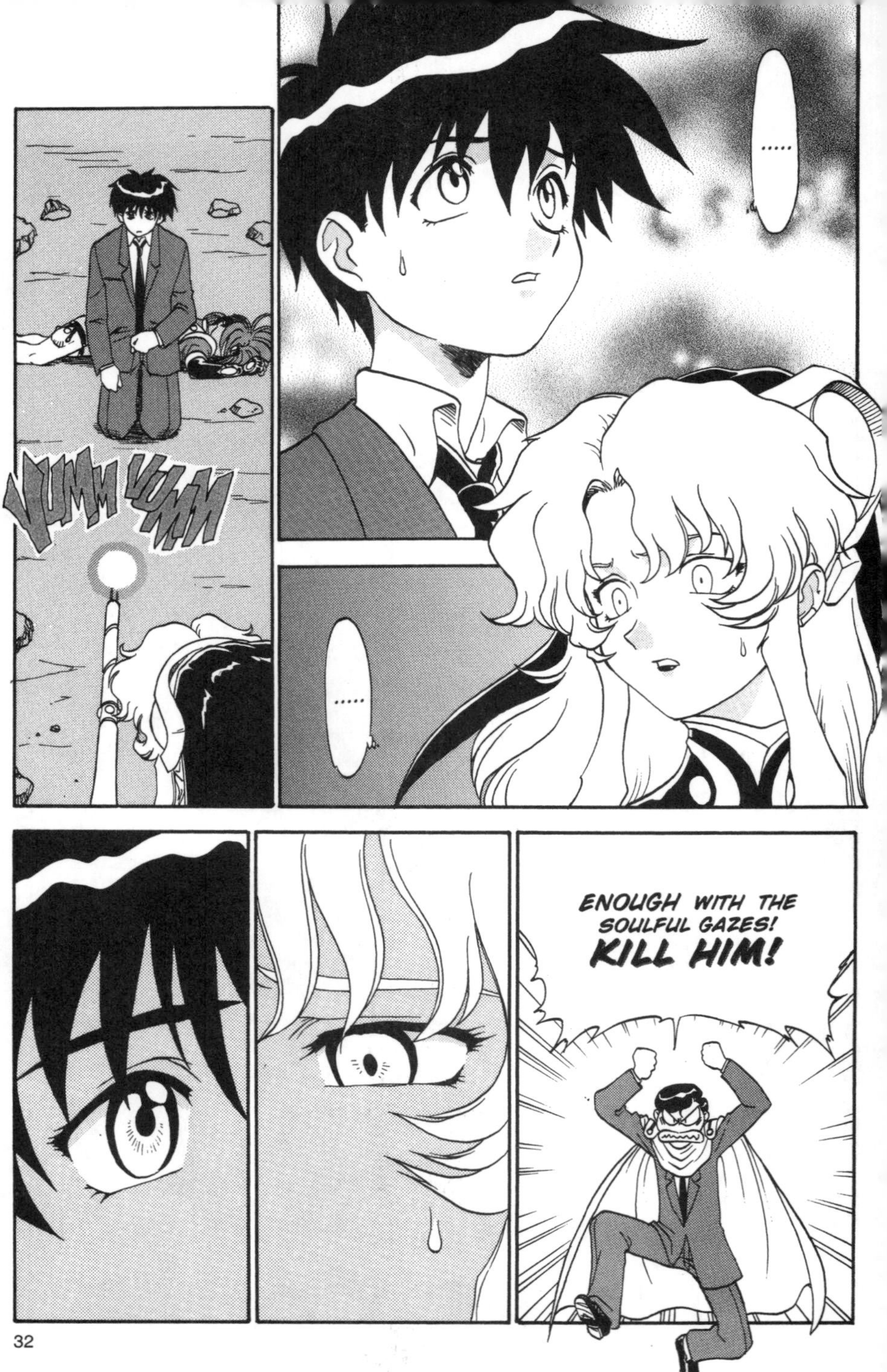
VUMM VUMM
......
......
ENOUGH WITH THE SOULFUL GAZES! KILL HIM!

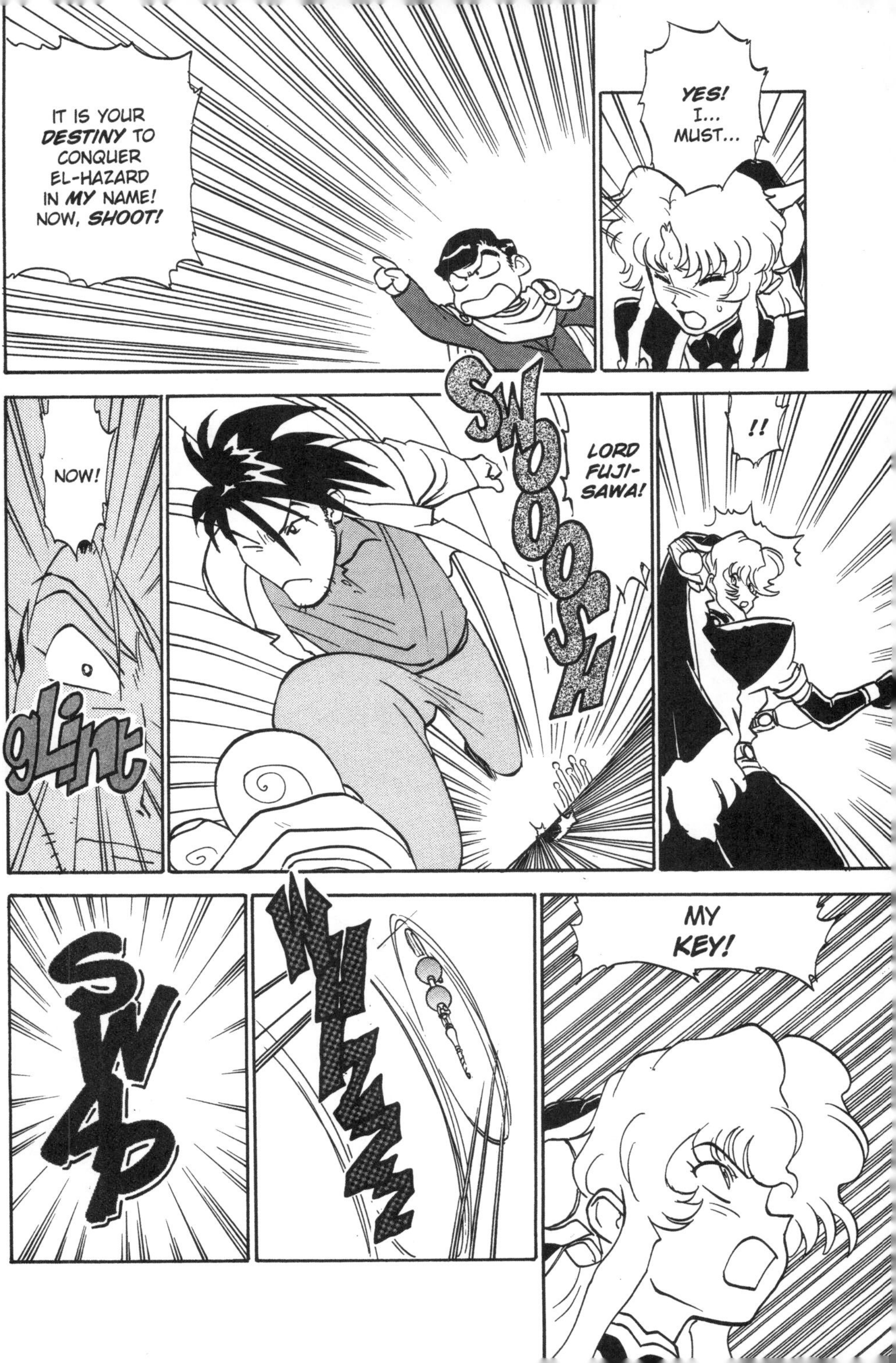
IT IS YOUR DESTINY TO CONQUER EL-HAZARD IN MY NAME! NOW, SHOOT!
YES! I... MUST...
NOW!
gLint
SWOOOSH
LORD FUJI-SAWA!
!!
SWAP
WHMMM
MY KEY!

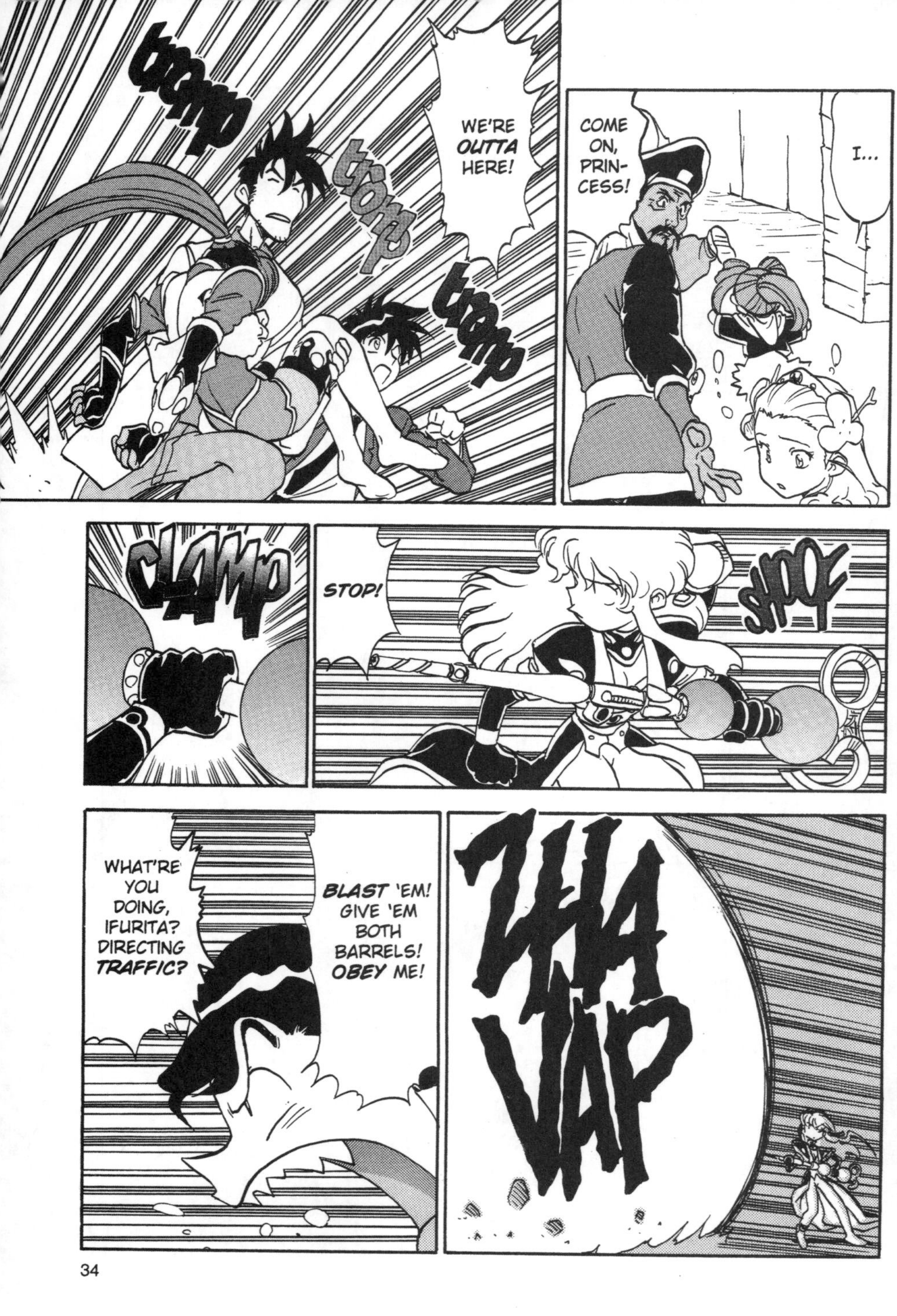
tromp
WE'RE OUTTA HERE!
tromp
tromp
COME ON, PRINCESS!
I...
CLAMP
STOP!
WHAT'RE YOU DOING, IFURITA? DIRECTING TRAFFIC?
BLAST 'EM! GIVE 'EM BOTH BARRELS! OBEY ME!
ZHA VAP

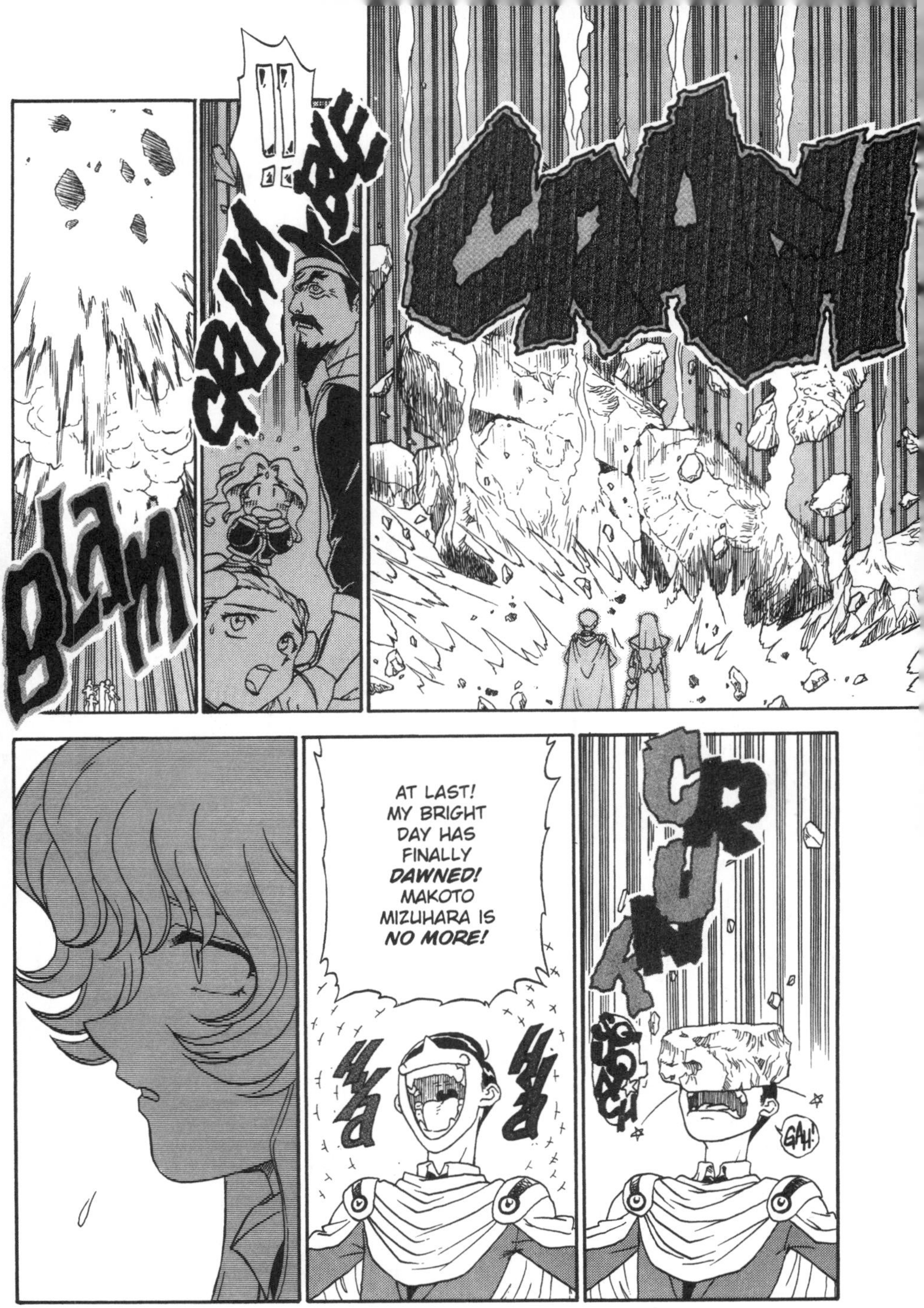

BLAM
!!
CRUMBLE
CRASH
AT LAST! MY BRIGHT DAY HAS FINALLY ***DAWNED!*** MAKOTO MIZUHARA IS ***NO MORE!***
CRUNK
GAH!

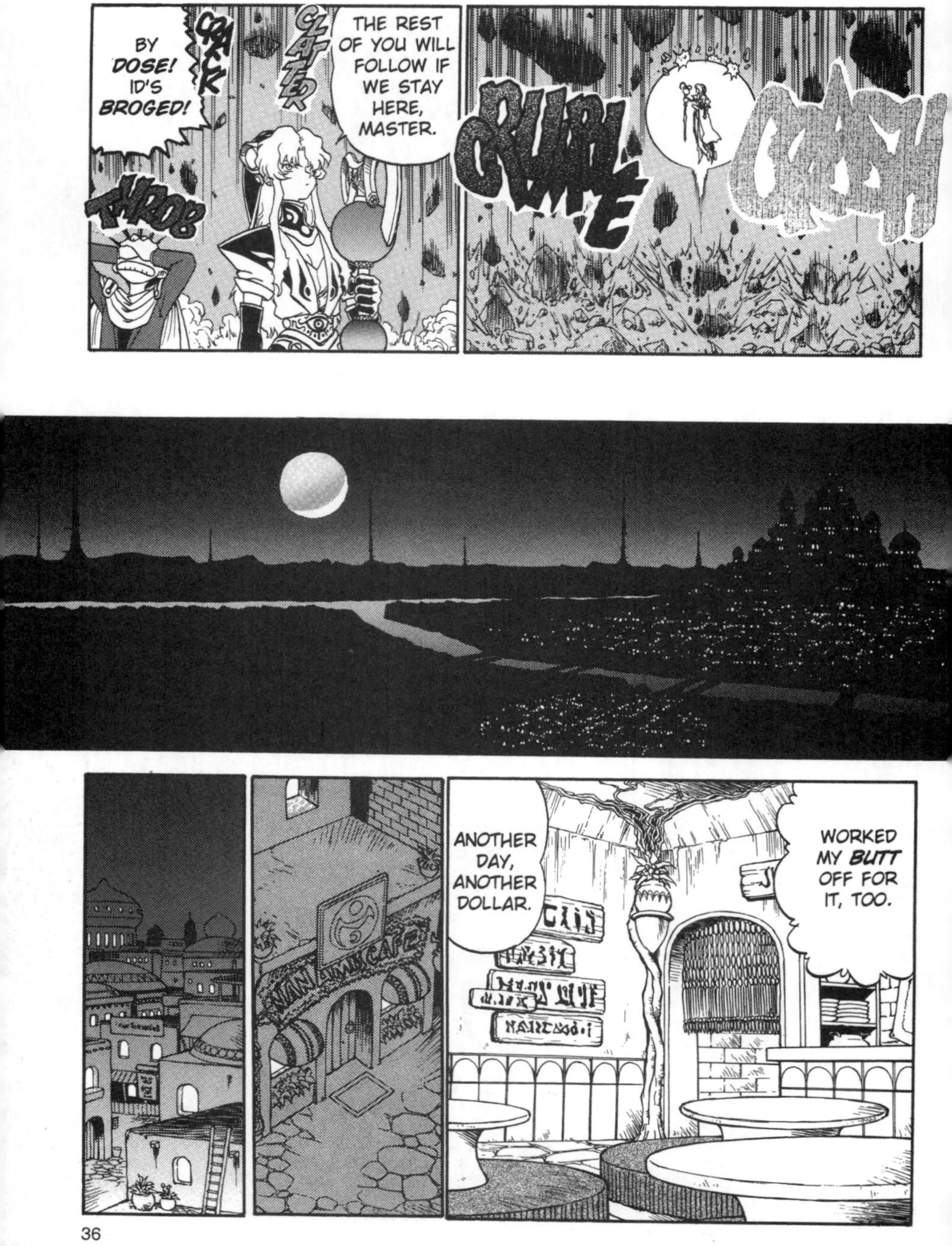
BY DOSE! ID'S BROGED!
CRACK
THROB
CLATTER
THE REST OF YOU WILL FOLLOW IF WE STAY HERE, MASTER.
CRUMBLE
CRASH
ANOTHER DAY, ANOTHER DOLLAR.
WORKED MY BUTT OFF FOR IT, TOO.

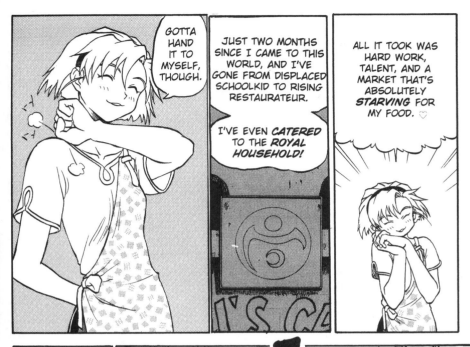

GOTTA HAND IT TO MYSELF, THOUGH.

JUST TWO MONTHS SINCE I CAME TO THIS WORLD, AND I'VE GONE FROM DISPLACED SCHOOLKID TO RISING RESTAURATEUR.

I'VE EVEN *CATERED* TO THE *ROYAL HOUSEHOLD!*

ALL IT TOOK WAS HARD WORK, TALENT, AND A MARKET THAT'S ABSOLUTELY *STARVING* FOR MY FOOD. ♡

BUT THIS SHOP'S JUST FOR STARTERS. NEXT UP: *FRANCHISING!*

CHA-

CHUG

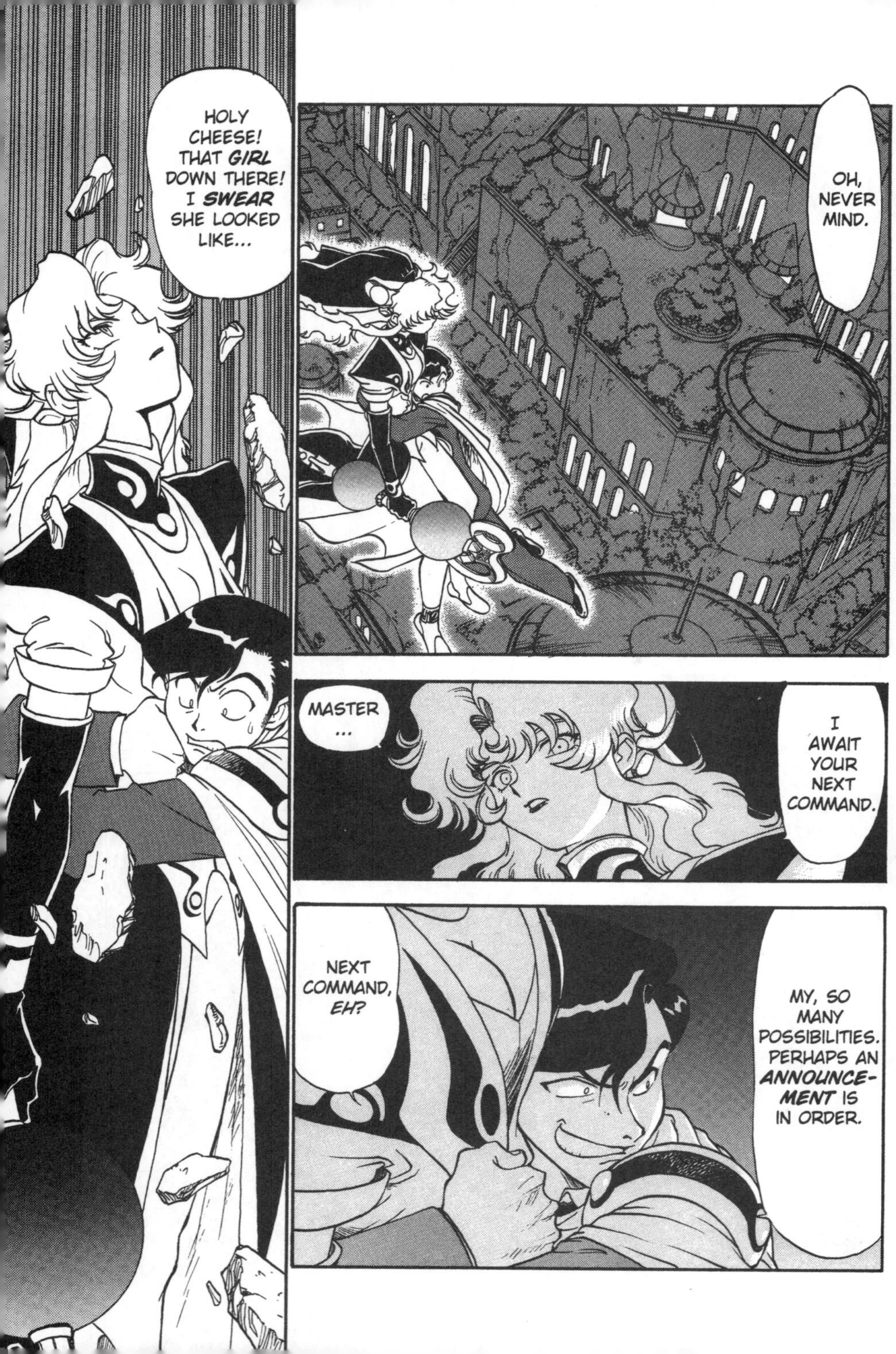
HOLY CHEESE! THAT GIRL DOWN THERE! I SWEAR SHE LOOKED LIKE...
OH, NEVER MIND.
MASTER ...
I AWAIT YOUR NEXT COMMAND.
NEXT COMMAND, EH?
MY, SO MANY POSSIBILITIES. PERHAPS AN ANNOUNCE-MENT IS IN ORDER.

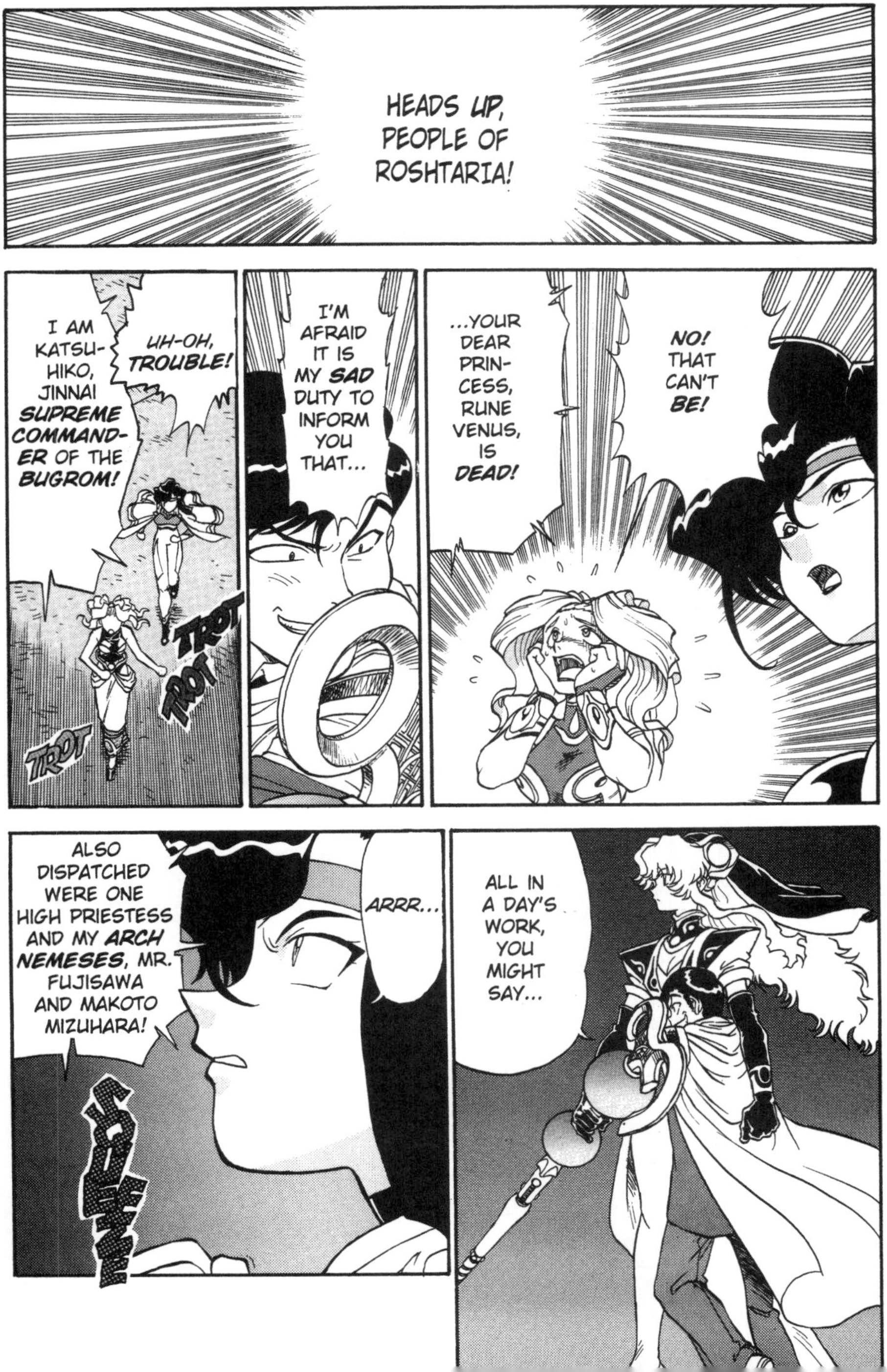
HEADS UP, PEOPLE OF ROSHTARIA!
I AM KATSUHIKO, JINNAI SUPREME COMMANDER OF THE BUGROM!
UH-OH, TROUBLE!
TROT
TROT
TROT
I'M AFRAID IT IS MY SAD DUTY TO INFORM YOU THAT...
...YOUR DEAR PRINCESS, RUNE VENUS, IS DEAD!
NO! THAT CAN'T BE!
ALSO DISPATCHED WERE ONE HIGH PRIESTESS AND MY ARCH NEMESES, MR. FUJISAWA AND MAKOTO MIZUHARA!
ARRR...
ALL IN A DAY'S WORK, YOU MIGHT SAY...

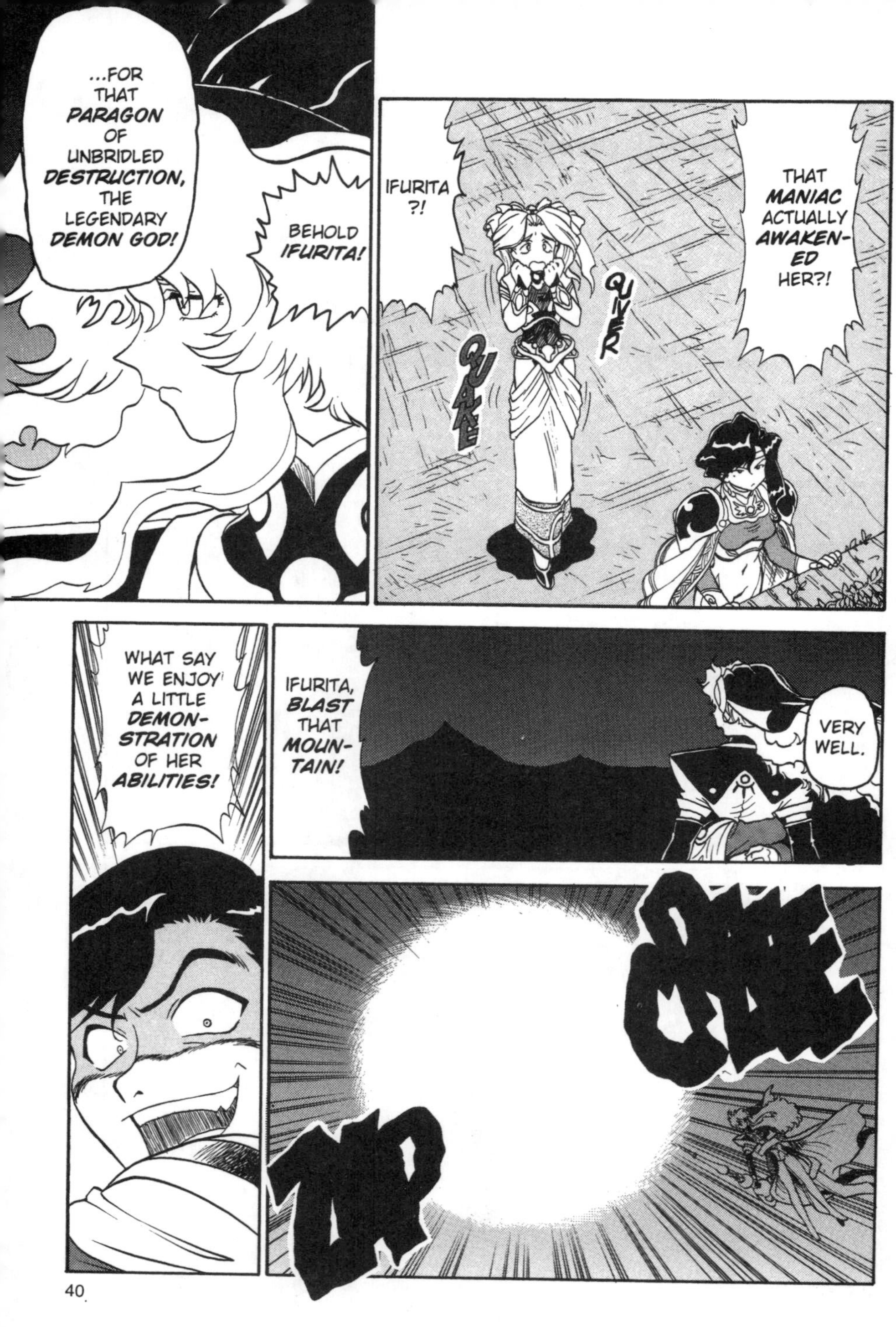

...FOR THAT PARAGON OF UNBRIDLED DESTRUCTION, THE LEGENDARY DEMON GOD!
BEHOLD IFURITA!
IFURITA ?!
THAT MANIAC ACTUALLY AWAKEN-ED HER?!
QUIVER
QUAKE
WHAT SAY WE ENJOY A LITTLE DEMON-STRATION OF HER ABILITIES!
IFURITA, BLAST THAT MOUN-TAIN!
VERY WELL.
ZAP

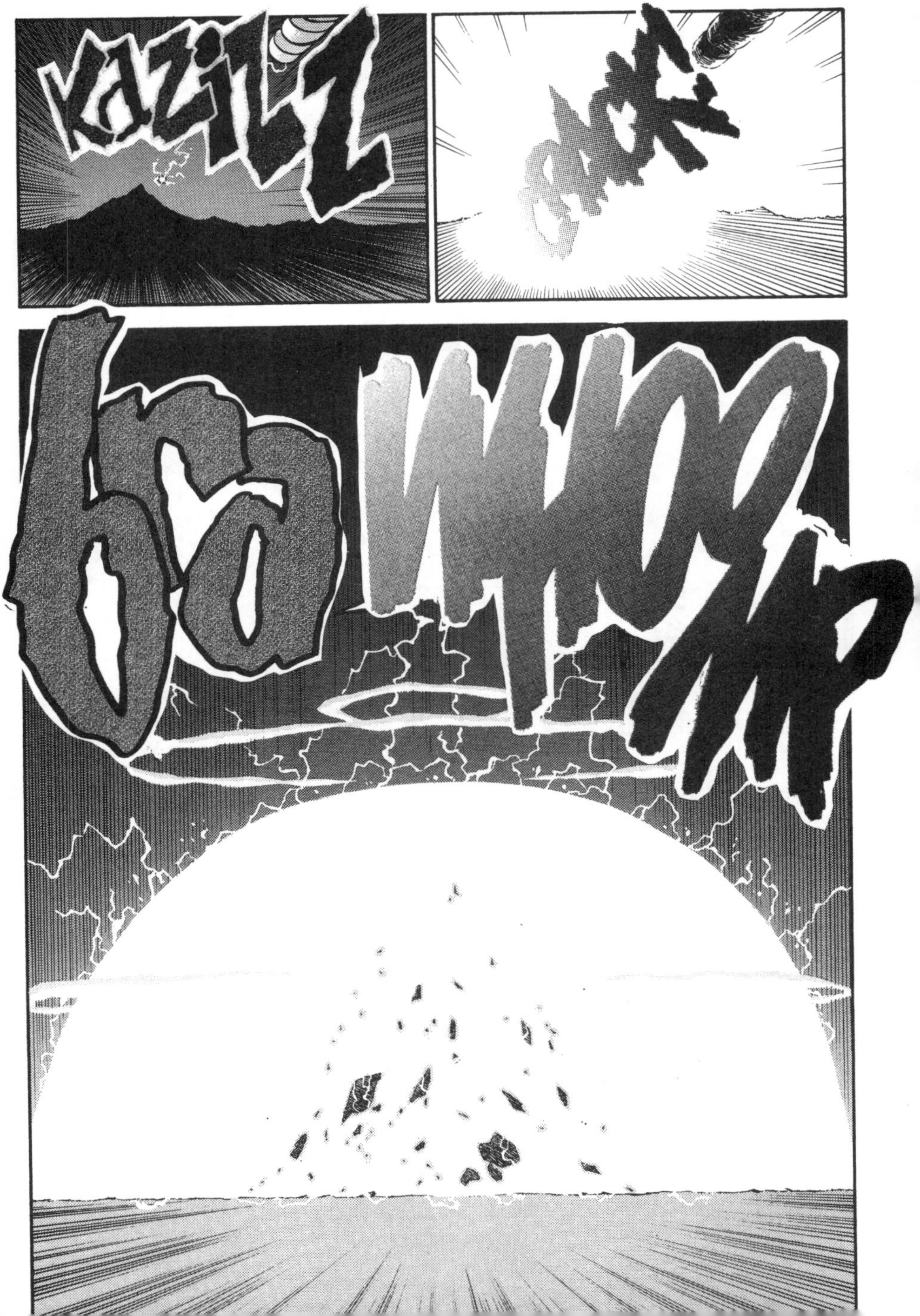
CRACK!

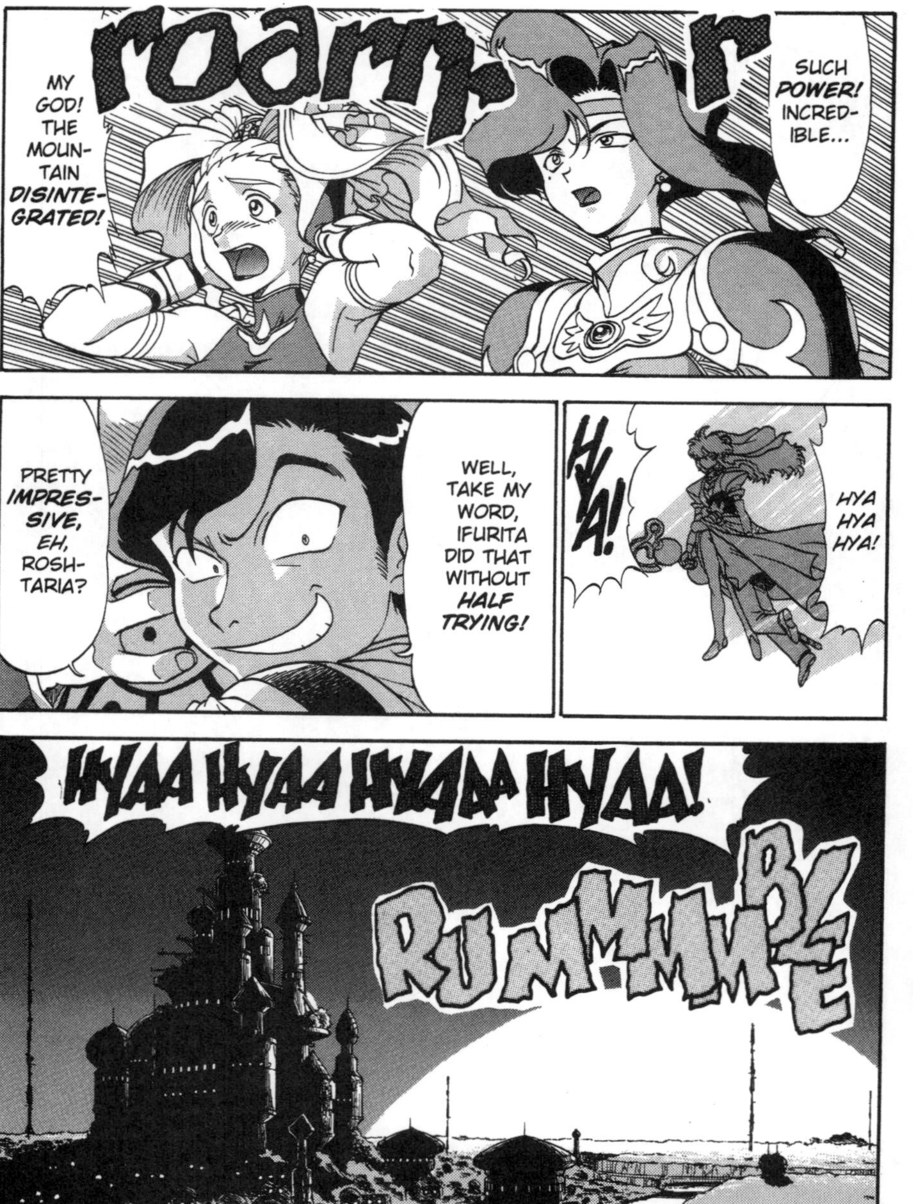
roarr...r
MY GOD! THE MOUNTAIN *DISINTEGRATED!*
SUCH *POWER!* INCREDIBLE...
PRETTY *IMPRESSIVE,* EH, ROSHTARIA?
WELL, TAKE MY WORD, IFURITA DID THAT WITHOUT *HALF TRYING!*
HYA!
HYA HYA HYA!
HYAA HYAA HYAAA HYAA!
RUMMMMBLE

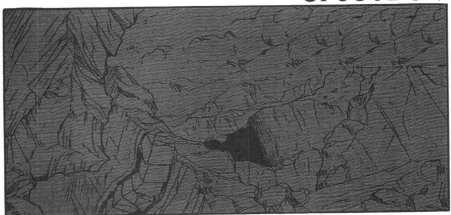

DAMN... UMPH... IT'S *DARK!*

IS THAT YOU, MR. FUJISAWA? ARE YOU OKAY?

I THINK SO, MAKOTO.

I'M OKAY, TOO.

ALIELLE... GOOD, THAT'S THREE. ANYONE ELSE?

PRINCESS? PRINCESS?

I'M HERE, LONDS. WHAT ABOUT SHAYLA SHAYLA?

SHE'S UNCON-SCIOUS, BUT ALIVE.

THAT'LL DO FOR THE MOMENT.

NOW, IF I STILL HAVE MY LIGHTER...

RUMMAGE RUMMAGE

AH, HERE IT IS. NOW, TO SHED A LITTLE LIGHT ON THE SUBJECT.

43

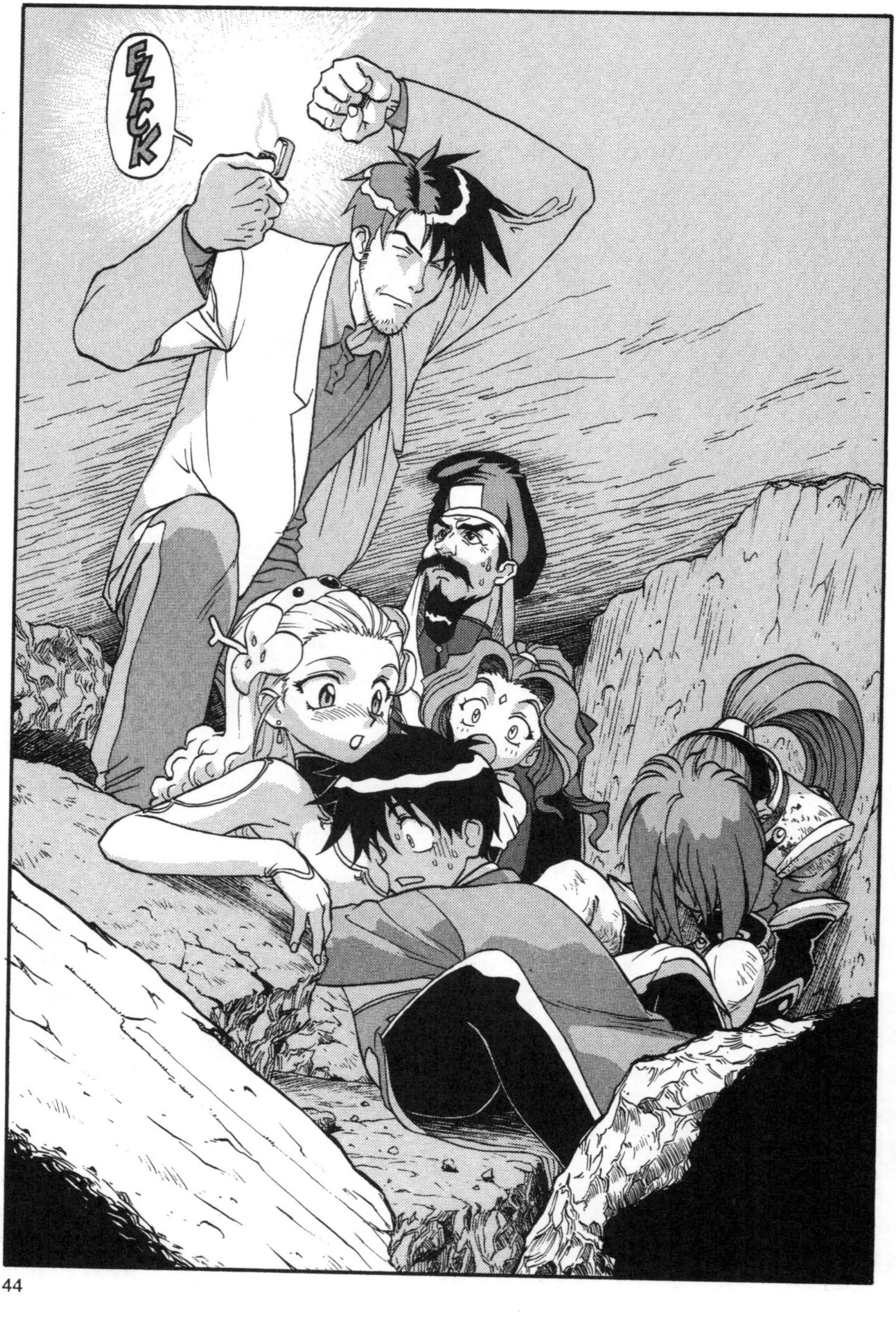
FZCK

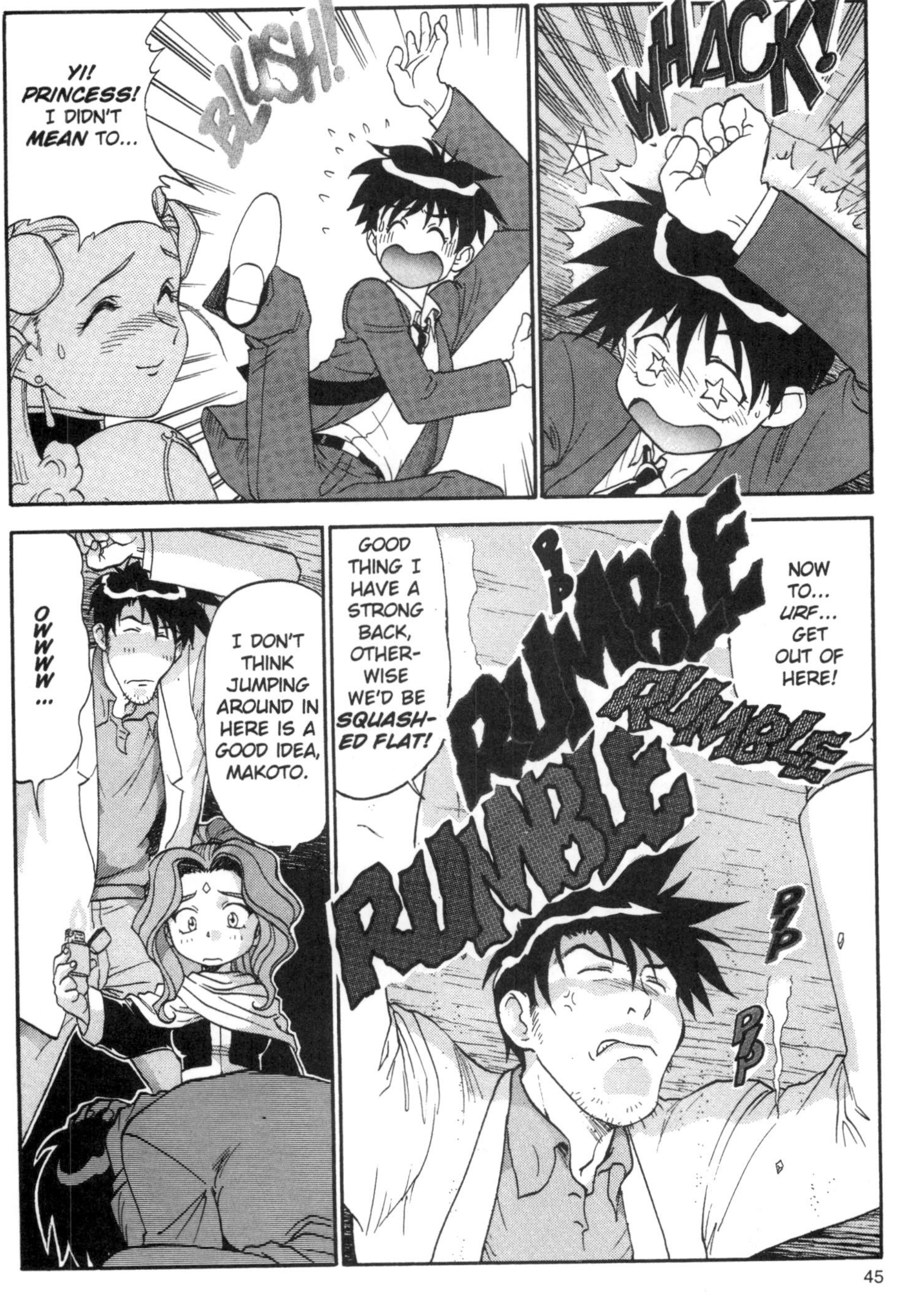
YI! PRINCESS! I DIDN'T MEAN TO...
BLUSH!
WHACK!
OWWWW...
I DON'T THINK JUMPING AROUND IN HERE IS A GOOD IDEA, MAKOTO.
GOOD THING I HAVE A STRONG BACK, OTHERWISE WE'D BE SQUASHED FLAT!
RIP
RUMBLE
RUMBLE
RUMBLE
NOW TO... URF... GET OUT OF HERE!
RIP
RIP

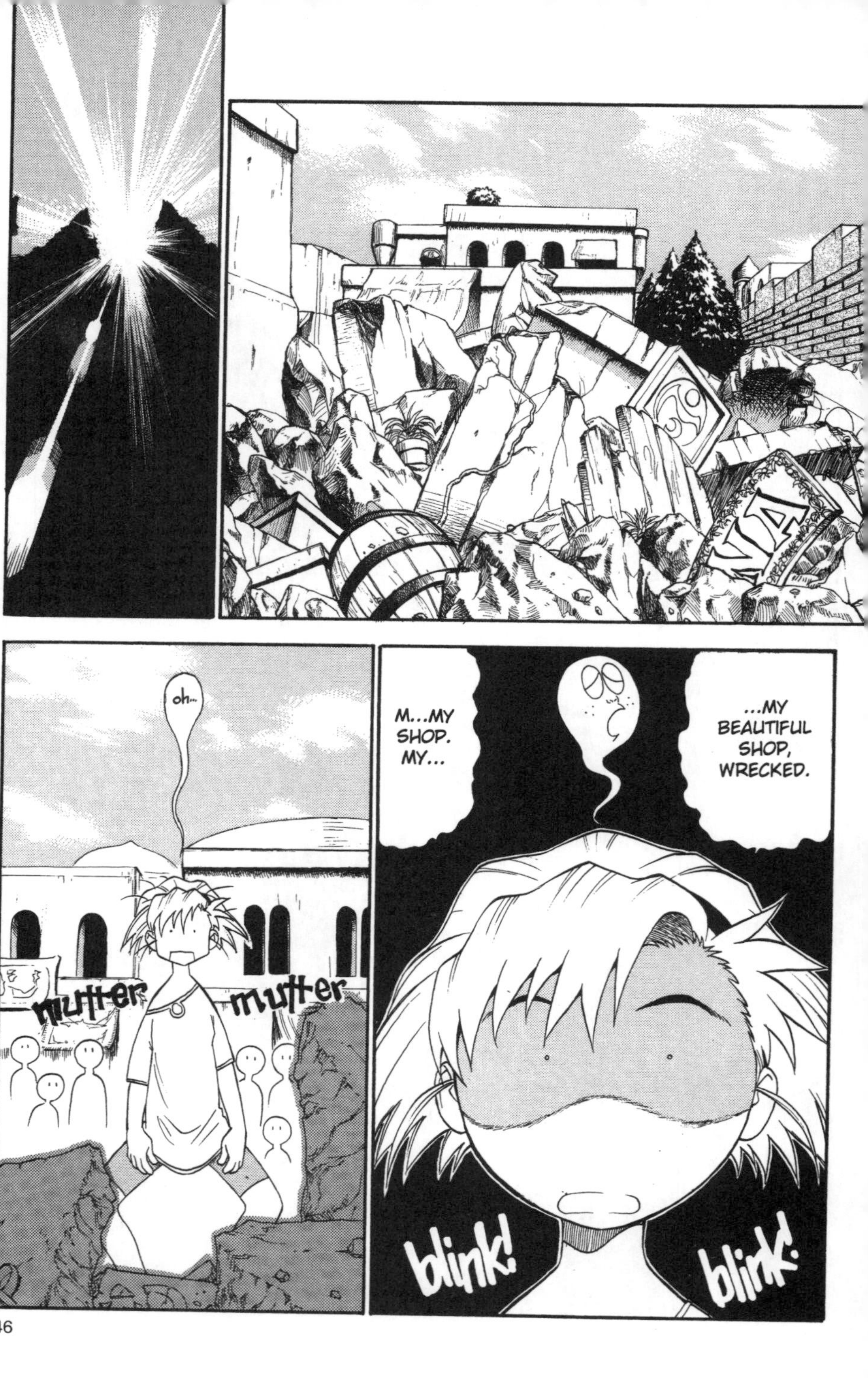
oh...
mutter
mutter
M...MY SHOP. MY...
...MY BEAUTIFUL SHOP, WRECKED.
blink!
blink!

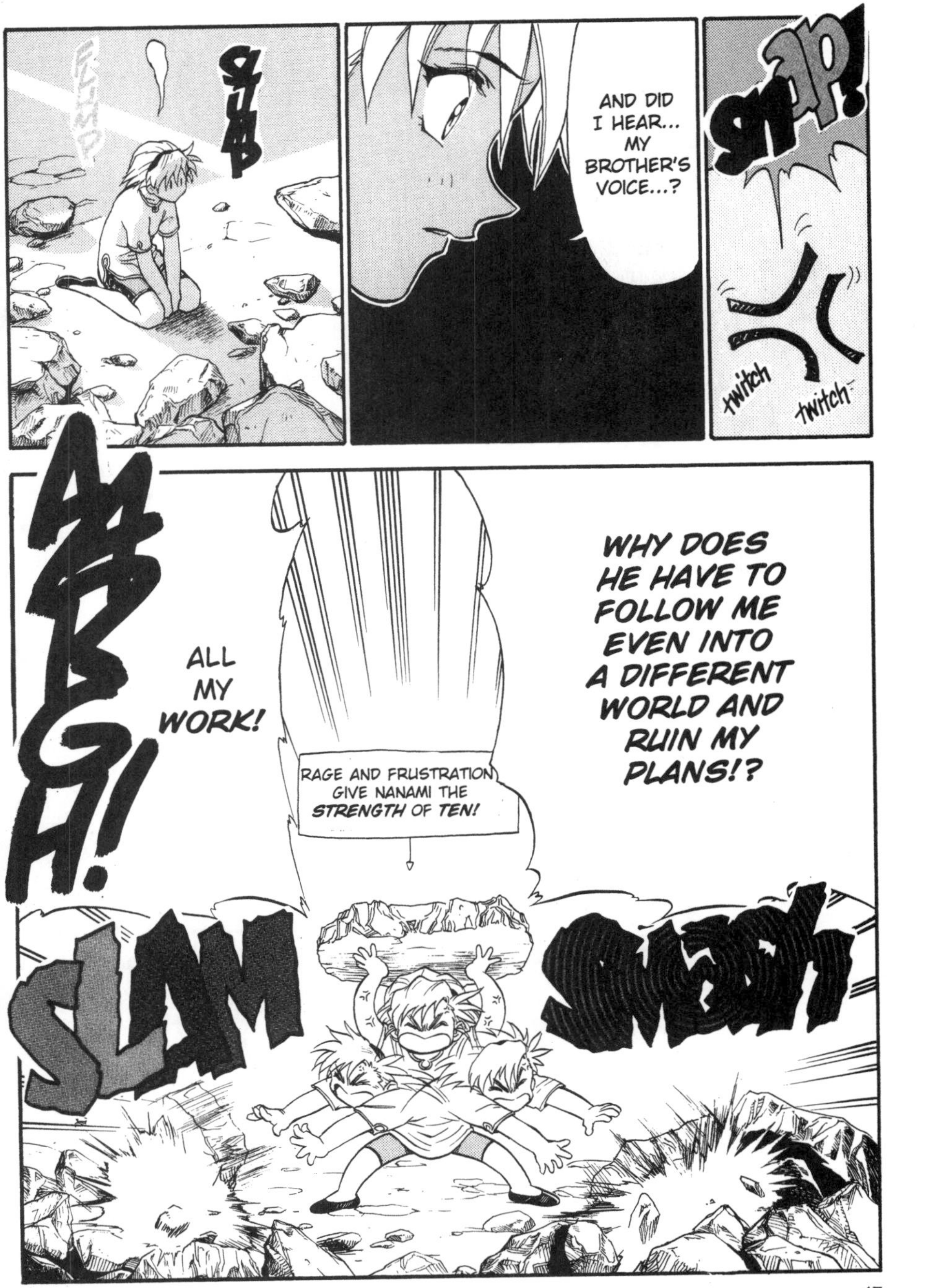
FLUMP
SLUMP
AND DID I HEAR... MY BROTHER'S VOICE...?
SNAP!
twitch
twitch
ALL MY WORK!
WHY DOES HE HAVE TO FOLLOW ME EVEN INTO A DIFFERENT WORLD AND RUIN MY PLANS!?
RAGE AND FRUSTRATION GIVE NANAMI THE STRENGTH OF TEN!
SLAM
SMASH

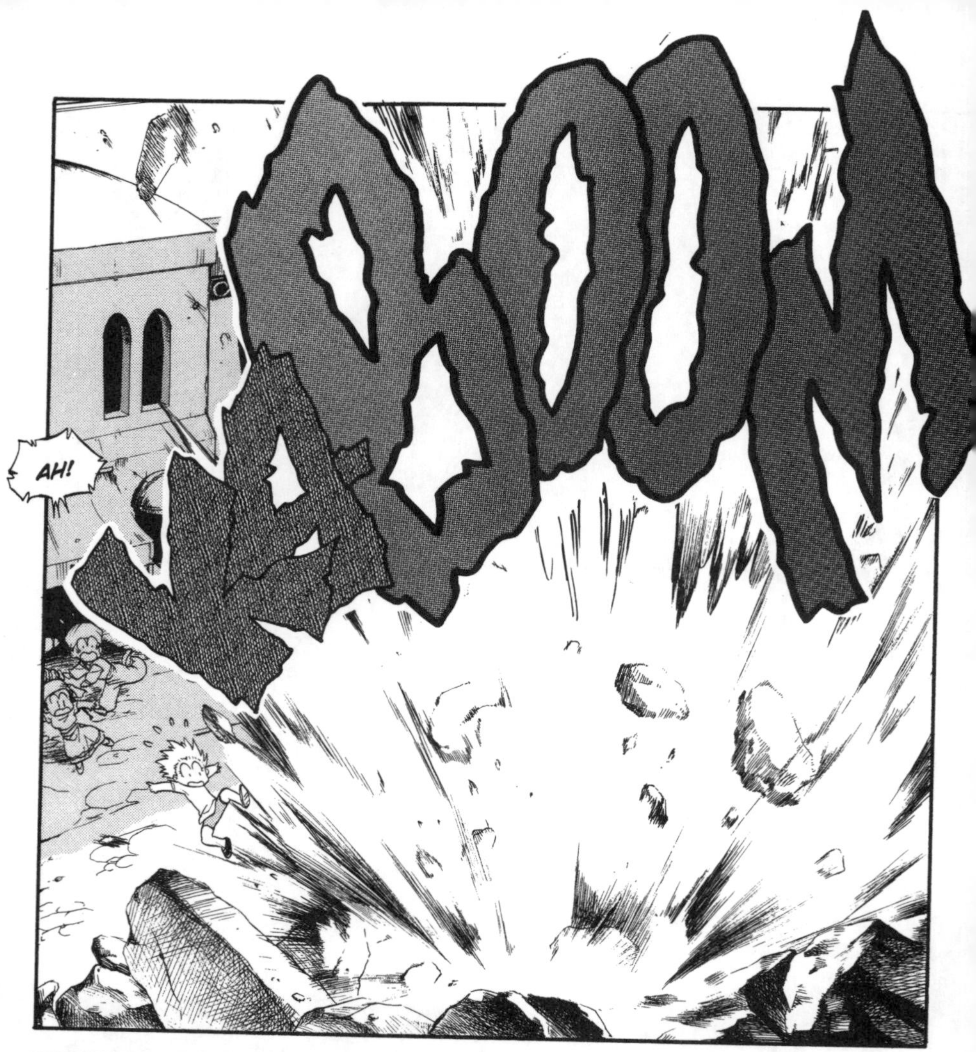
AH!
KA-BOOM
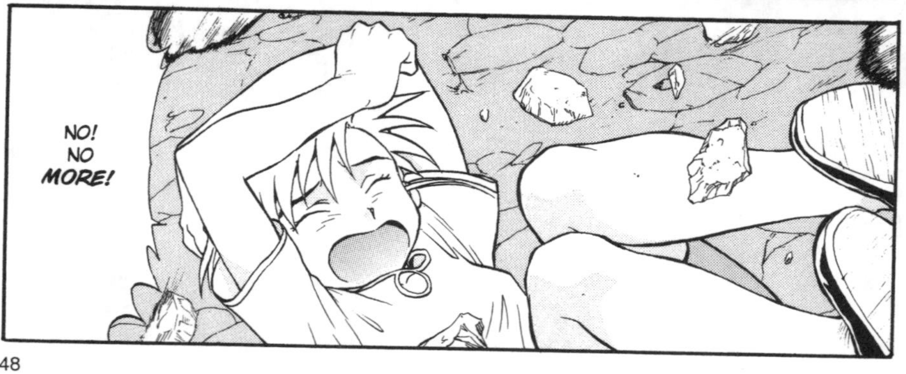
NO!
NO
MORE!

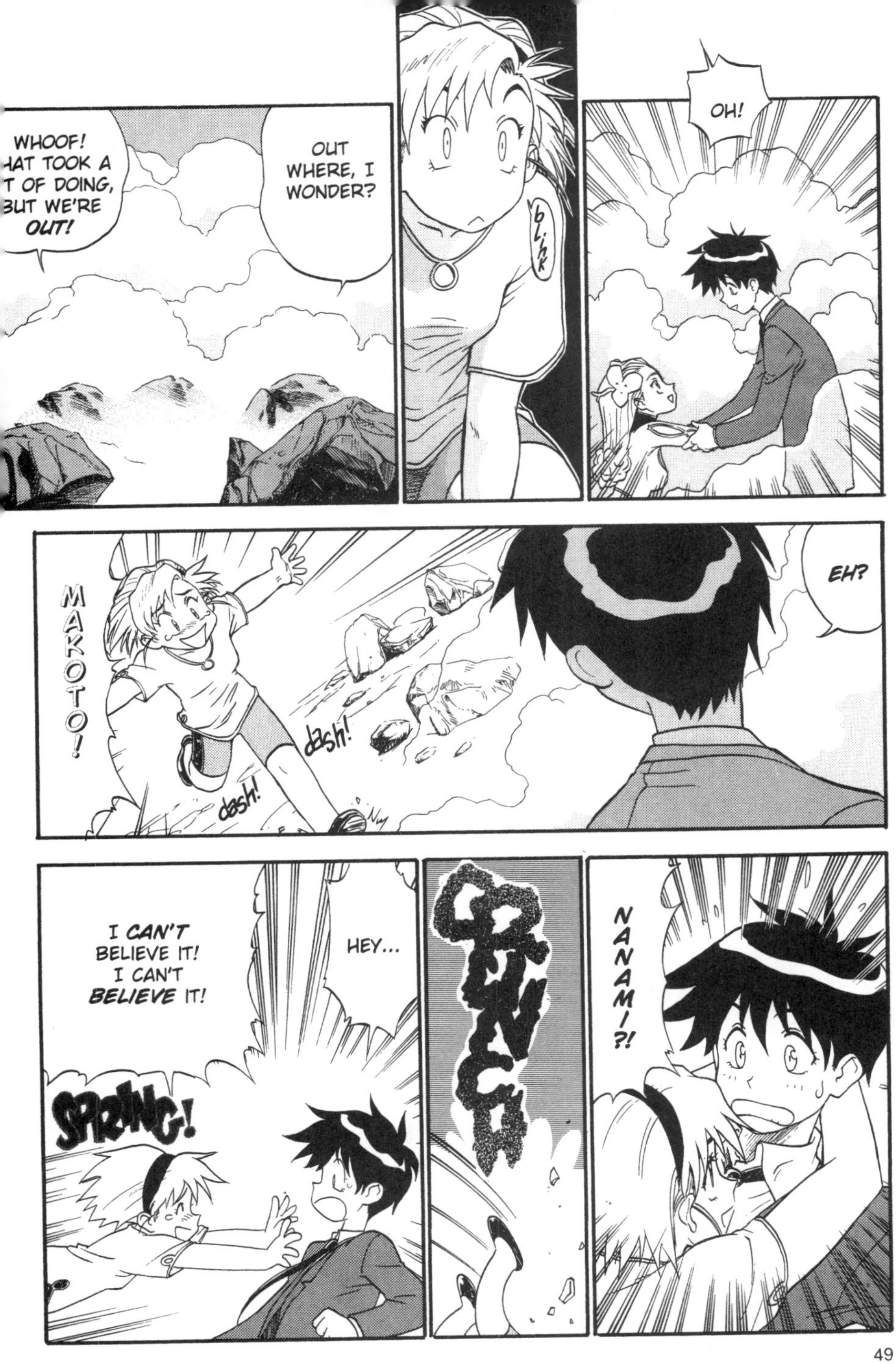
WHOOF! HAT TOOK A T OF DOING, BUT WE'RE OUT!
OUT WHERE, I WONDER?
blink
OH!
MAKOTO!
dash!
dash!
EH?
I CAN'T BELIEVE IT! I CAN'T BELIEVE IT!
HEY...
SPRING!
NANAMI?!

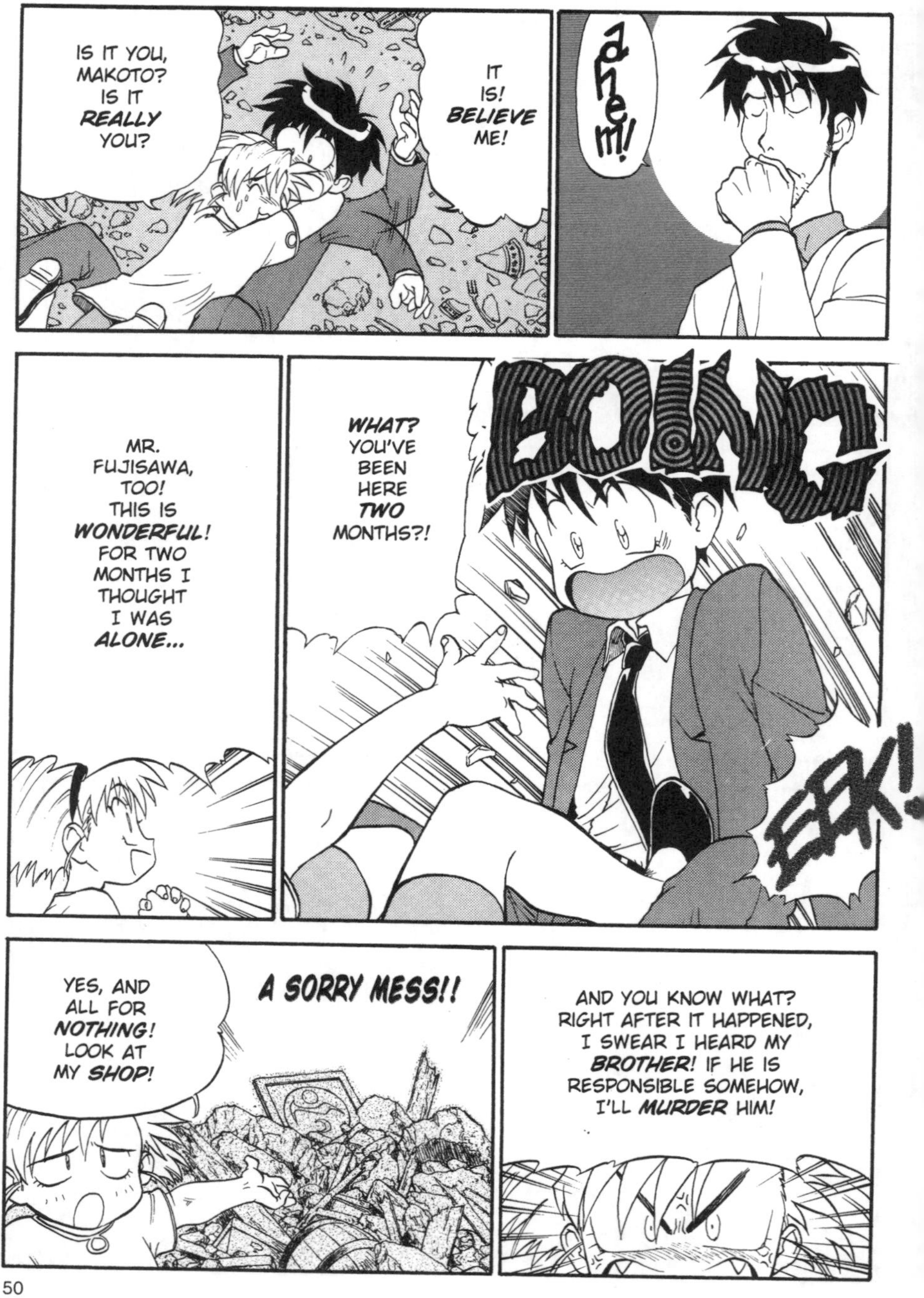
IS IT YOU, MAKOTO? IS IT REALLY YOU?
IT IS! BELIEVE ME!
ahem!
MR. FUJISAWA, TOO! THIS IS WONDERFUL! FOR TWO MONTHS I THOUGHT I WAS ALONE...
WHAT? YOU'VE BEEN HERE TWO MONTHS?!
BOING
EEK!
YES, AND ALL FOR NOTHING! LOOK AT MY SHOP!
A SORRY MESS!!
AND YOU KNOW WHAT? RIGHT AFTER IT HAPPENED, I SWEAR I HEARD MY BROTHER! IF HE IS RESPONSIBLE SOMEHOW, I'LL MURDER HIM!

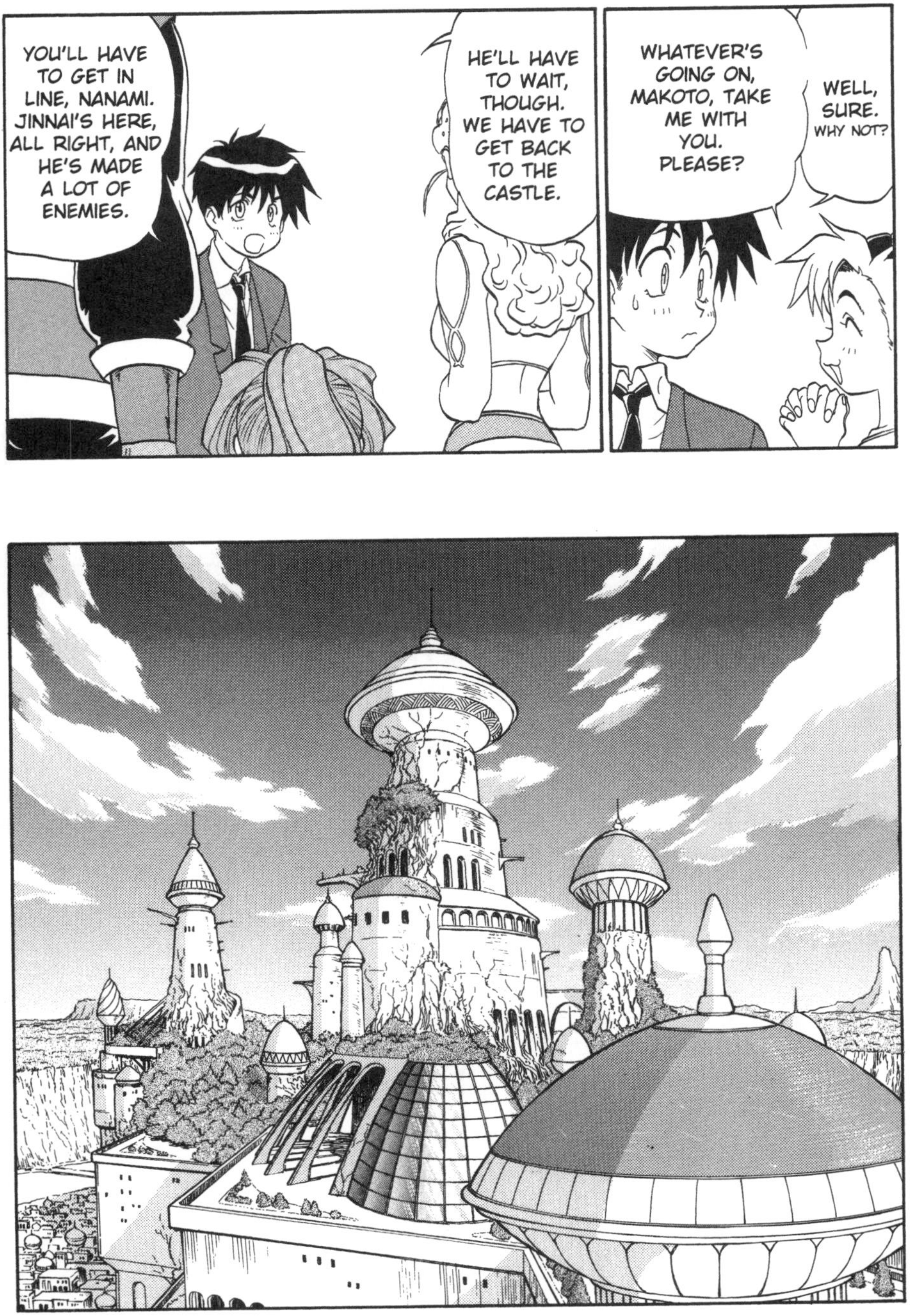
YOU'LL HAVE TO GET IN LINE, NANAMI. JINNAI'S HERE, ALL RIGHT, AND HE'S MADE A LOT OF ENEMIES.
HE'LL HAVE TO WAIT, THOUGH. WE HAVE TO GET BACK TO THE CASTLE.
WHATEVER'S GOING ON, MAKOTO, TAKE ME WITH YOU. PLEASE?
WELL, SURE. WHY NOT?

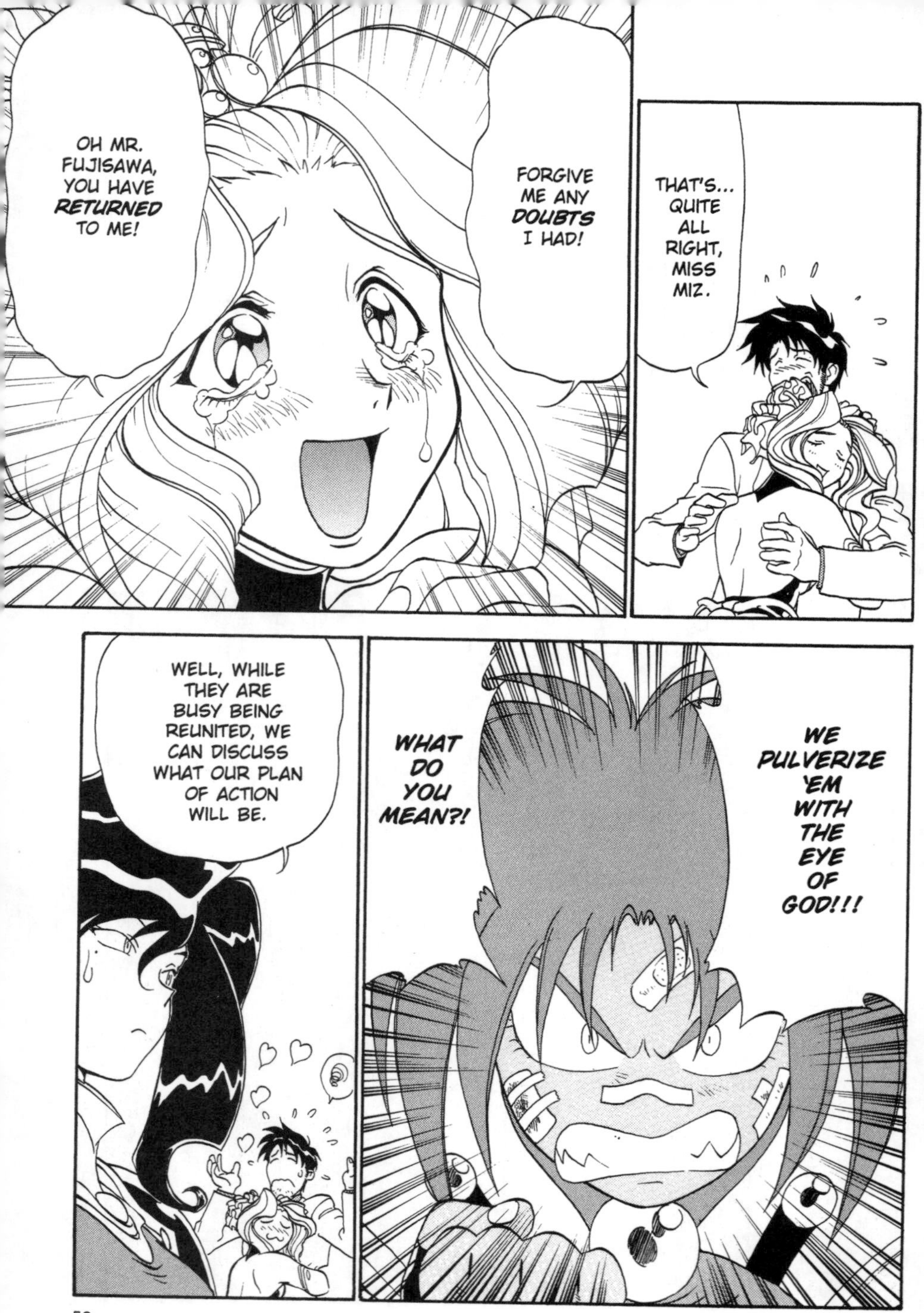
OH MR. FUJISAWA, YOU HAVE **RETURNED** TO ME!
FORGIVE ME ANY **DOUBTS** I HAD!
THAT'S... QUITE ALL RIGHT, MISS MIZ.
WELL, WHILE THEY ARE BUSY BEING REUNITED, WE CAN DISCUSS WHAT OUR PLAN OF ACTION WILL BE.
WHAT DO YOU MEAN?!
WE PULVERIZE 'EM WITH THE EYE OF GOD!!!

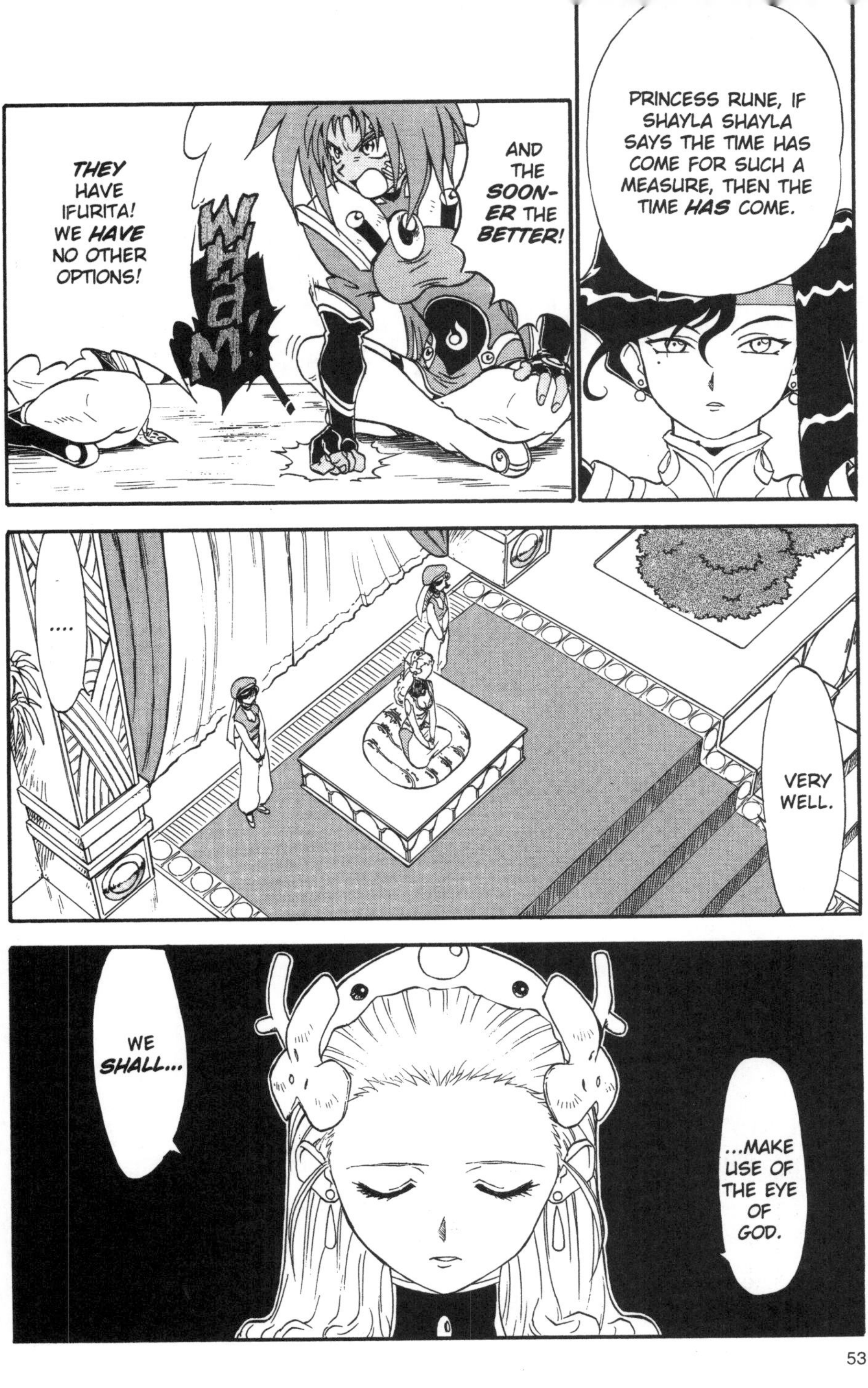
THEY HAVE IFURITA! WE HAVE NO OTHER OPTIONS!
WHAM!
AND THE SOONER THE BETTER!
PRINCESS RUNE, IF SHAYLA SHAYLA SAYS THE TIME HAS COME FOR SUCH A MEASURE, THEN THE TIME HAS COME.
....
VERY WELL.
WE SHALL...
...MAKE USE OF THE EYE OF GOD.

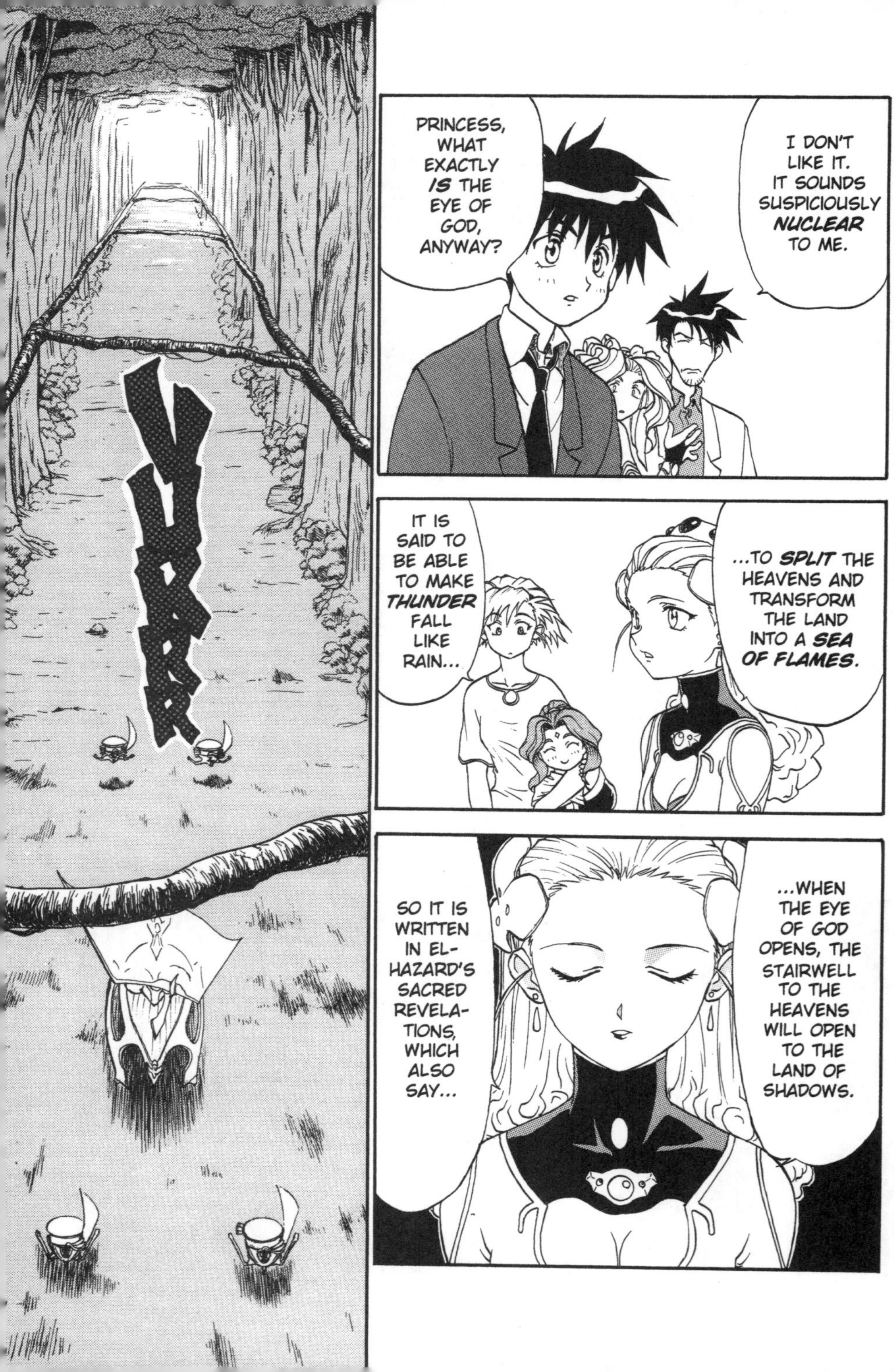
VURRR
PRINCESS, WHAT EXACTLY *IS* THE EYE OF GOD, ANYWAY?
I DON'T LIKE IT. IT SOUNDS SUSPICIOUSLY ***NUCLEAR*** TO ME.
IT IS SAID TO BE ABLE TO MAKE ***THUNDER*** FALL LIKE RAIN...
...TO ***SPLIT*** THE HEAVENS AND TRANSFORM THE LAND INTO A ***SEA OF FLAMES***.
SO IT IS WRITTEN IN EL-HAZARD'S SACRED REVELATIONS, WHICH ALSO SAY...
...WHEN THE EYE OF GOD OPENS, THE STAIRWELL TO THE HEAVENS WILL OPEN TO THE LAND OF SHADOWS.

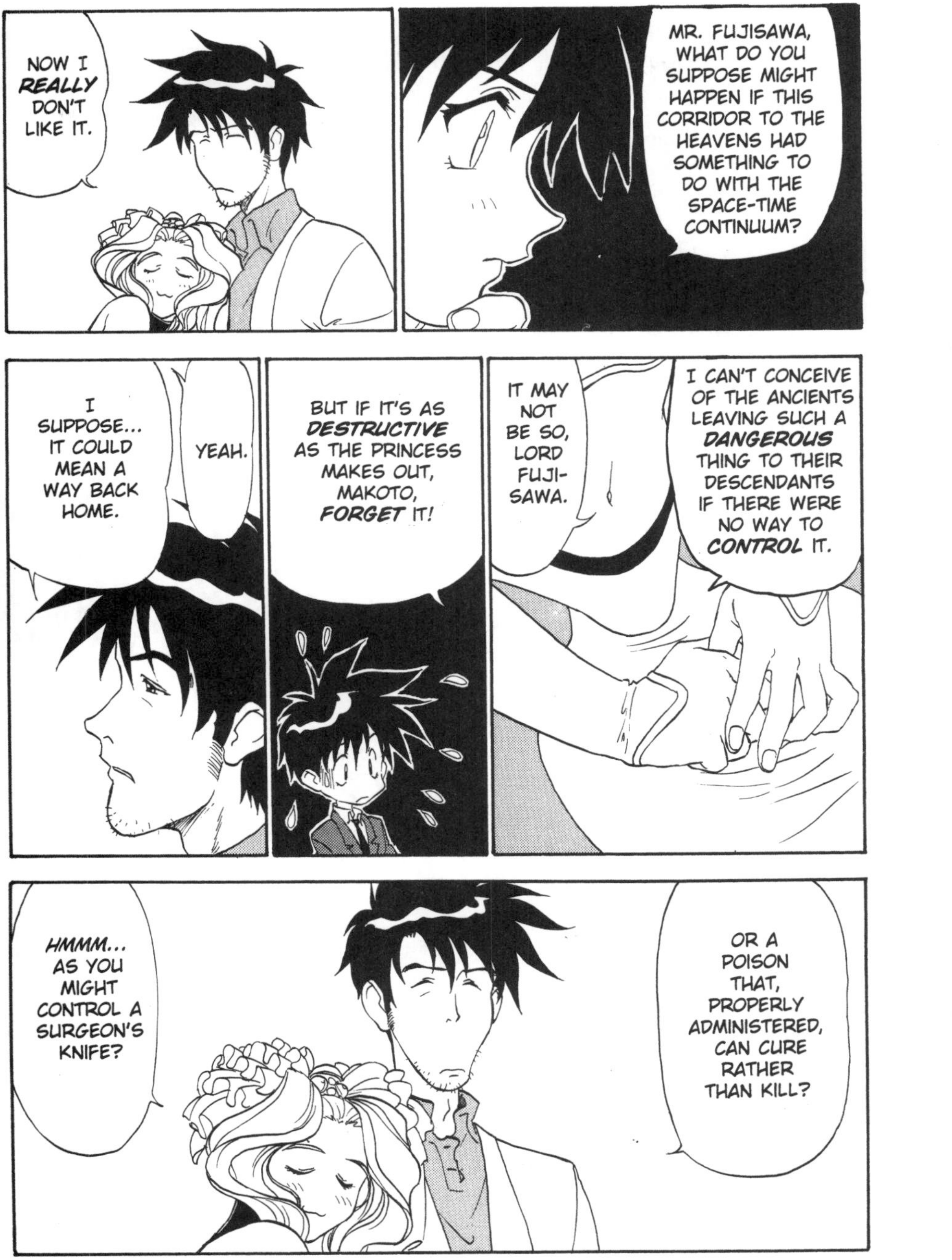
NOW I REALLY DON'T LIKE IT.
MR. FUJISAWA, WHAT DO YOU SUPPOSE MIGHT HAPPEN IF THIS CORRIDOR TO THE HEAVENS HAD SOMETHING TO DO WITH THE SPACE-TIME CONTINUUM?
I SUPPOSE... IT COULD MEAN A WAY BACK HOME.
YEAH.
BUT IF IT'S AS DESTRUCTIVE AS THE PRINCESS MAKES OUT, MAKOTO, FORGET IT!
IT MAY NOT BE SO, LORD FUJI-SAWA.
I CAN'T CONCEIVE OF THE ANCIENTS LEAVING SUCH A DANGEROUS THING TO THEIR DESCENDANTS IF THERE WERE NO WAY TO CONTROL IT.
HMMM... AS YOU MIGHT CONTROL A SURGEON'S KNIFE?
OR A POISON THAT, PROPERLY ADMINISTERED, CAN CURE RATHER THAN KILL?

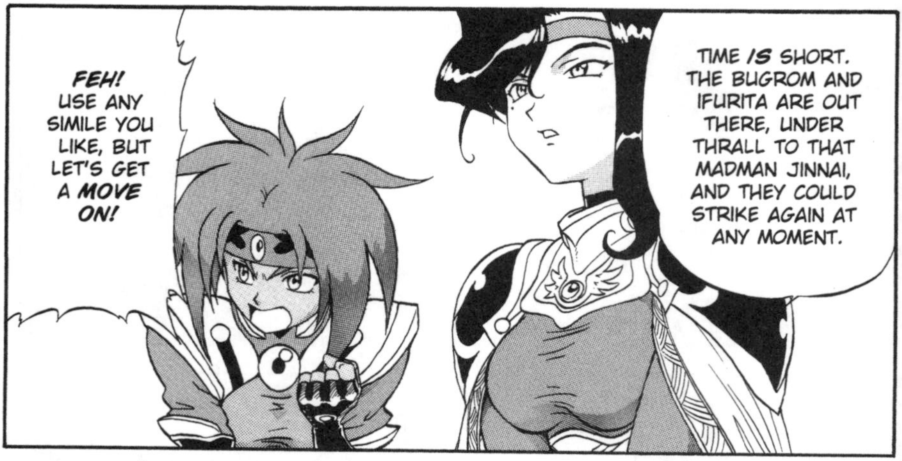
FEH! USE ANY SIMILE YOU LIKE, BUT LET'S GET A **MOVE** ON!
TIME **IS** SHORT. THE BUGROM AND IFURITA ARE OUT THERE, UNDER THRALL TO THAT MADMAN JINNAI, AND THEY COULD STRIKE AGAIN AT ANY MOMENT.
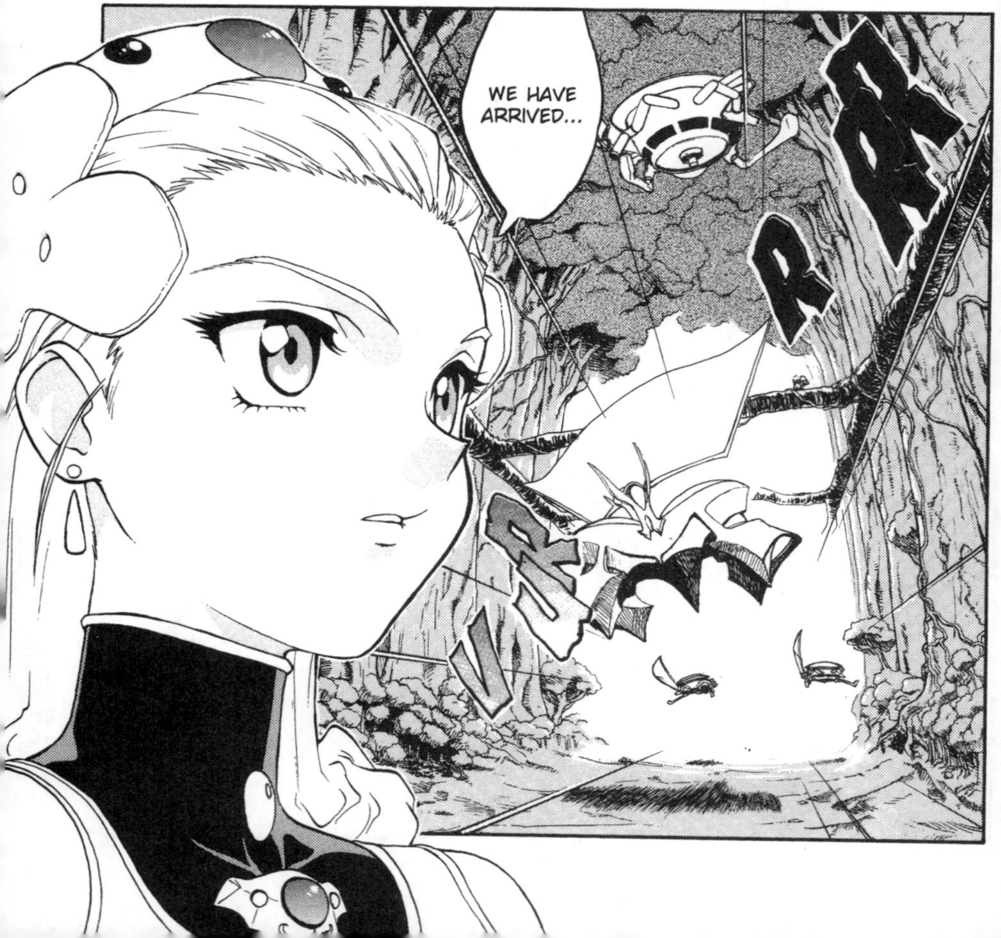
WE HAVE ARRIVED...
RRR
VRR

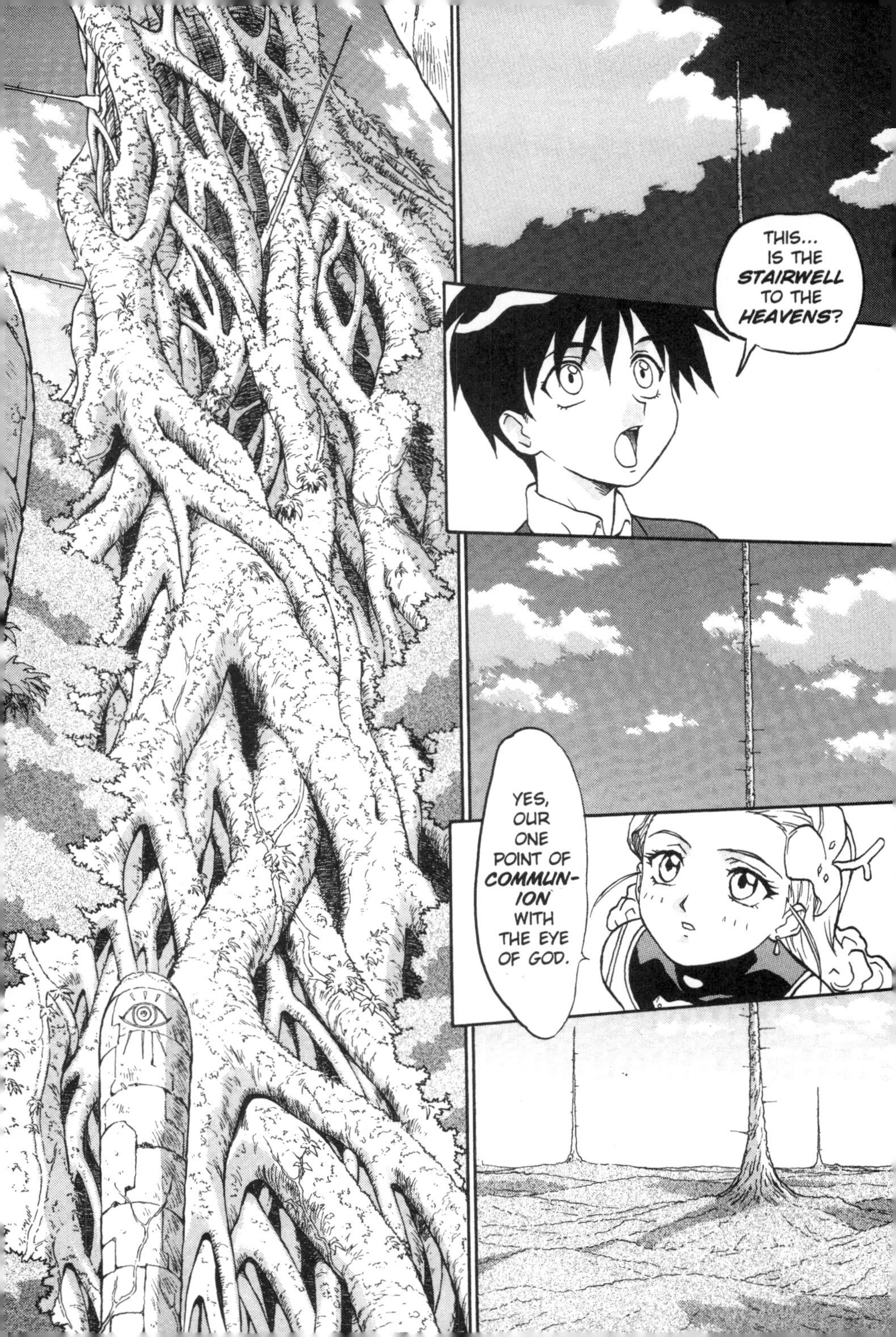
THIS... IS THE STAIRWELL TO THE HEAVENS?
YES, OUR ONE POINT OF COMMUNION WITH THE EYE OF GOD.

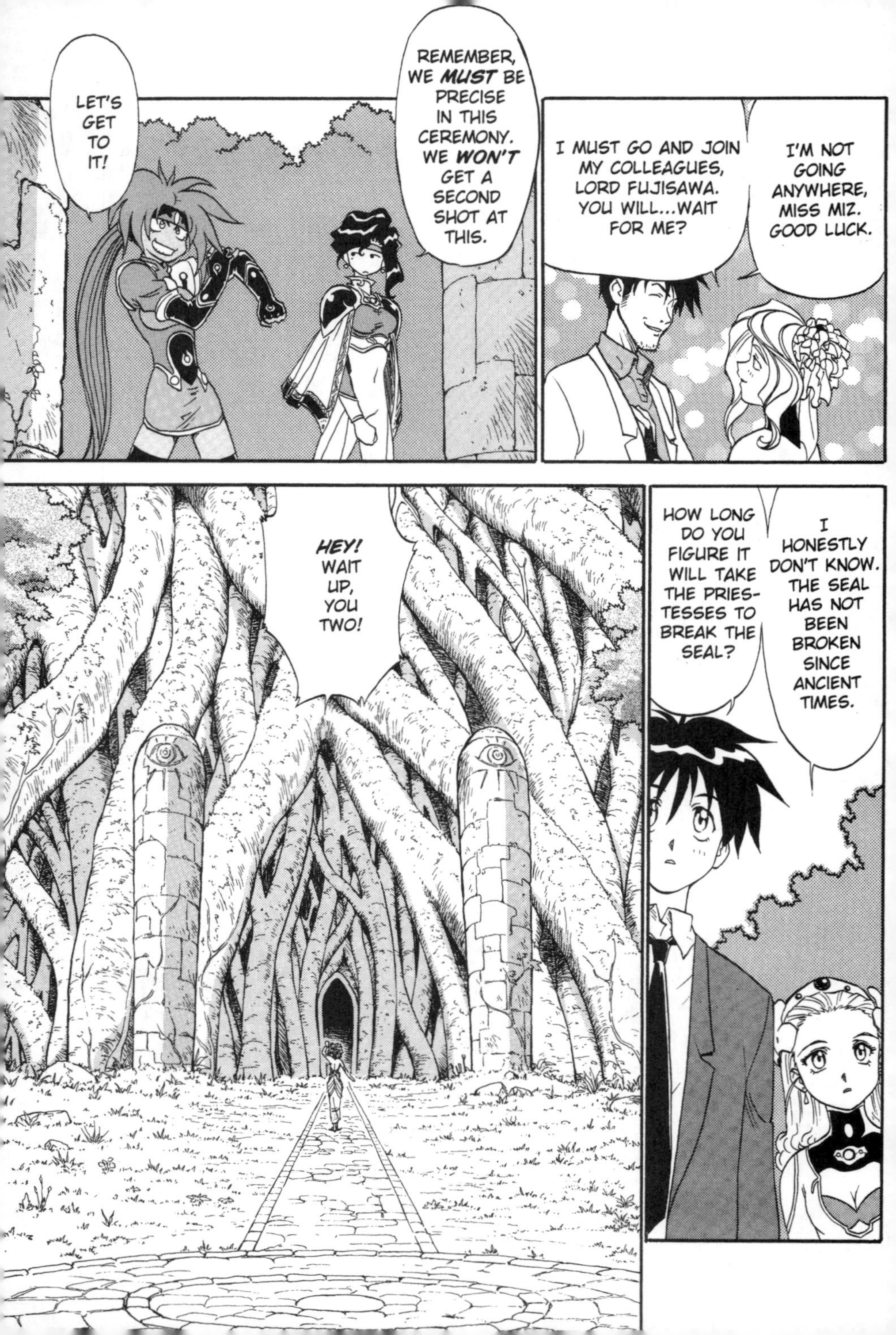
LET'S GET TO IT!
REMEMBER, WE *MUST* BE PRECISE IN THIS CEREMONY. WE *WON'T* GET A SECOND SHOT AT THIS.
I MUST GO AND JOIN MY COLLEAGUES, LORD FUJISAWA. YOU WILL...WAIT FOR ME?
I'M NOT GOING ANYWHERE, MISS MIZ. GOOD LUCK.
HEY! WAIT UP, YOU TWO!
HOW LONG DO YOU FIGURE IT WILL TAKE THE PRIES-TESSES TO BREAK THE SEAL?
I HONESTLY DON'T KNOW. THE SEAL HAS NOT BEEN BROKEN SINCE ANCIENT TIMES.

MAKOTO...

YES?

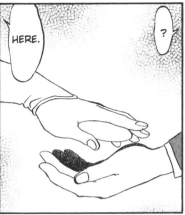

HERE.

?

WHAT'S THIS?

AN AMULET OF PROTECTION PASSED DOWN THROUGH THE ROYAL FAMILY.

IT'S A TOKEN OF MY GRATITUDE... FOR ALL YOU'VE DONE.

PRINCESS, I DON'T KNOW... WHAT TO SAY...

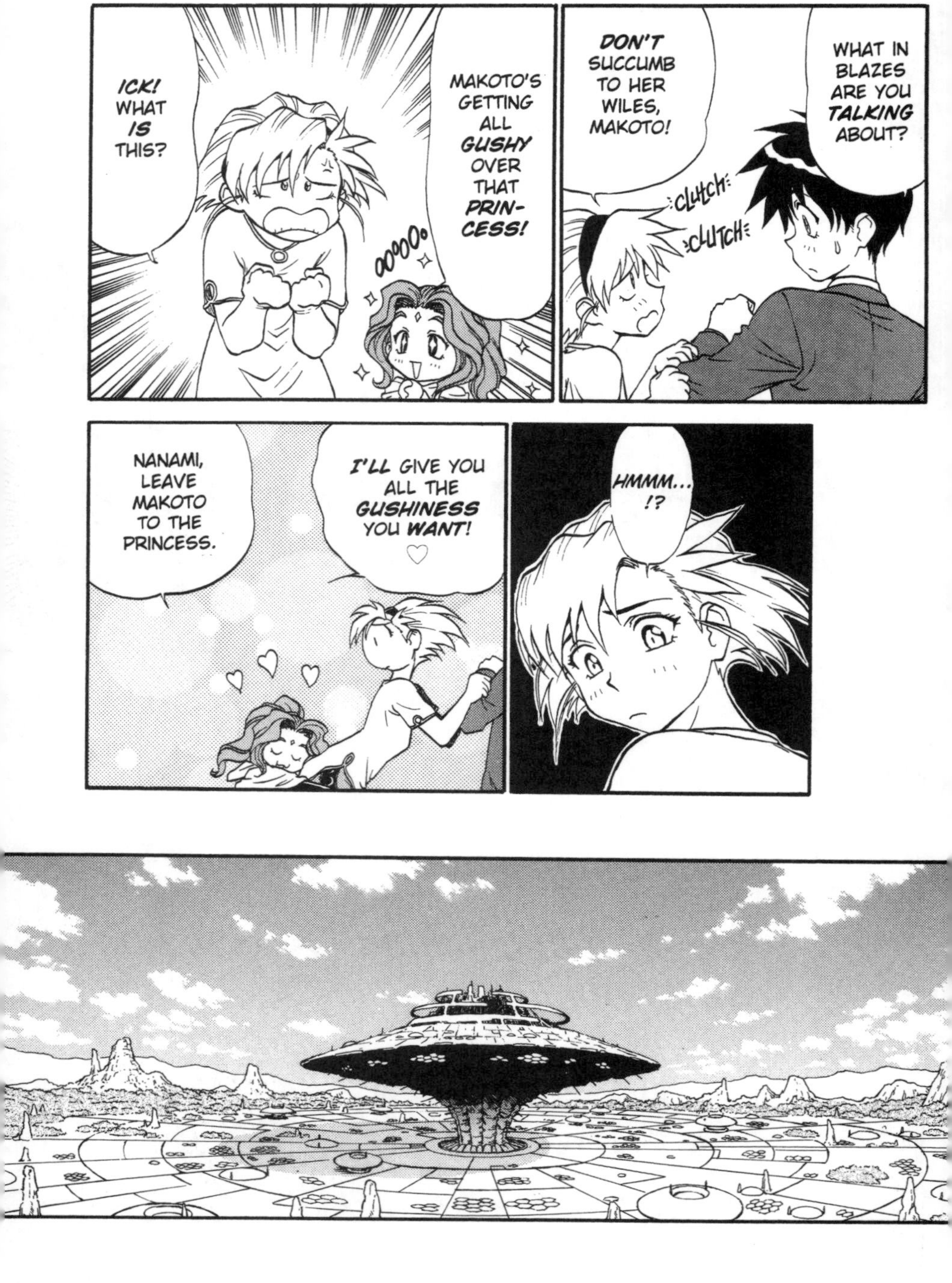
ICK! WHAT IS THIS?
MAKOTO'S GETTING ALL GUSHY OVER THAT PRIN-CESS!
OOOOOO
DON'T SUCCUMB TO HER WILES, MAKOTO!
WHAT IN BLAZES ARE YOU TALKING ABOUT?
CLUTCH
CLUTCH
NANAMI, LEAVE MAKOTO TO THE PRINCESS.
I'LL GIVE YOU ALL THE GUSHINESS YOU WANT! ♡
HMMM... !?

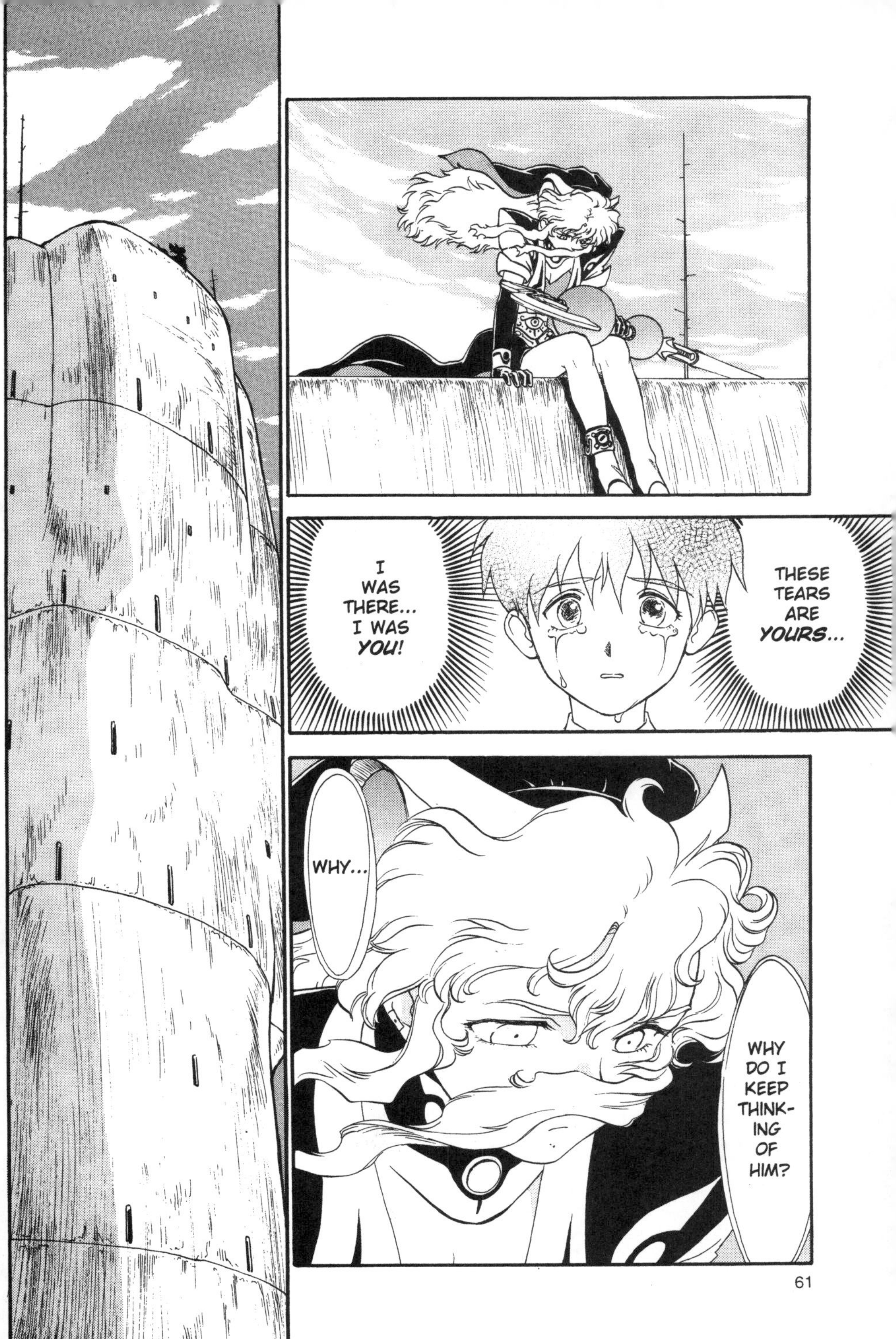
I WAS THERE... I WAS *YOU*!
THESE TEARS ARE *YOURS*...
WHY...
WHY DO I KEEP THINKING OF HIM?

BECAUSE I COULD NOT CONFIRM HIS DEATH.

NO!

I **HAD** THE OPPORTUNITY, BUT DID NOT END HIS LIFE...

WHY DIDN'T I DO IT?

WHY DIDN'T I?

WHY...?

BECAUSE HE TOUCHED MY MEMORY?

NO...!

HIS EYES...

THOSE EYES...

...RE-VEALED NEITHER TERROR NOR FEAR...

...NO PITY... NO HATRED...

HIS EYES REVEALED TO ME... ANGER AND INFINITE SADNESS WRAPPED AROUND YET ANOTHER EMOTION...

I FEARED HIS EYES AND THAT UNNAMED EMOTION...

I COULD NOT KILL... HIM

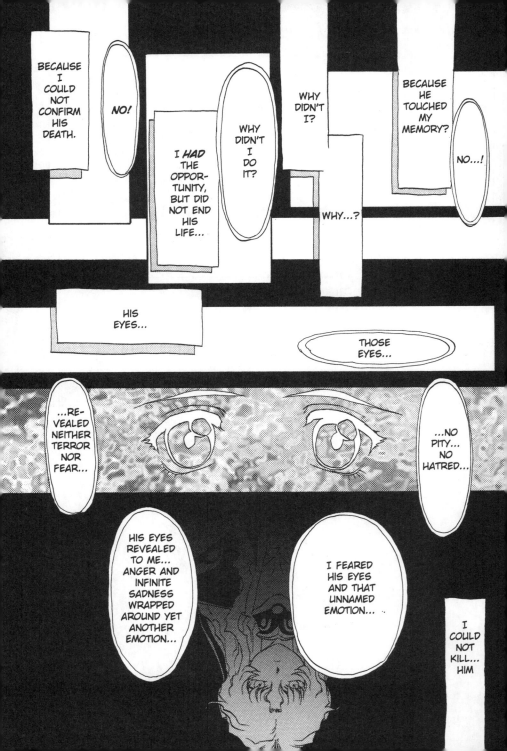

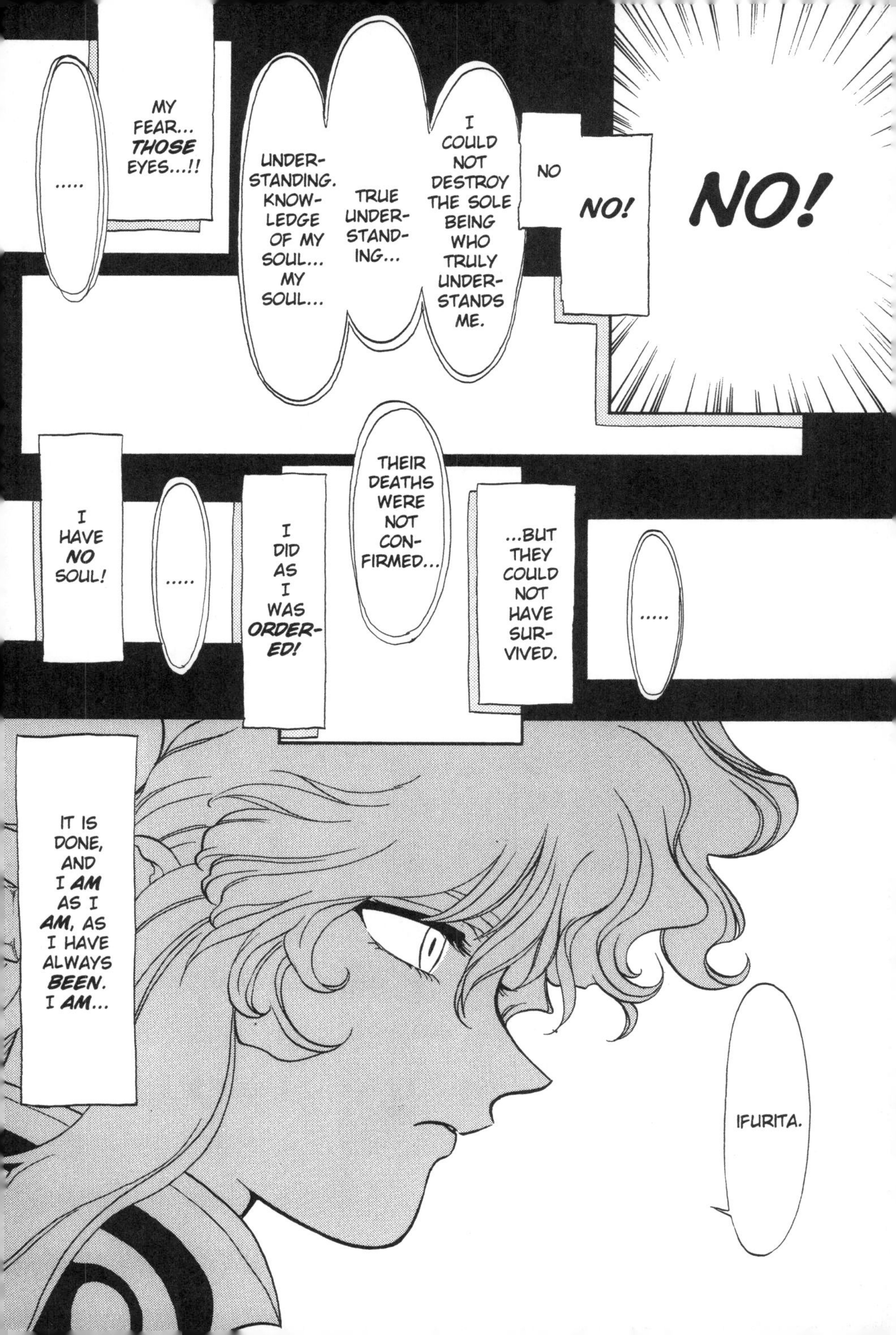
.....
MY FEAR... *THOSE* EYES...!!
UNDER-STANDING. KNOW-LEDGE OF MY SOUL... MY SOUL...
TRUE UNDER-STAND-ING...
I COULD NOT DESTROY THE SOLE BEING WHO TRULY UNDER-STANDS ME.
NO
NO!
NO!
I HAVE *NO* SOUL!
.....
I DID AS I WAS *ORDER-ED!*
THEIR DEATHS WERE NOT CON-FIRMED...
...BUT THEY COULD NOT HAVE SUR-VIVED.
.....
IT IS DONE, AND I *AM* AS I *AM*, AS I HAVE ALWAYS *BEEN*. I *AM*...
IFURITA.

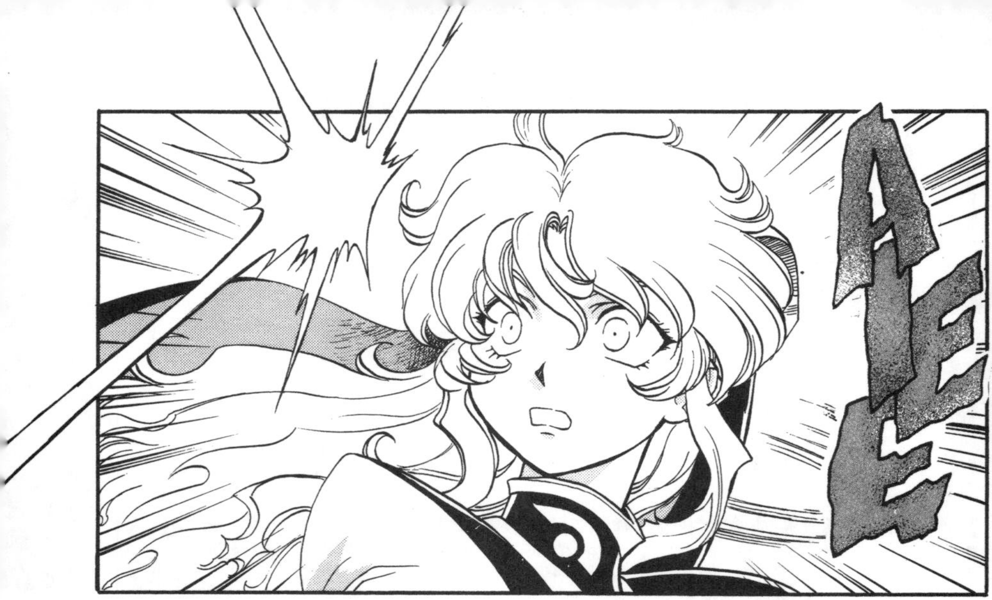
AEEE

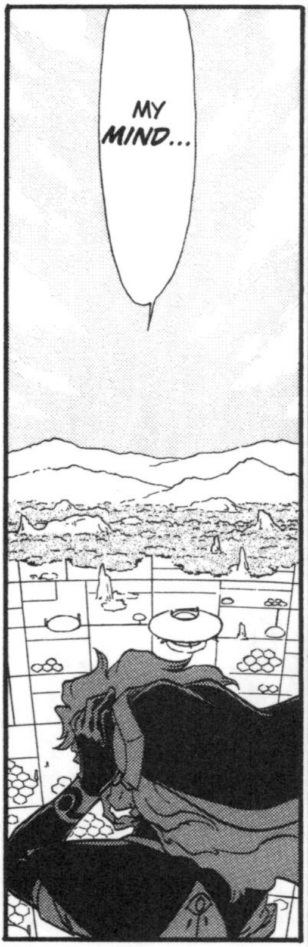
MY *MIND*...

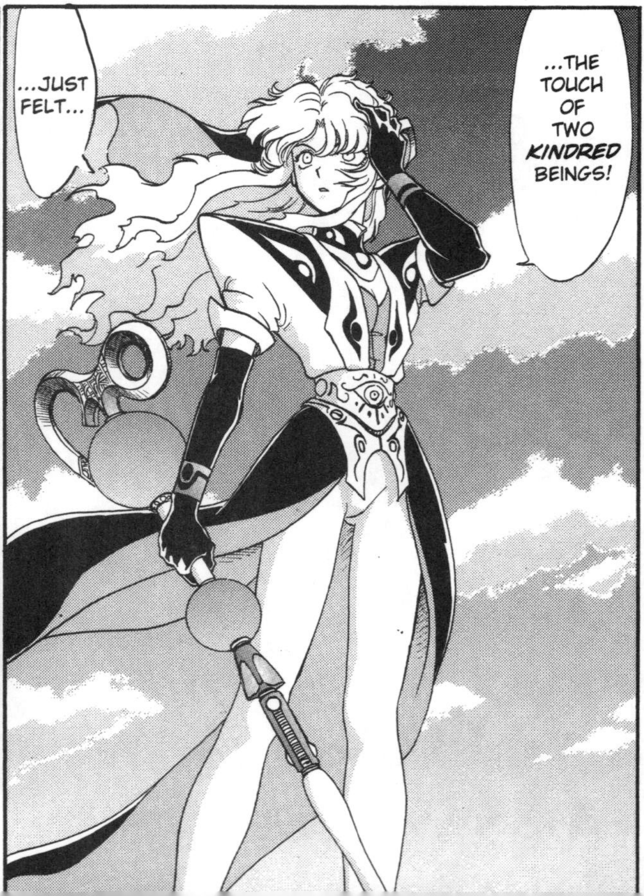
...JUST FELT...
...THE TOUCH OF TWO *KINDRED* BEINGS!

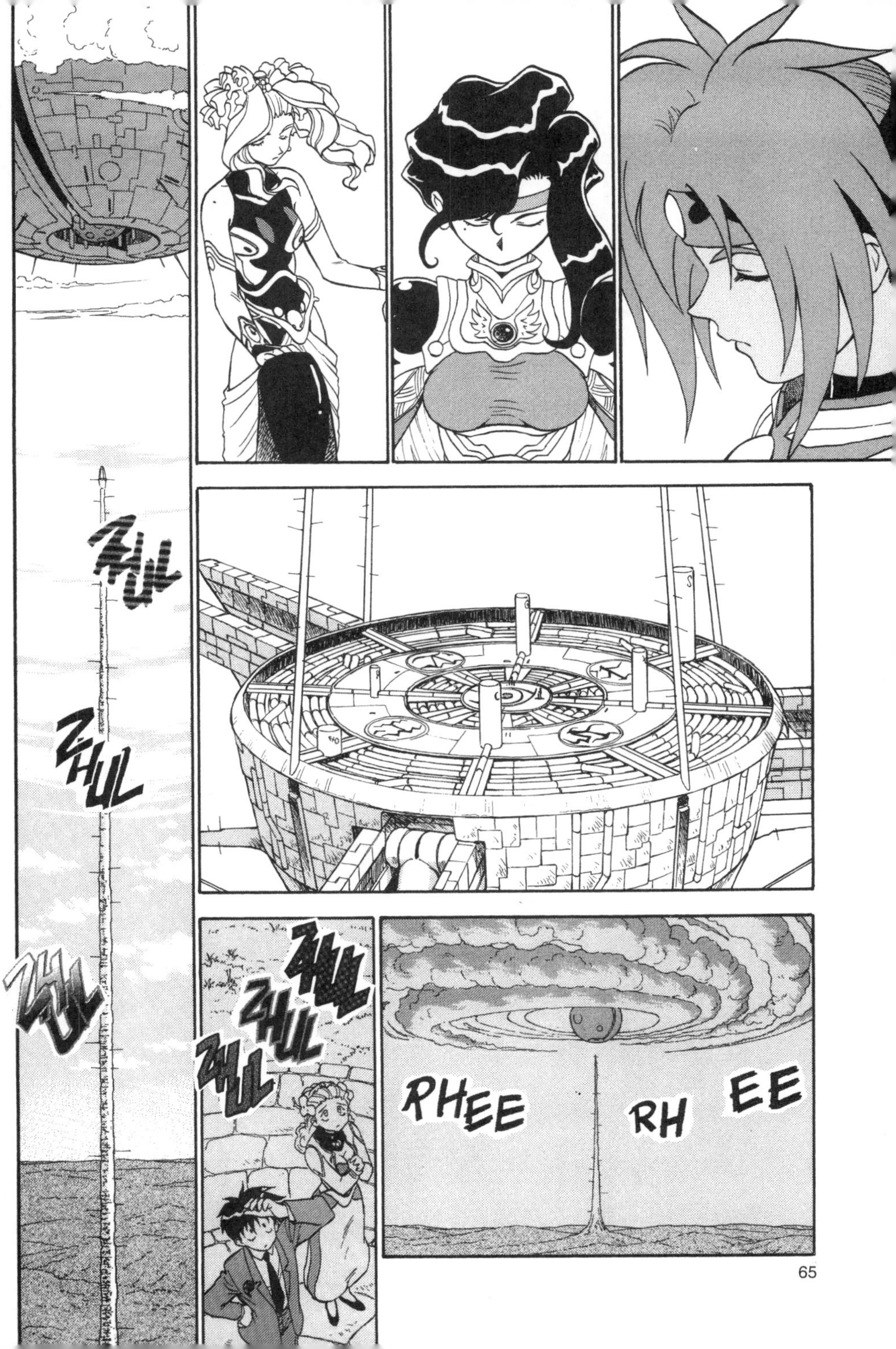
ZHUL
ZHUL
ZHUL
ZHUL
ZHUL
ZHUL
RHEE
RH
EE

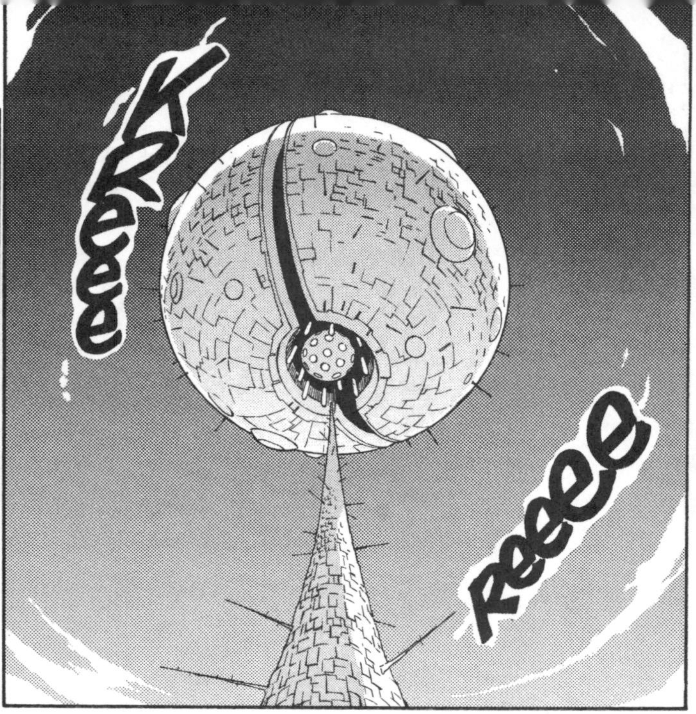
KREEEE
REEEE
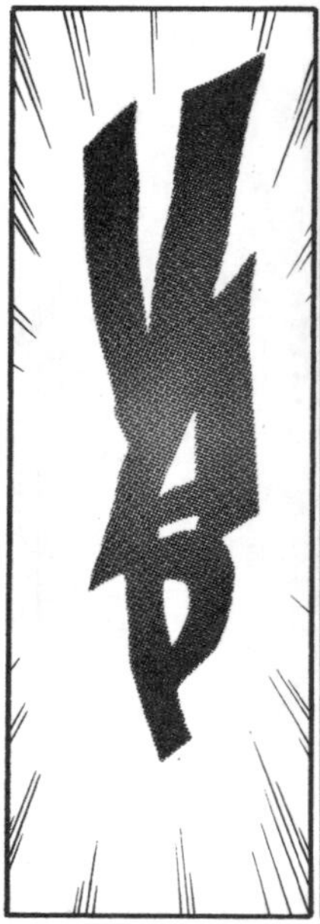
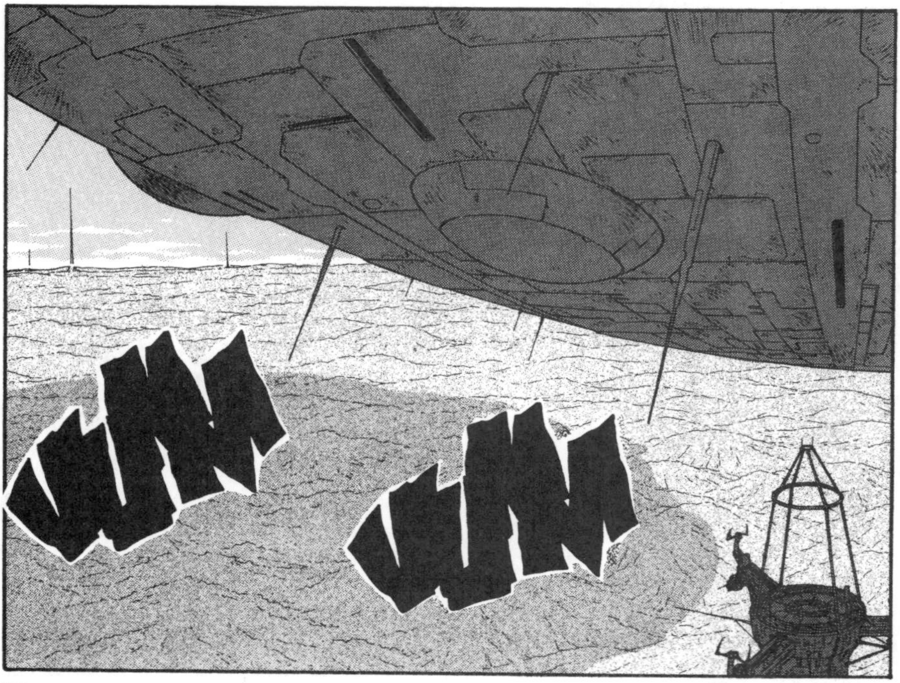
VUM
VUM

WELL...

IT IS DONE.

SO, OLD TIMER, SENILITY DID NOT PREVENT YOU FROM REMEMBER-ING THE CEREMONY.

NEITHER DID JUVENILE INEXPERIENCE CAUSE YOU TO MAKE A BLUNDERING MISTAKE!

REGARD-LESS... IT'S *DONE!*

KABOOM

!!

IFURITA? ALREADY?

MY GOD! IFURITA'S *ATTACKING* THE *CITY CENTER!*

ON *JINNAI'S* ORDER, NO DOUBT!

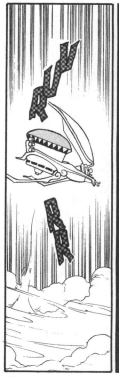

I CAN'T LET HER DO IT!

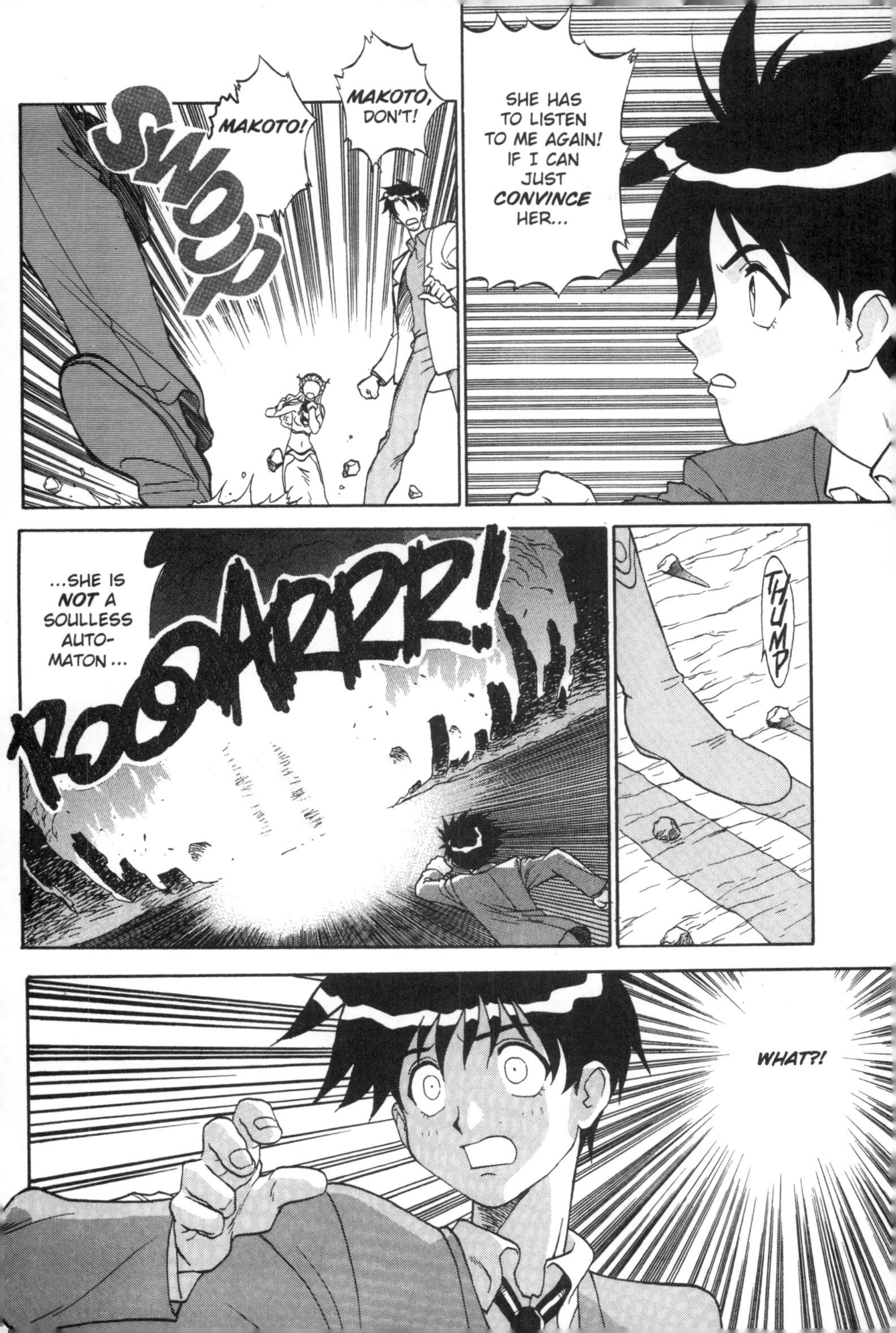
SWOOP
MAKOTO!
MAKOTO, DON'T!
SHE HAS TO LISTEN TO ME AGAIN! IF I CAN JUST CONVINCE HER...
...SHE IS NOT A SOULLESS AUTO-MATON...
ROOOARRR!
THUMP
WHAT?!

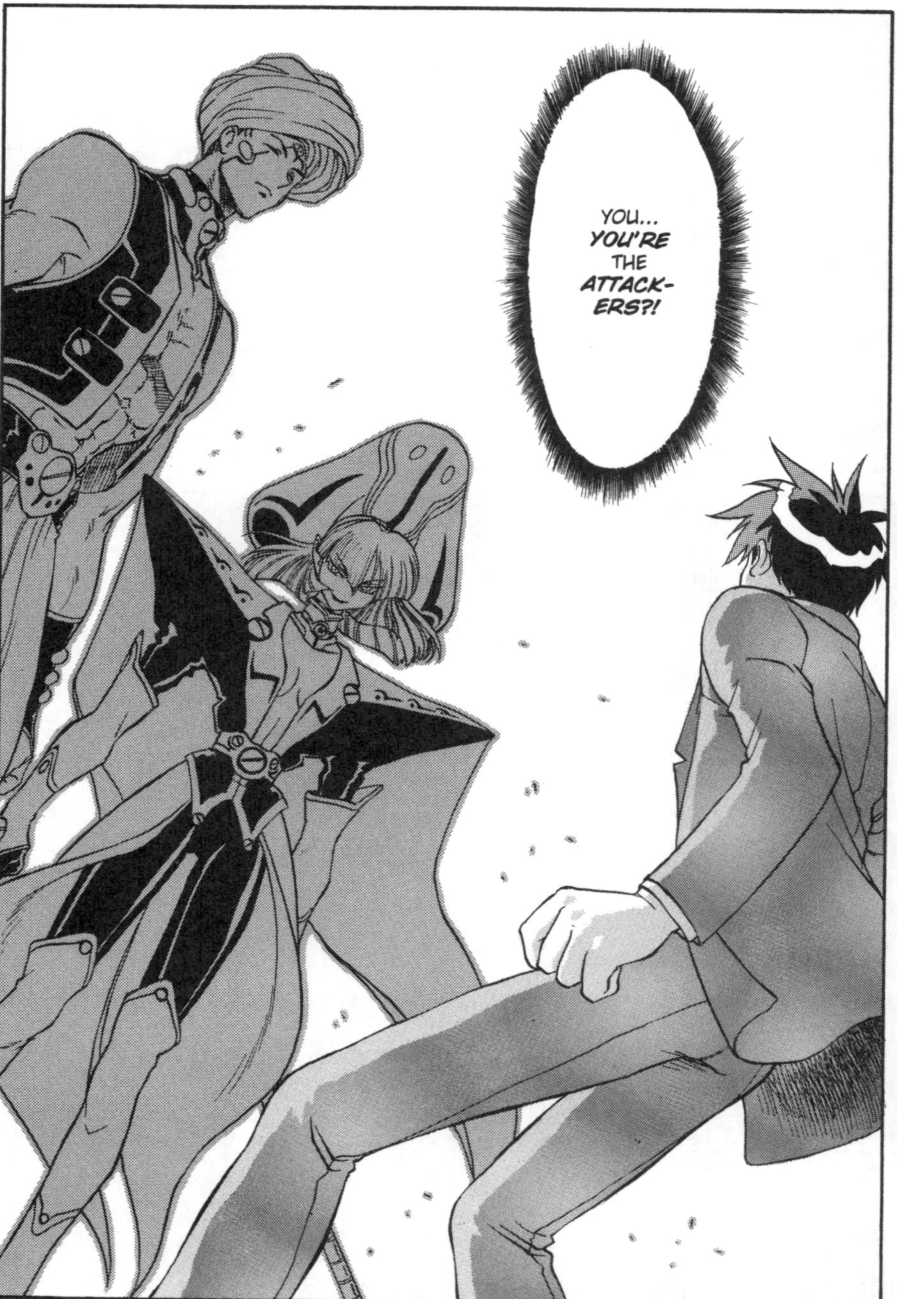
YOU... YOU'RE THE ATTACKERS?!

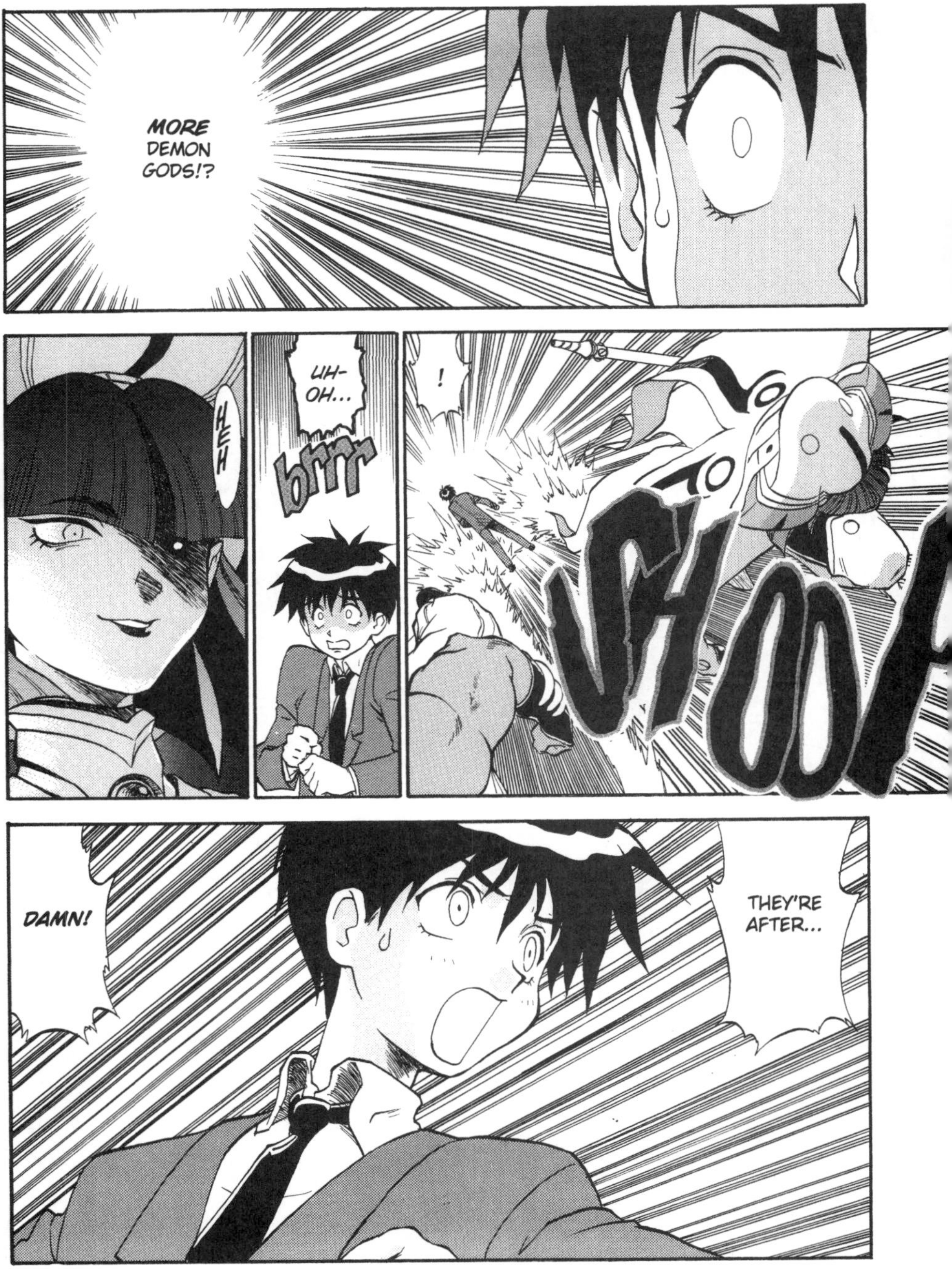
MORE DEMON GODS!?
HEH
UH-OH...
brrr
!
DAMN!
THEY'RE AFTER...

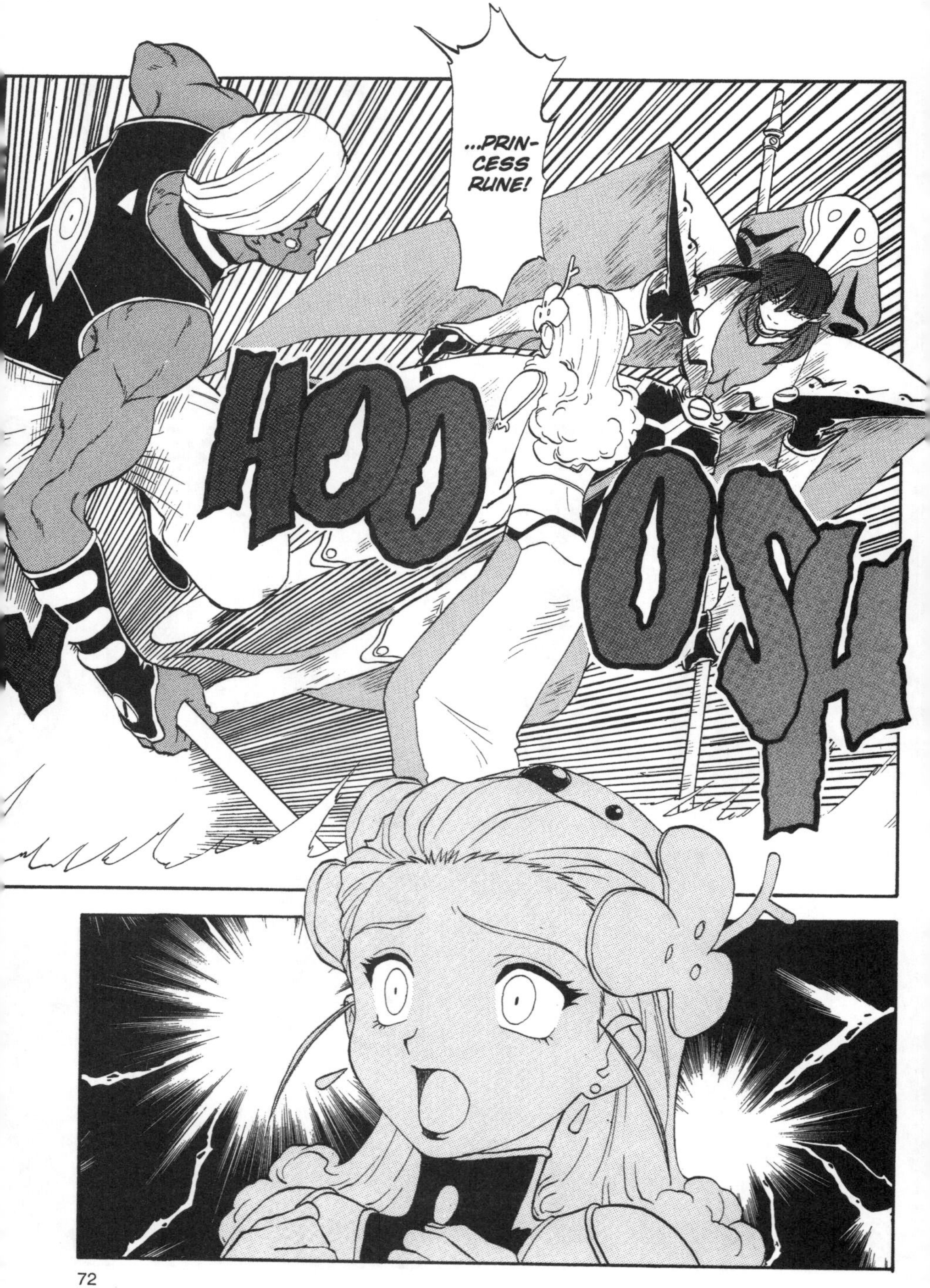
...PRIN-CESS RUNE!
HOOOSH

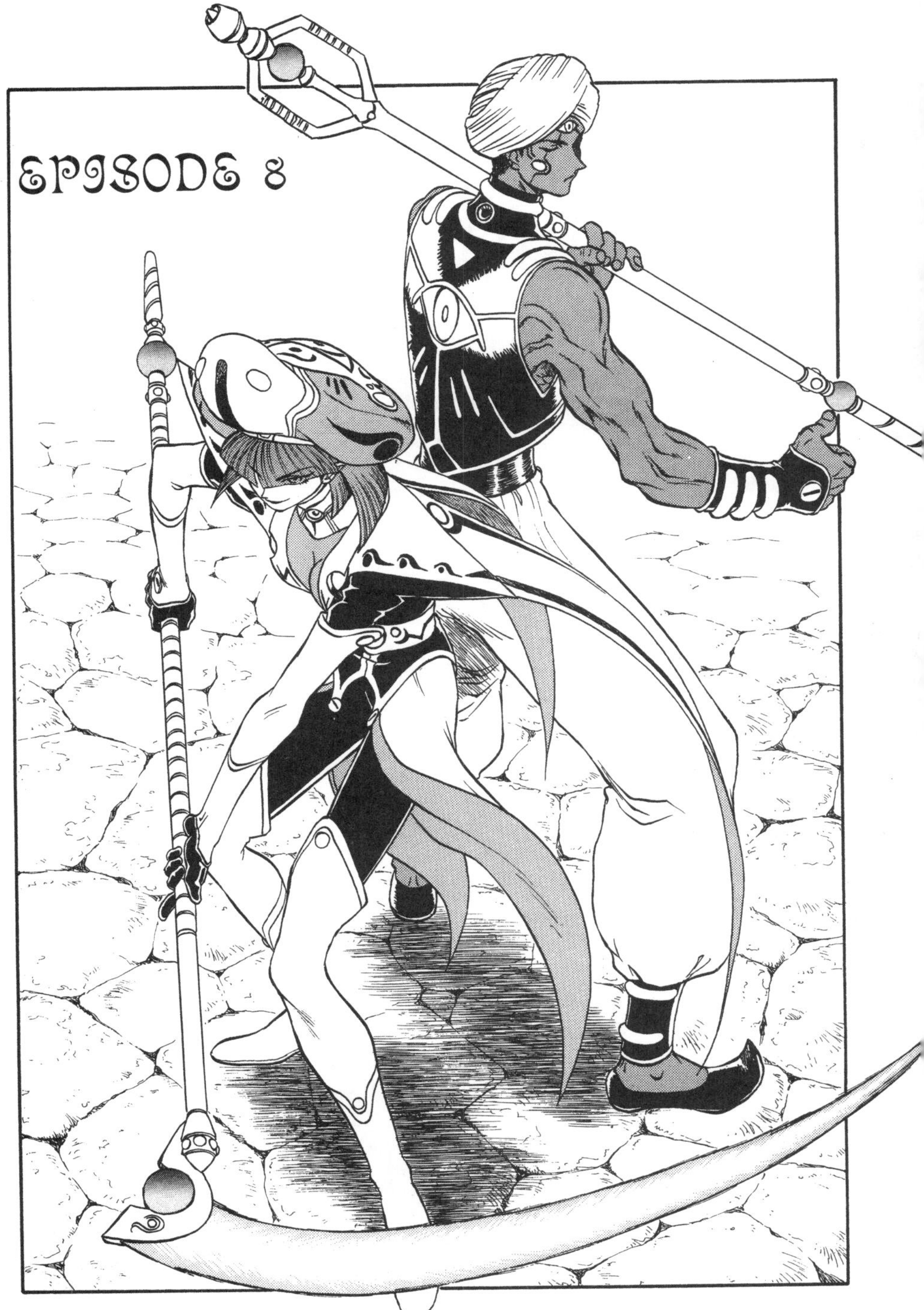
EPISODE 8

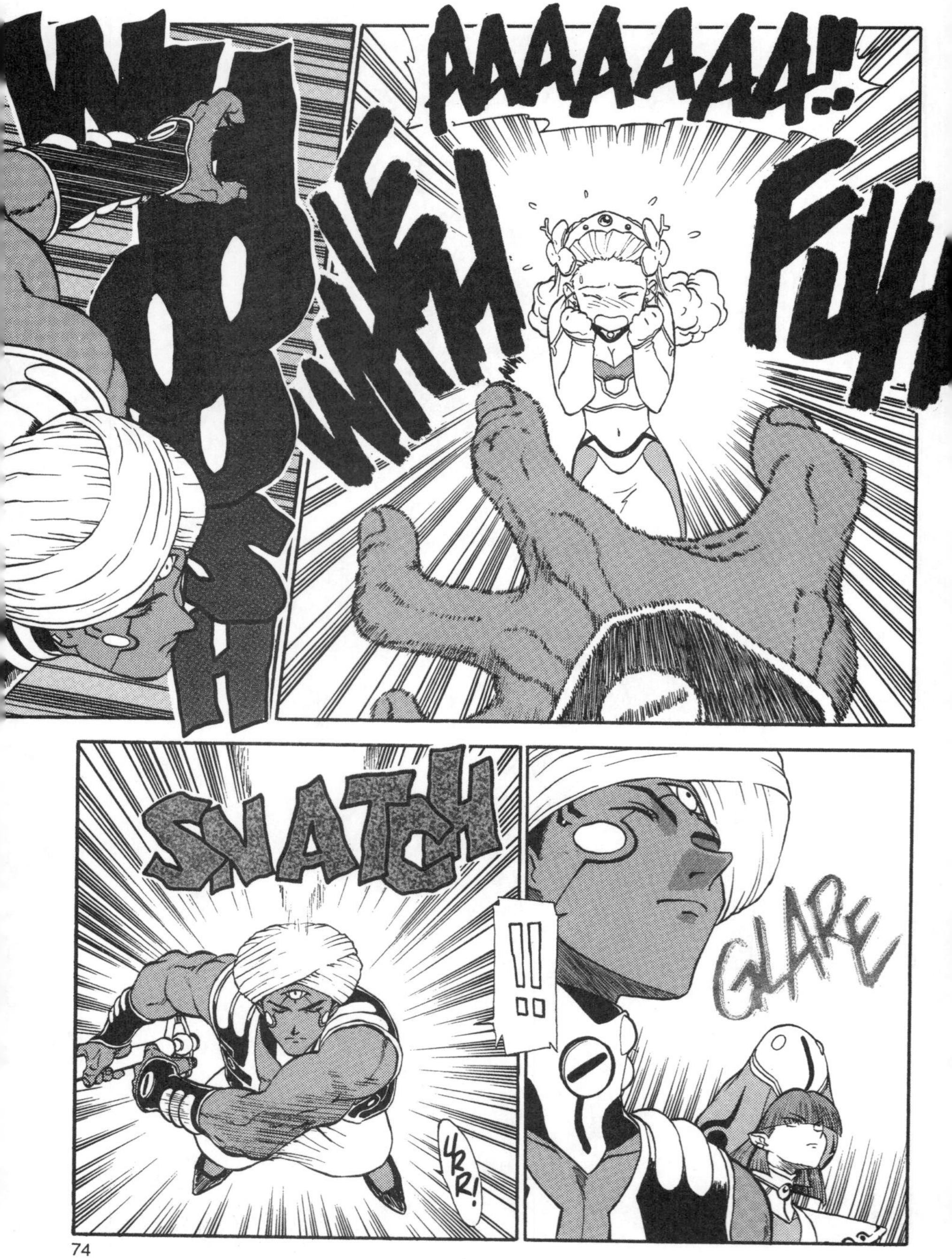
AAAAAAA!!
SNATCH
URR!
!!
GLARE

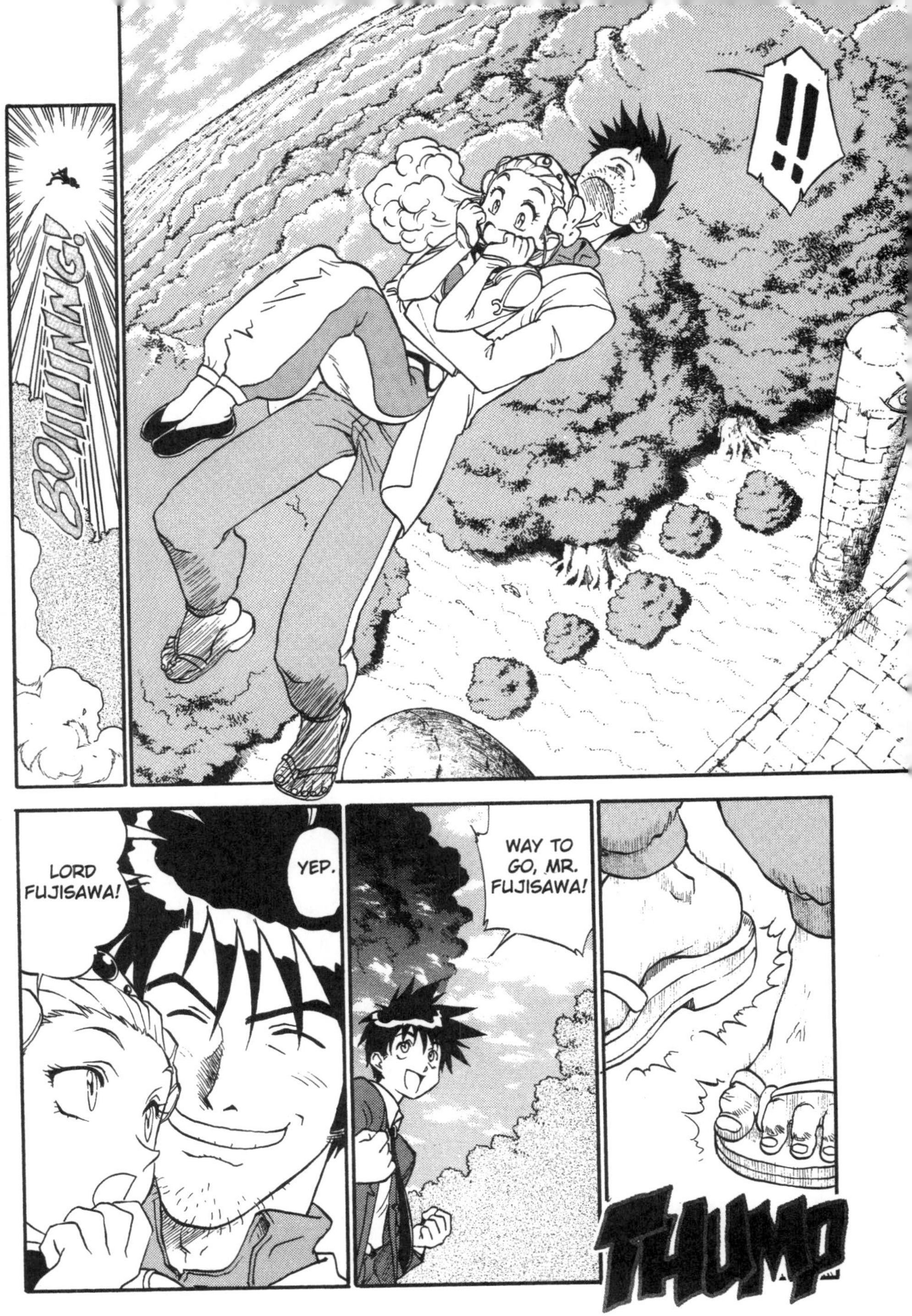
BOIIIIING!
!!
LORD FUJISAWA!
YEP.
WAY TO GO, MR. FUJISAWA!
THUMP

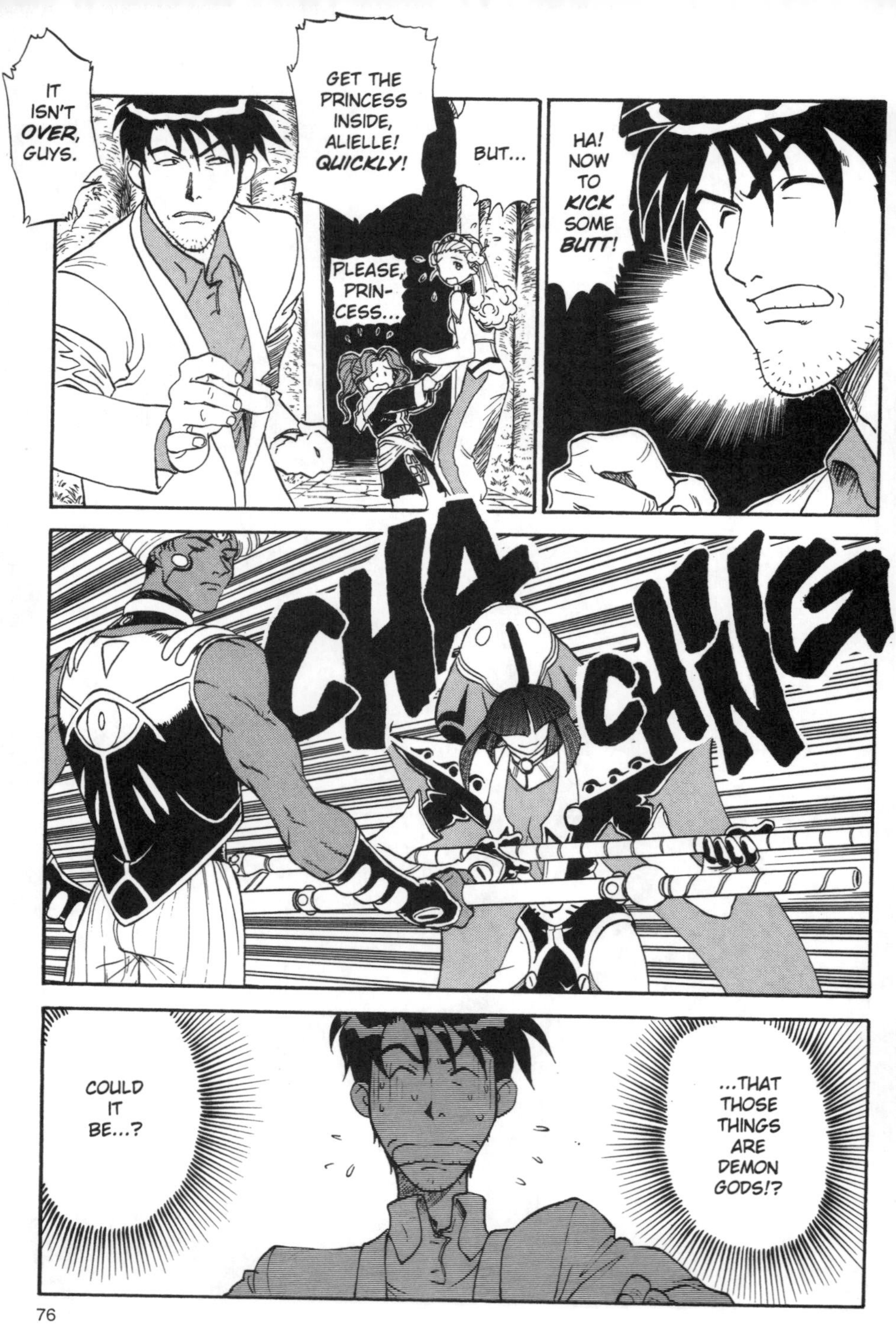
IT ISN'T OVER, GUYS.
GET THE PRINCESS INSIDE, ALIELLE! QUICKLY!
BUT...
PLEASE, PRIN-CESS...
HA! NOW TO KICK SOME BUTT!
CHA CHING
COULD IT BE...?
...THAT THOSE THINGS ARE DEMON GODS!?

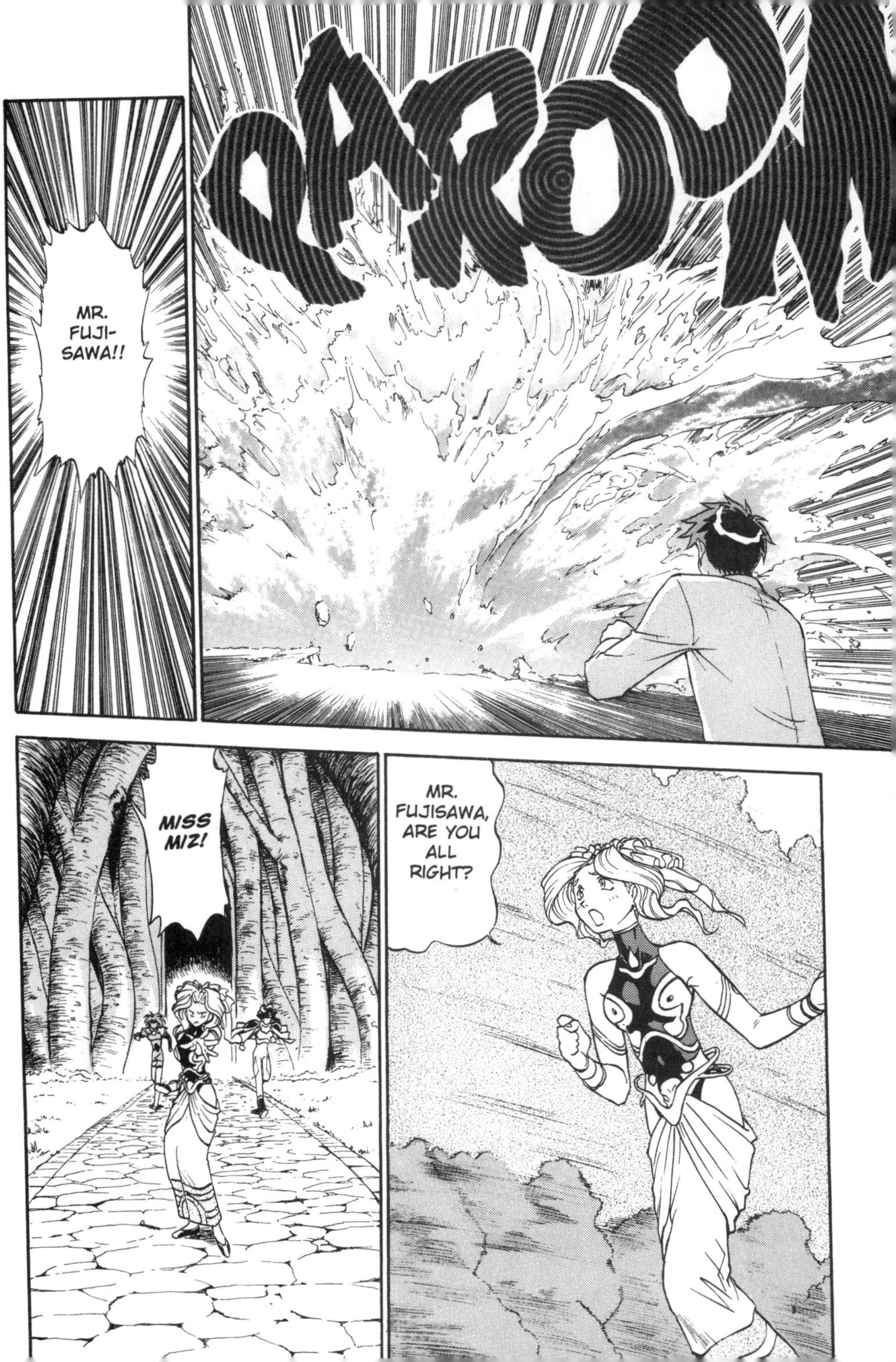
MR. FUJI-SAWA!!
MISS MIZ!
MR. FUJISAWA, ARE YOU ALL RIGHT?

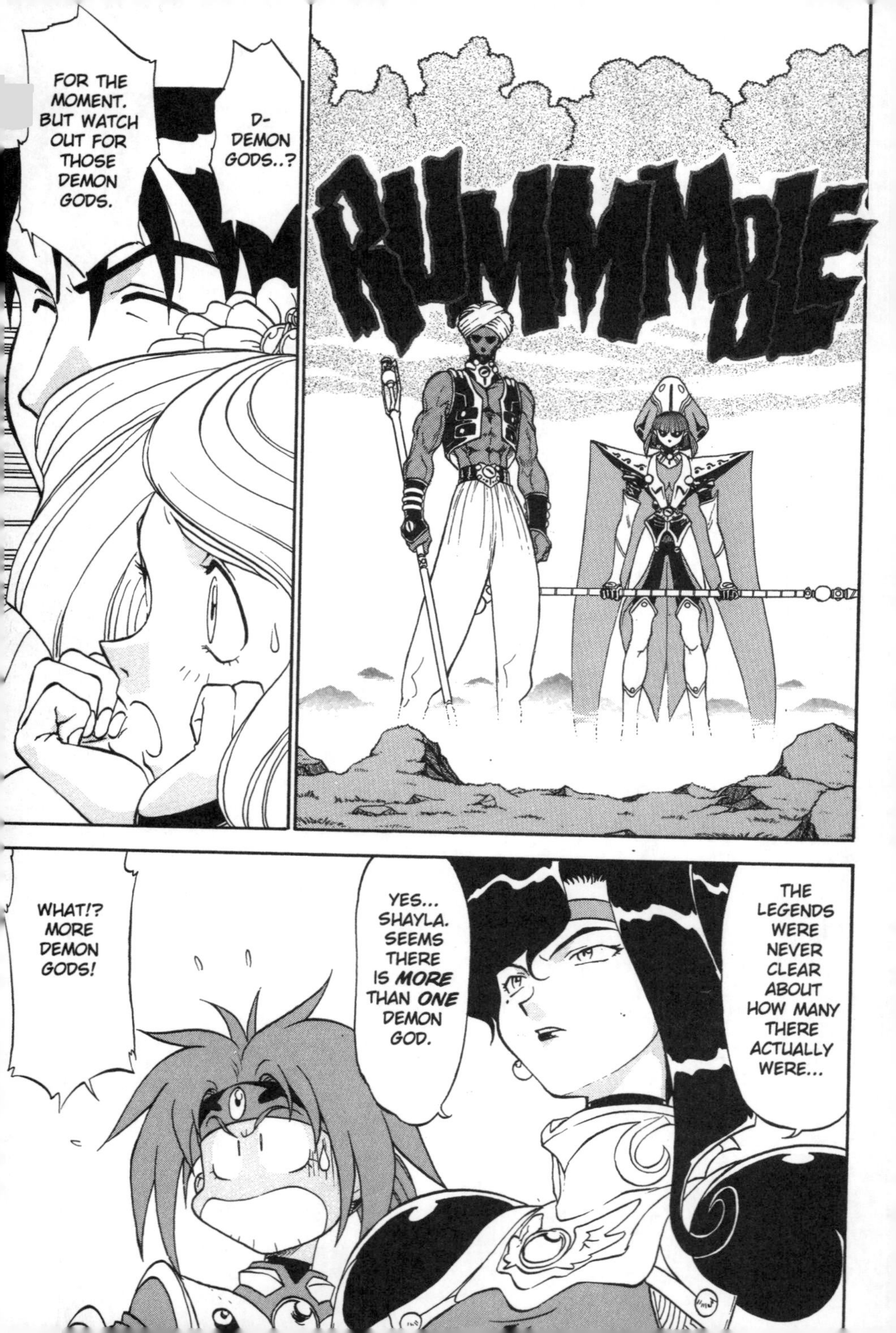
FOR THE MOMENT. BUT WATCH OUT FOR THOSE DEMON GODS.
D-DEMON GODS..?
RUMMMMBLE
WHAT!? MORE DEMON GODS!
YES... SHAYLA. SEEMS THERE IS ***MORE*** THAN ***ONE*** DEMON GOD.
THE LEGENDS WERE NEVER CLEAR ABOUT HOW MANY THERE ACTUALLY WERE...

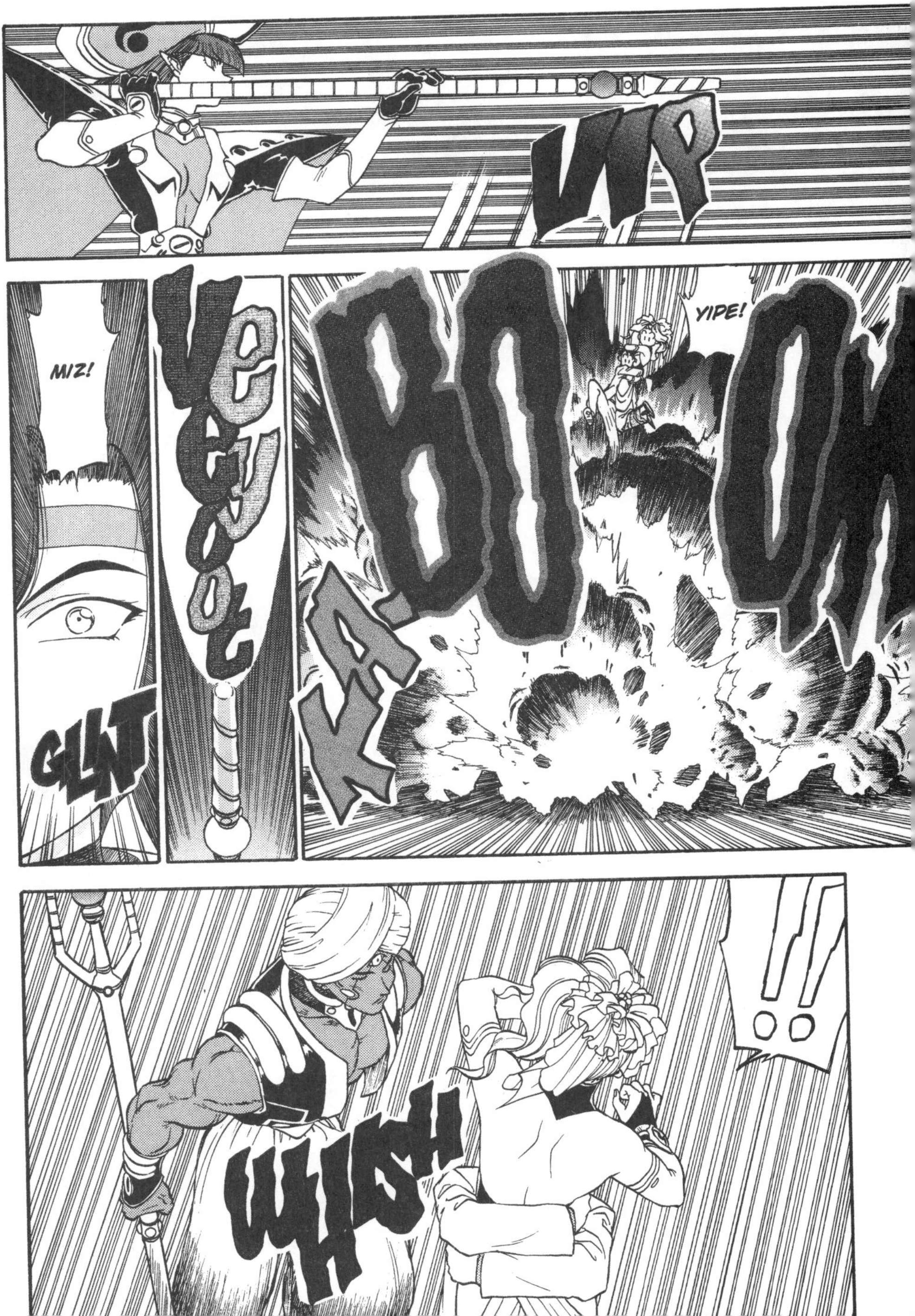
VIP
MIZ!
GLINT
KA BOO
YIPE!
WHISH
!!

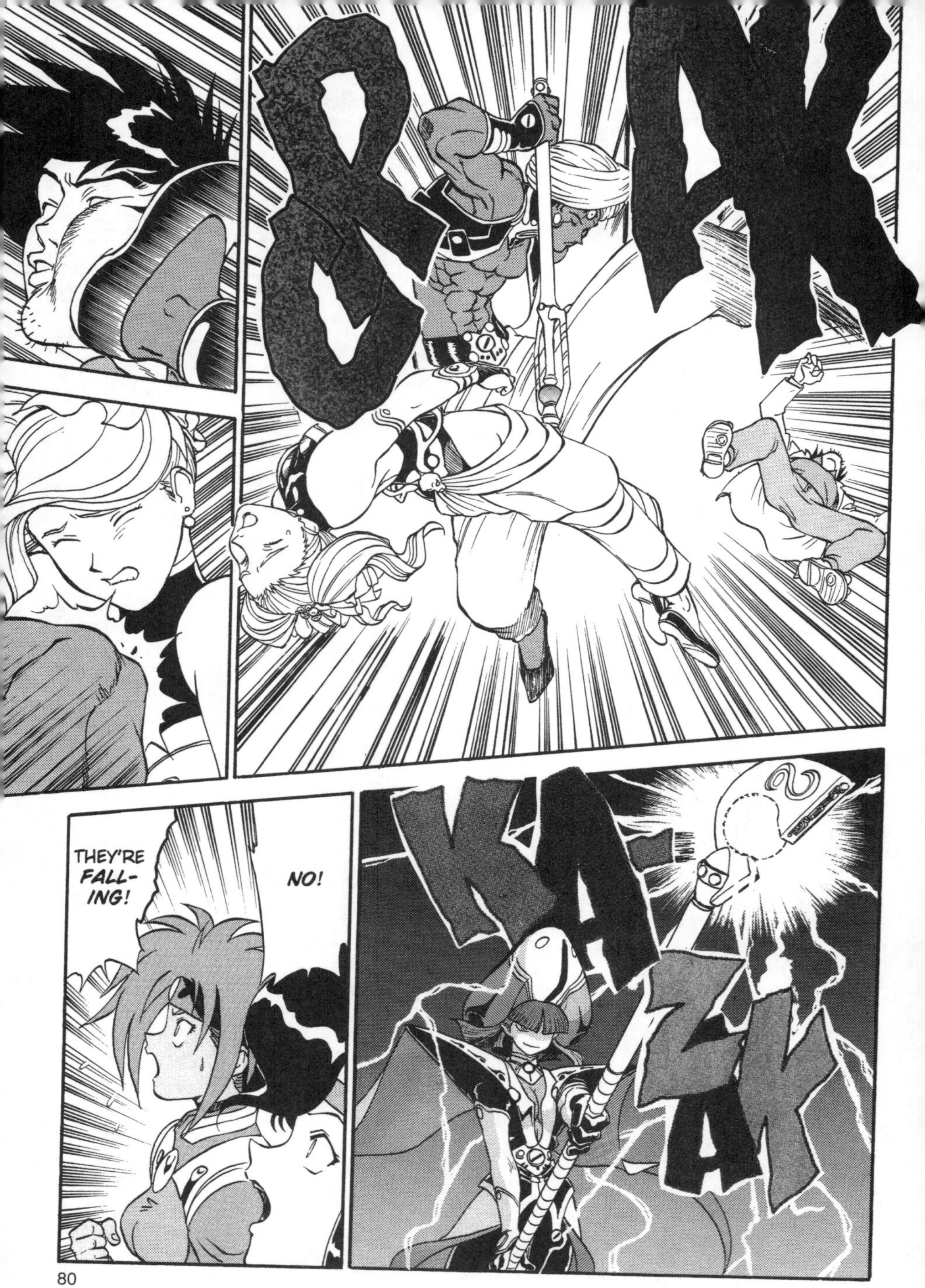
THEY'RE *FALL-ING!*
NO!

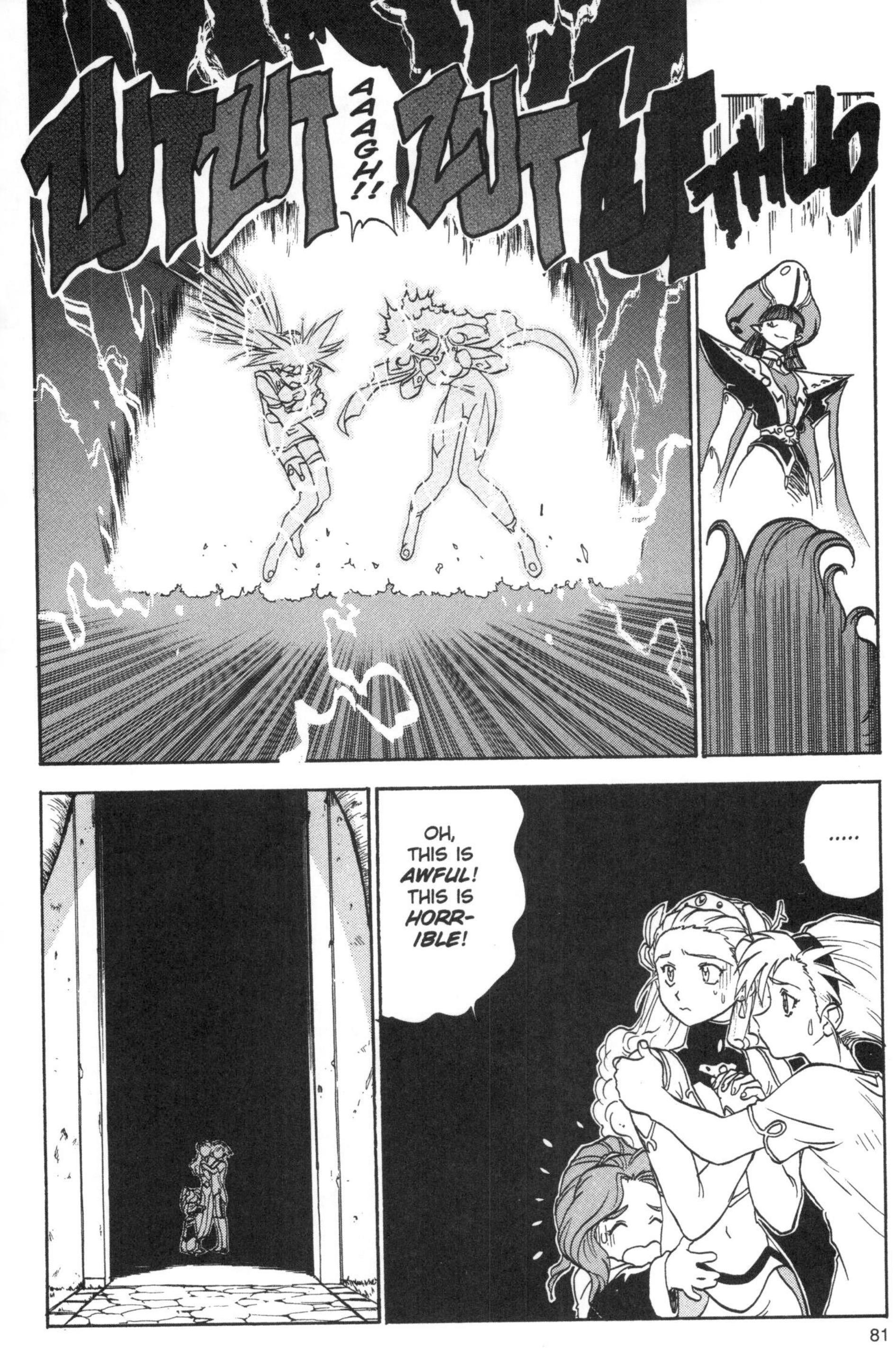
AAAGH!!
THUD
OH, THIS IS AWFUL! THIS IS HORRIBLE!
.....

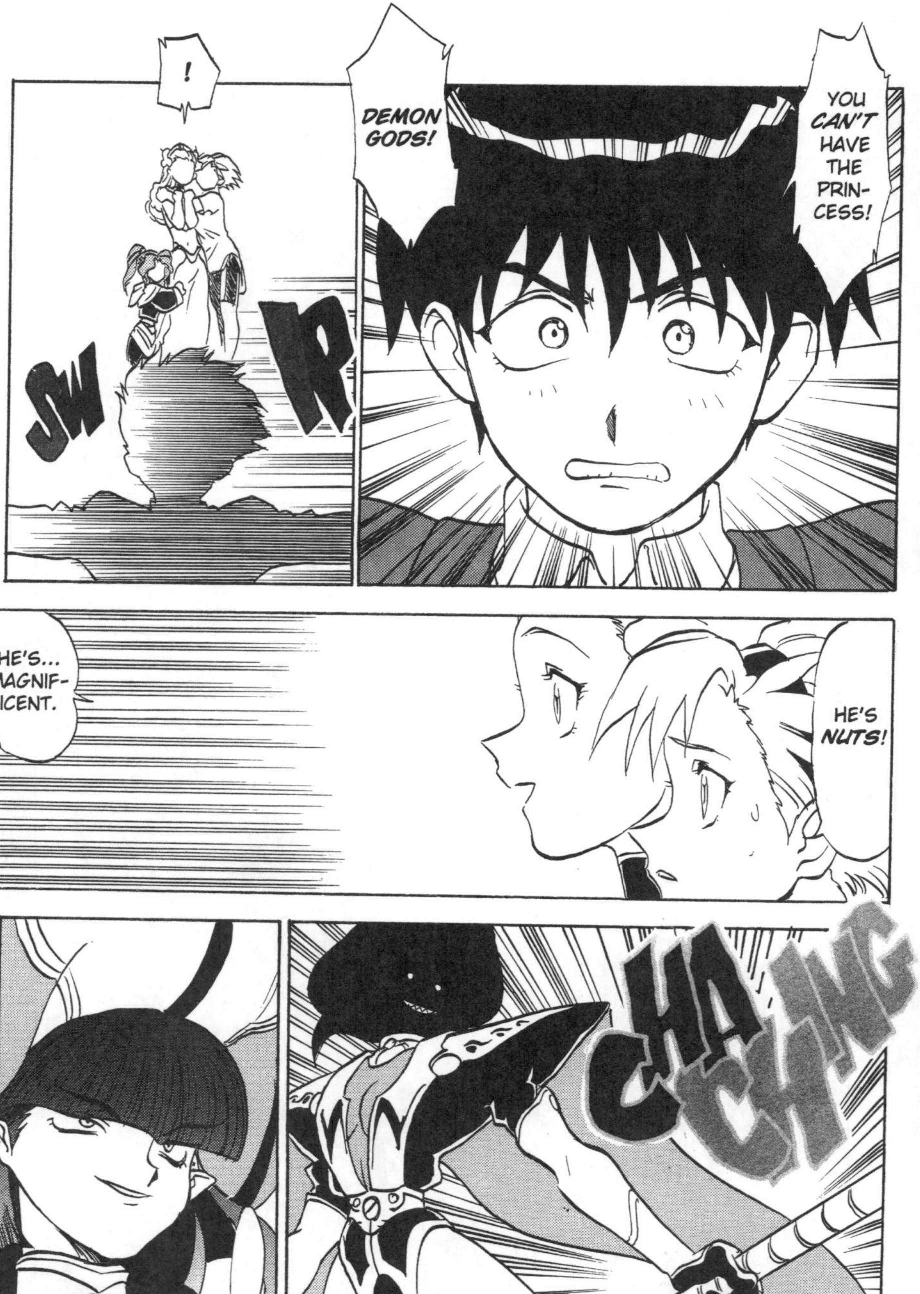
!
SW
IP
DEMON GODS!
YOU CAN'T HAVE THE PRIN-CESS!
HE'S... MAGNIF-ICENT.
HE'S NUTS!
CHA
CHING

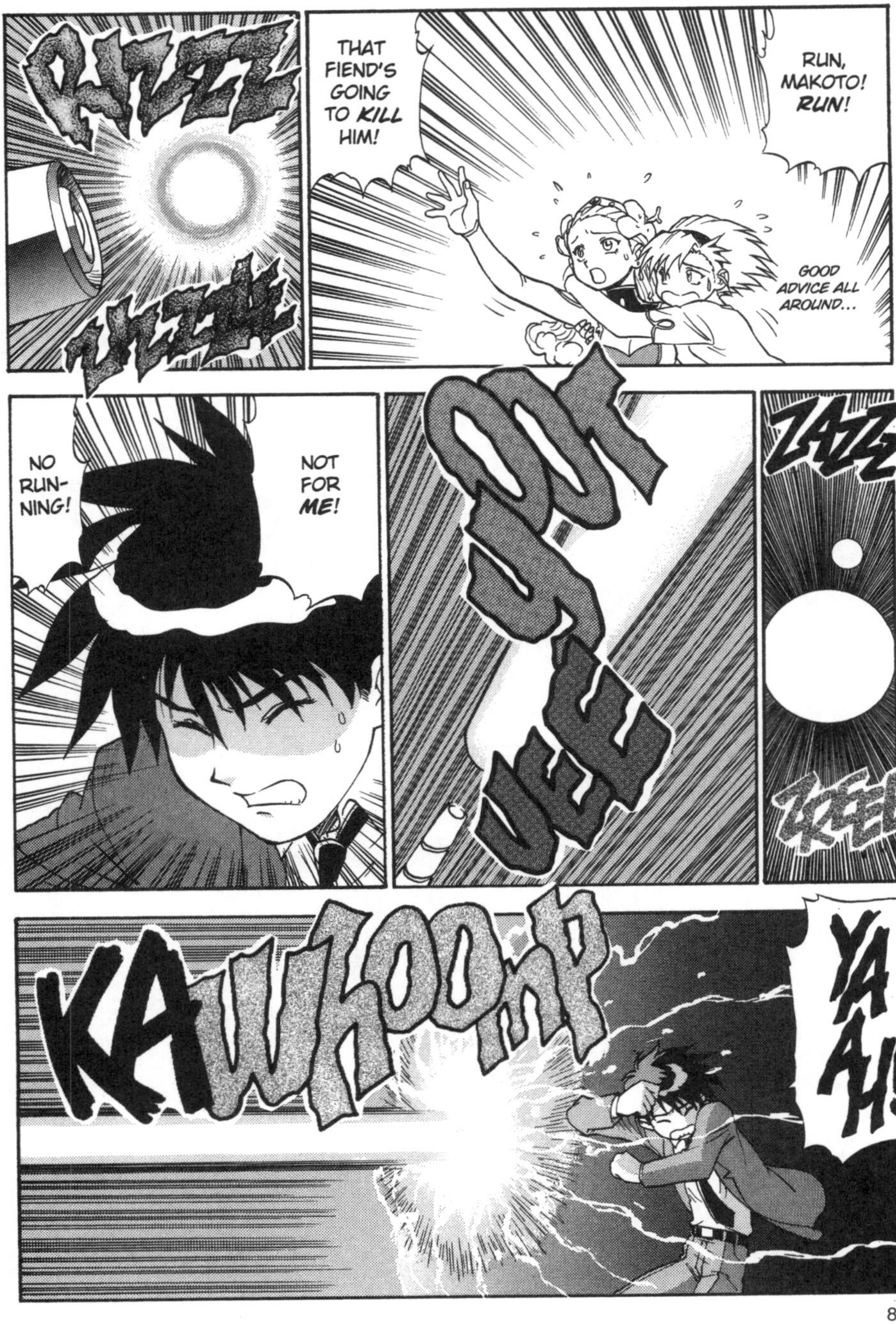
THAT FIEND'S GOING TO *KILL* HIM!
RUN, MAKOTO! *RUN*!
GOOD ADVICE ALL AROUND...
NO RUN-NING!
NOT FOR *ME*!
KAWHOOMP
YAAH!

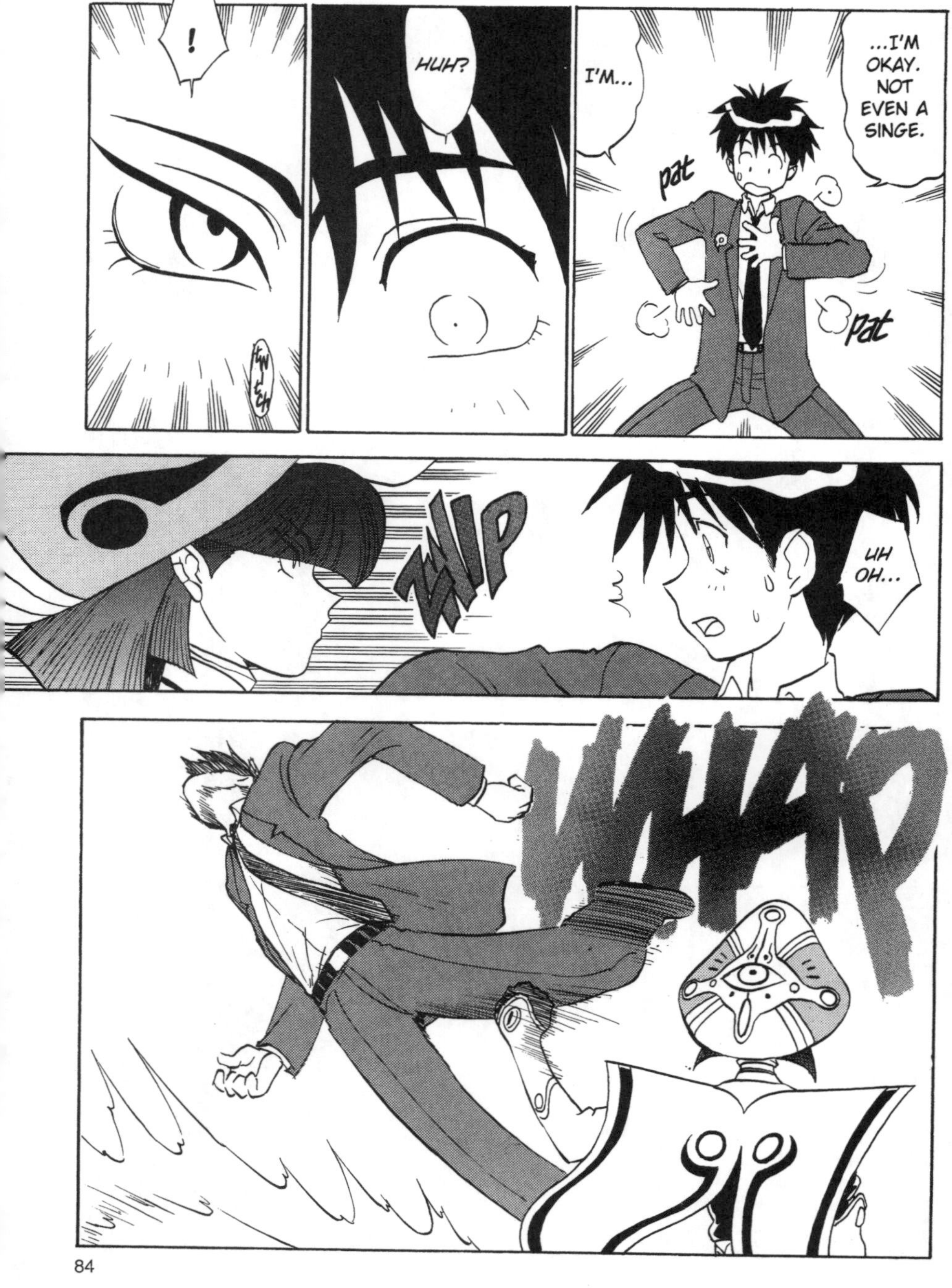
!
twitch
HUH?
I'M...
...I'M OKAY. NOT EVEN A SINGE.
pat
pat
ZWIP
UH OH...
WHAP

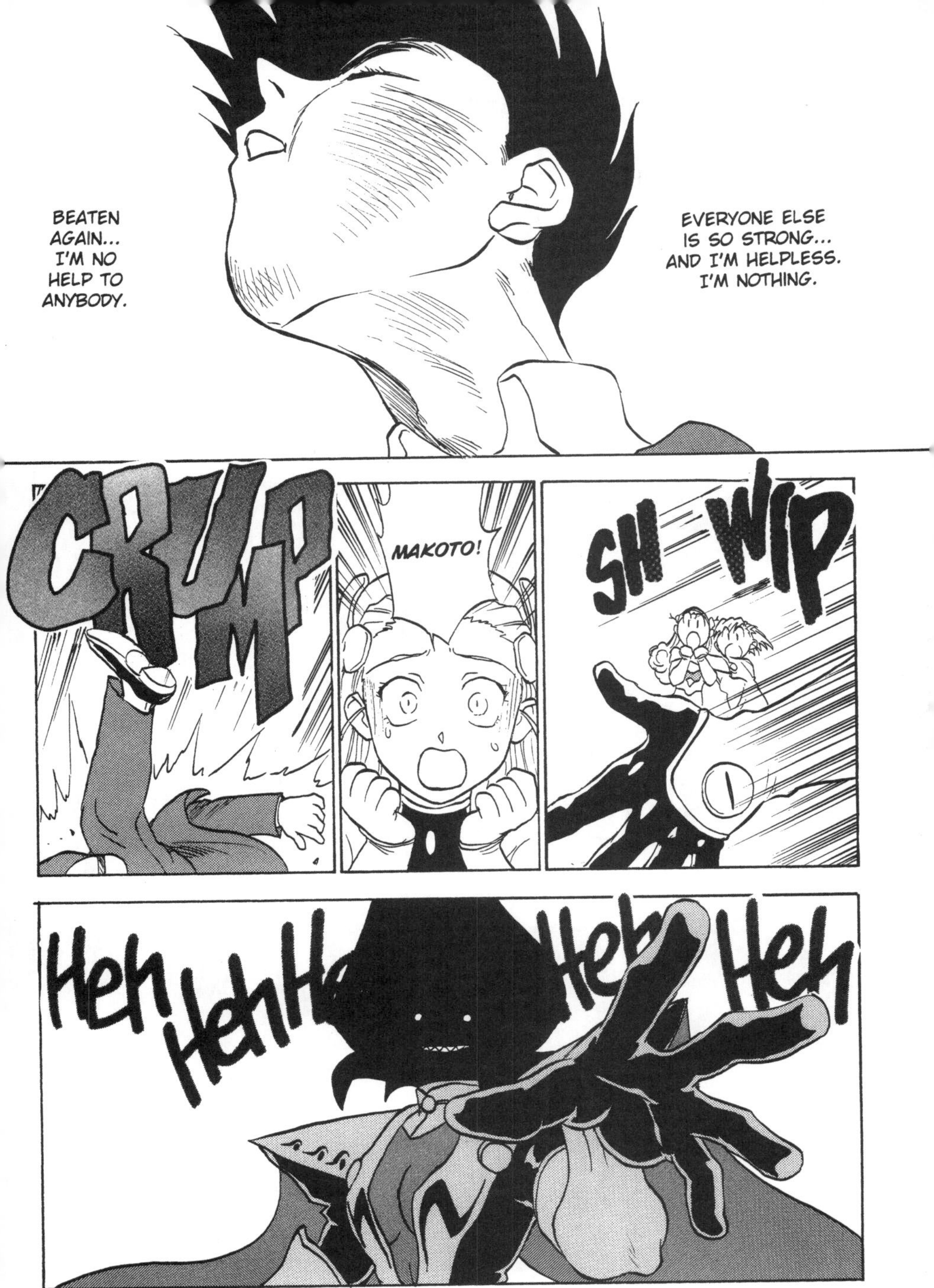

BEATEN AGAIN... I'M NO HELP TO ANYBODY.
EVERYONE ELSE IS SO STRONG... AND I'M HELPLESS. I'M NOTHING.
CRUMP
MAKOTO!
SH WIP
Heh Heh Heh Heh Heh

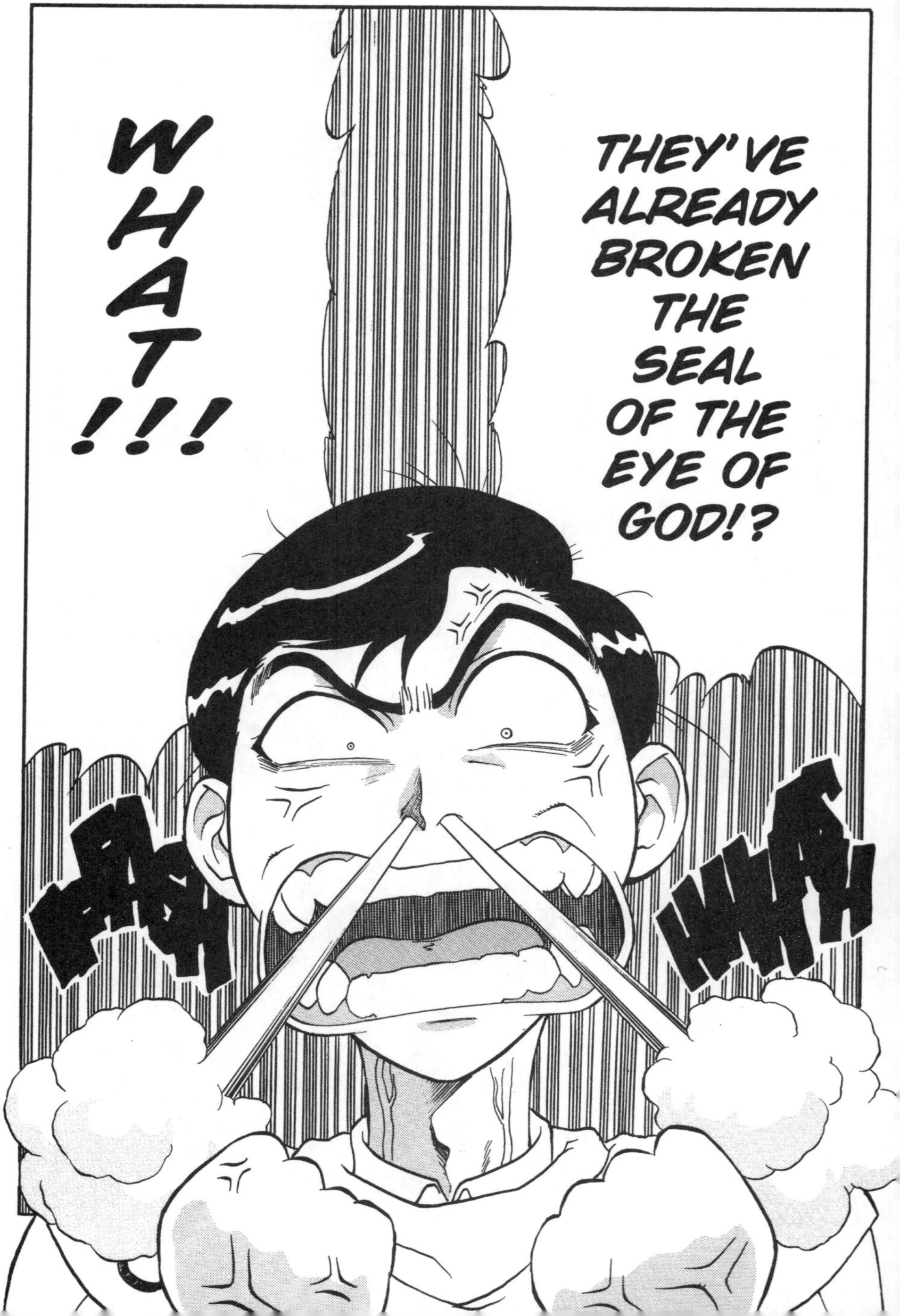
THEY'VE ALREADY BROKEN THE SEAL OF THE EYE OF GOD!?
WHAT!!!

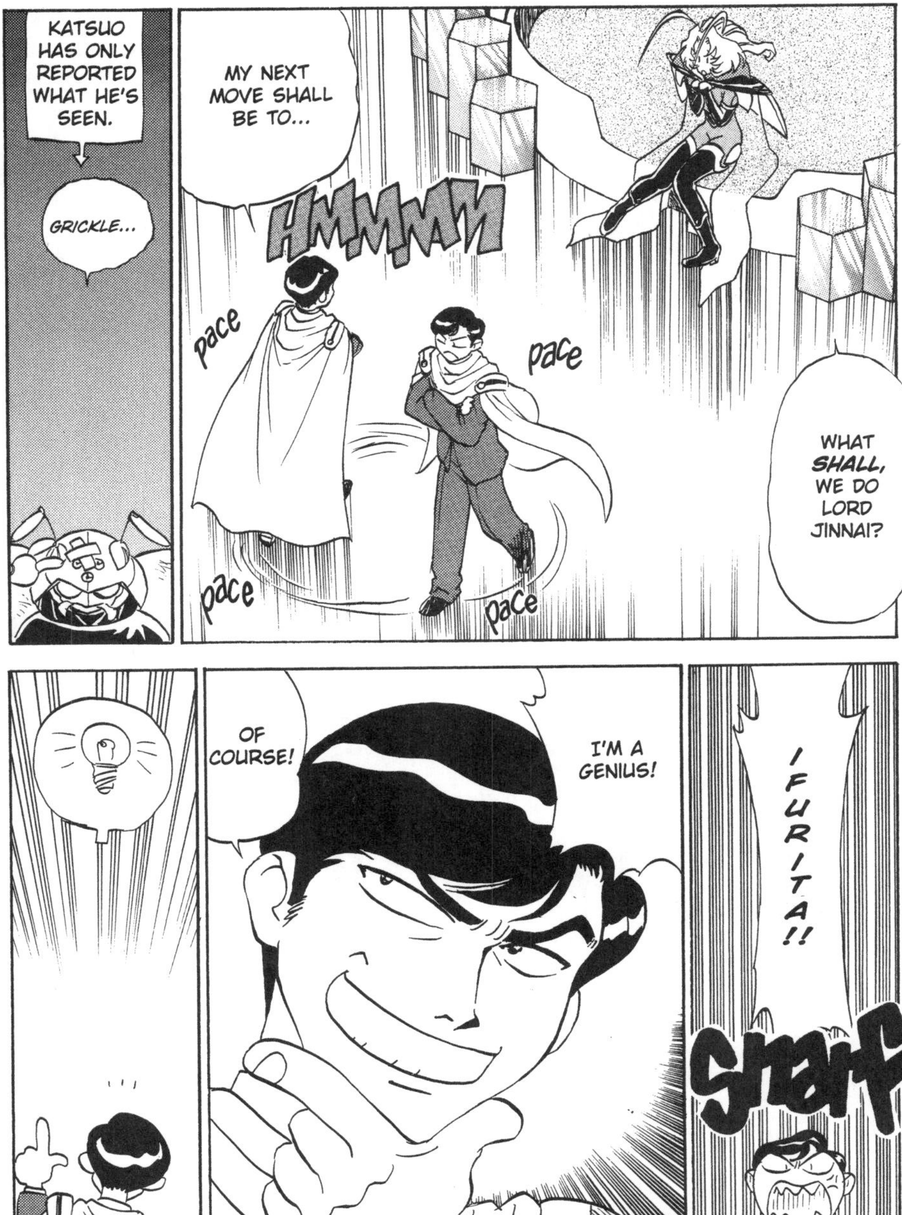
KATSUO HAS ONLY REPORTED WHAT HE'S SEEN.
GRICKLE...
MY NEXT MOVE SHALL BE TO...
HMMMM
pace
pace
pace
pace
WHAT SHALL, WE DO LORD JINNAI?
OF COURSE!
I'M A GENIUS!
IFURITA!!
Snarf

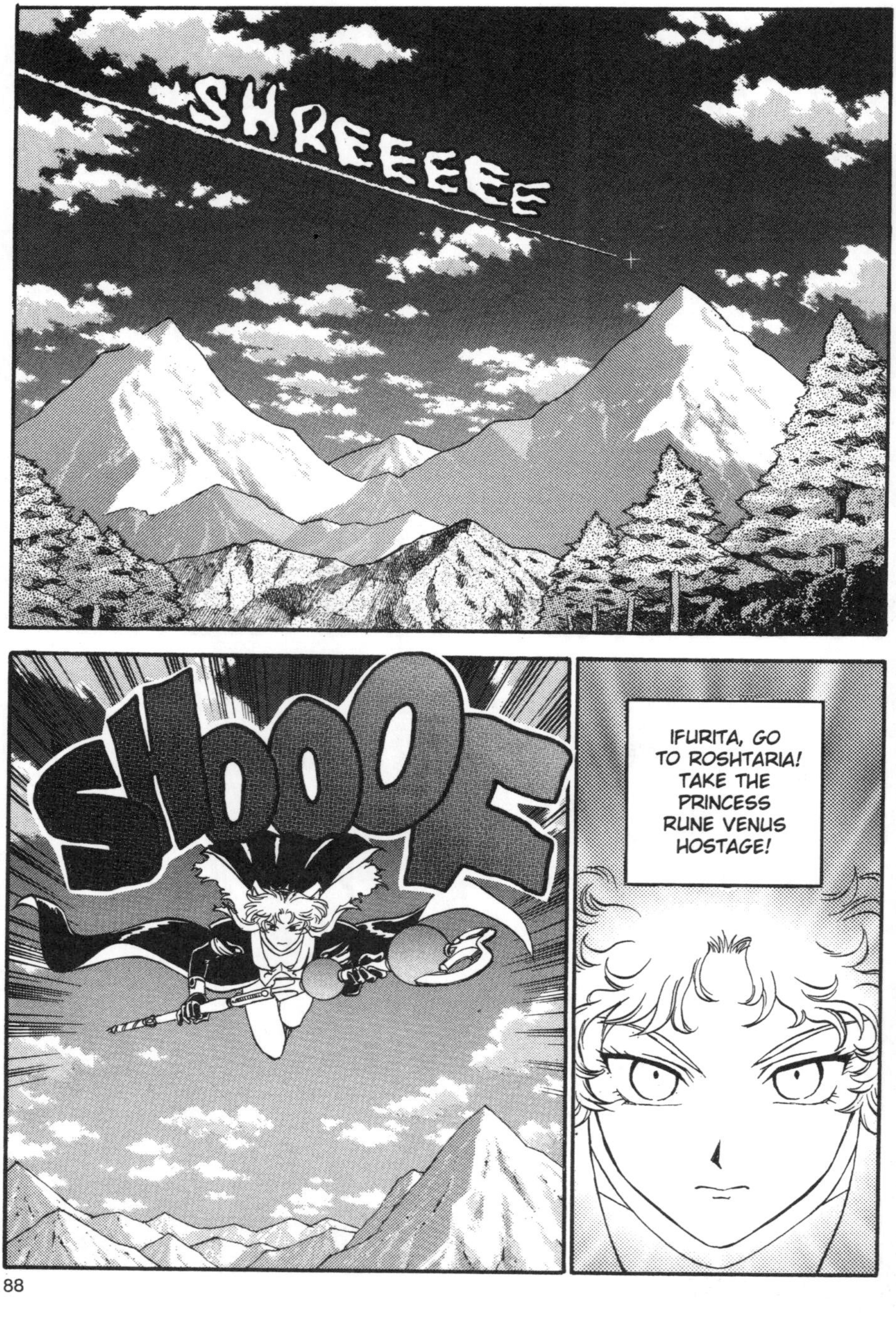
SHREEEEEE
SHOOOF
IFURITA, GO TO ROSHTARIA! TAKE THE PRINCESS RUNE VENUS HOSTAGE!

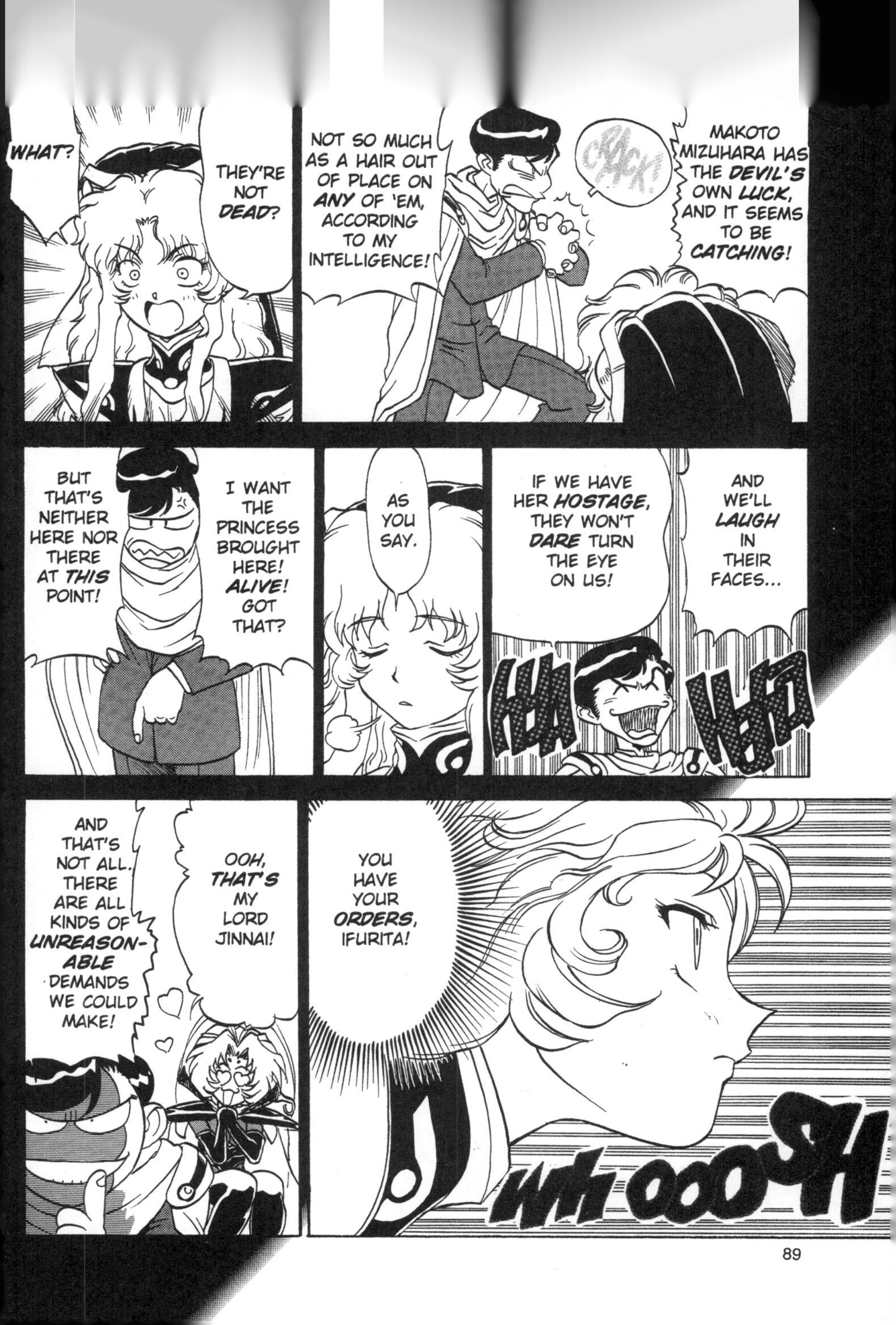
WHAT?
THEY'RE NOT DEAD?
NOT SO MUCH AS A HAIR OUT OF PLACE ON ANY OF 'EM, ACCORDING TO MY INTELLIGENCE!
CRACK!
MAKOTO MIZUHARA HAS THE DEVIL'S OWN LUCK, AND IT SEEMS TO BE CATCHING!
BUT THAT'S NEITHER HERE NOR THERE AT THIS POINT!
I WANT THE PRINCESS BROUGHT HERE! ALIVE! GOT THAT?
AS YOU SAY.
IF WE HAVE HER HOSTAGE, THEY WON'T DARE TURN THE EYE ON US!
AND WE'LL LAUGH IN THEIR FACES...
HA HA
HA HA
AND THAT'S NOT ALL. THERE ARE ALL KINDS OF UNREASON-ABLE DEMANDS WE COULD MAKE!
OOH, THAT'S MY LORD JINNAI!
YOU HAVE YOUR ORDERS, IFURITA!
WHOOOSH

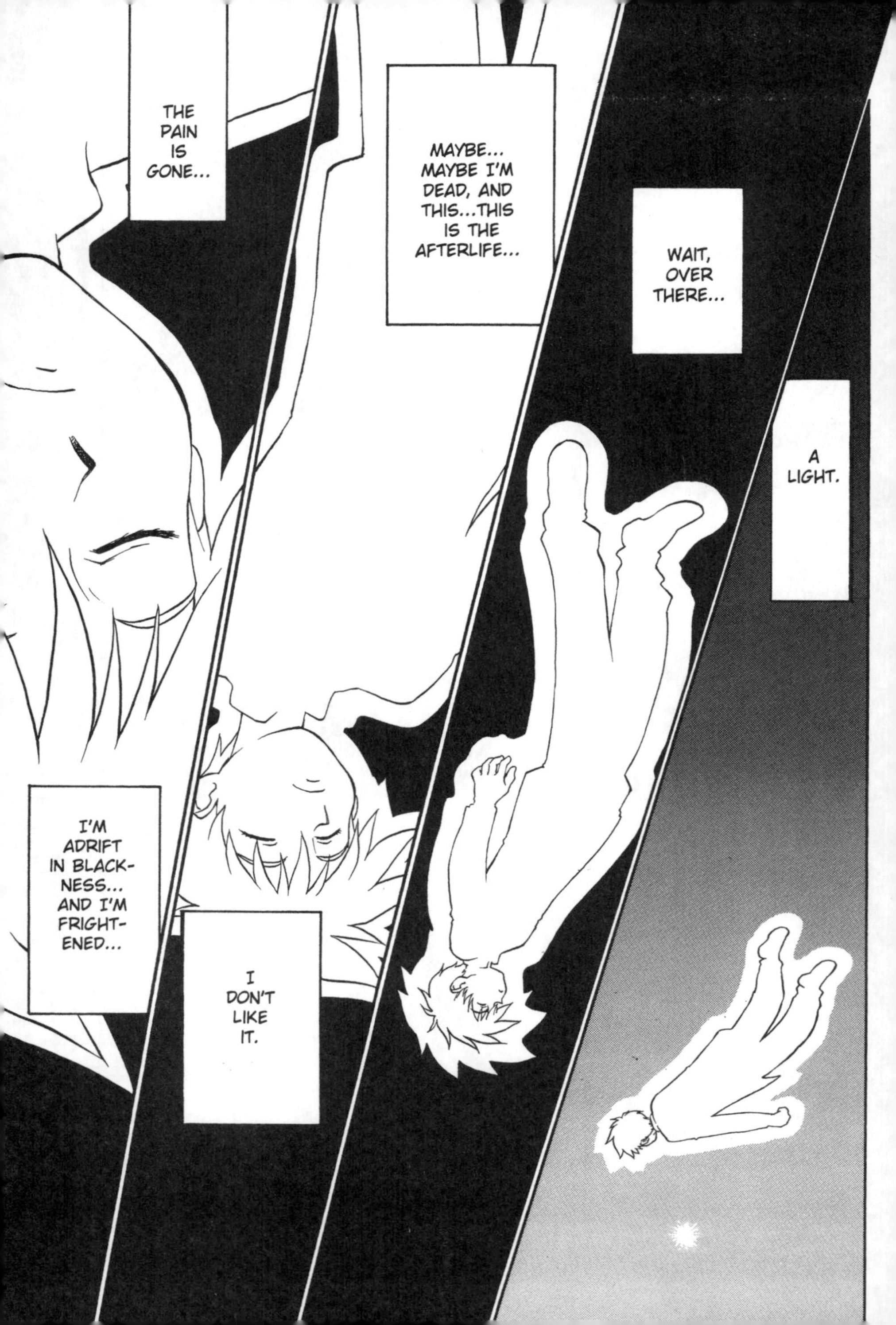
THE PAIN IS GONE...
I'M ADRIFT IN BLACKNESS... AND I'M FRIGHTENED...
MAYBE... MAYBE I'M DEAD, AND THIS...THIS IS THE AFTERLIFE...
I DON'T LIKE IT.
WAIT, OVER THERE...
A LIGHT.

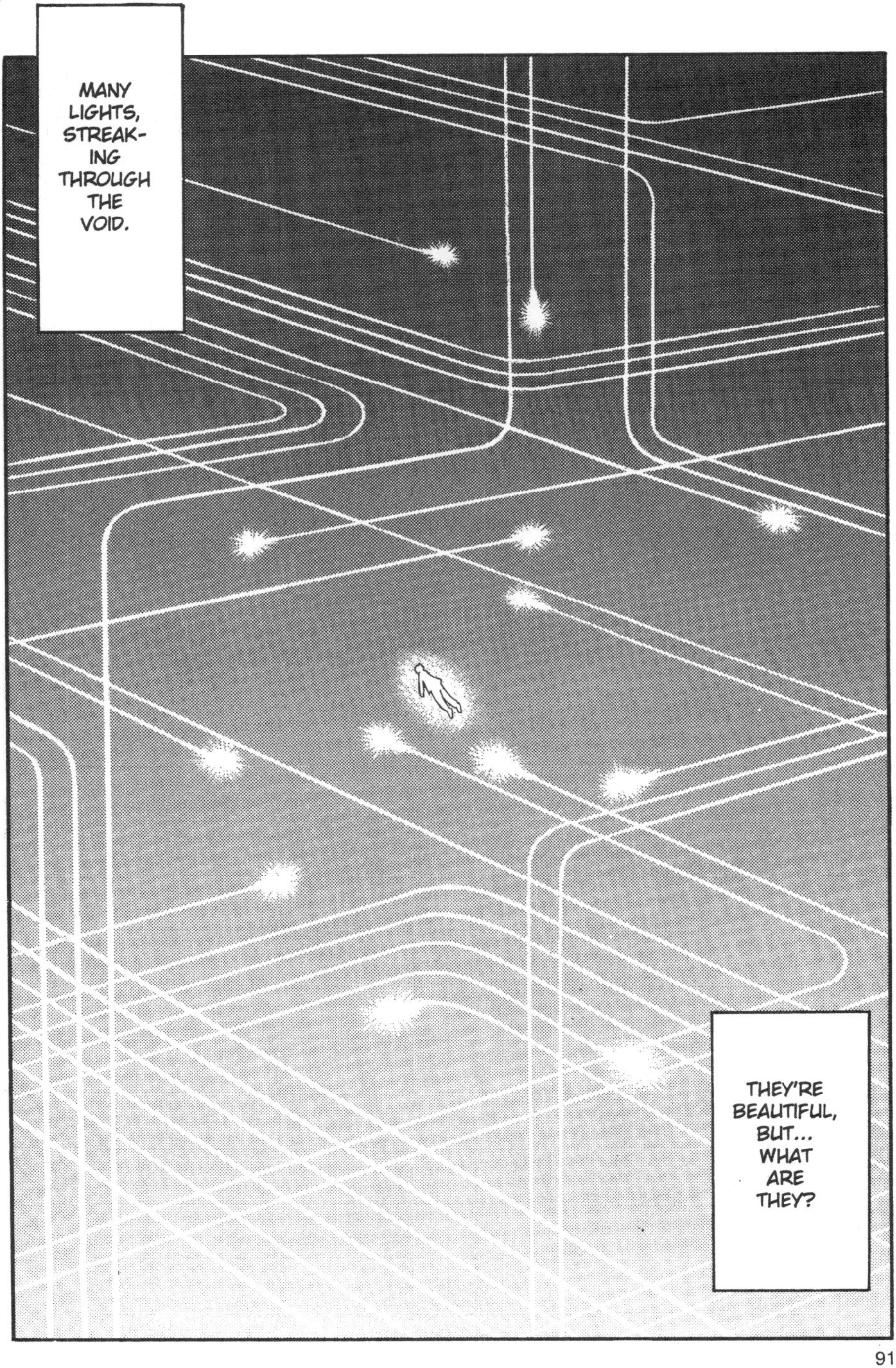
MANY LIGHTS, STREAK-ING THROUGH THE VOID.
THEY'RE BEAUTIFUL, BUT... WHAT ARE THEY?

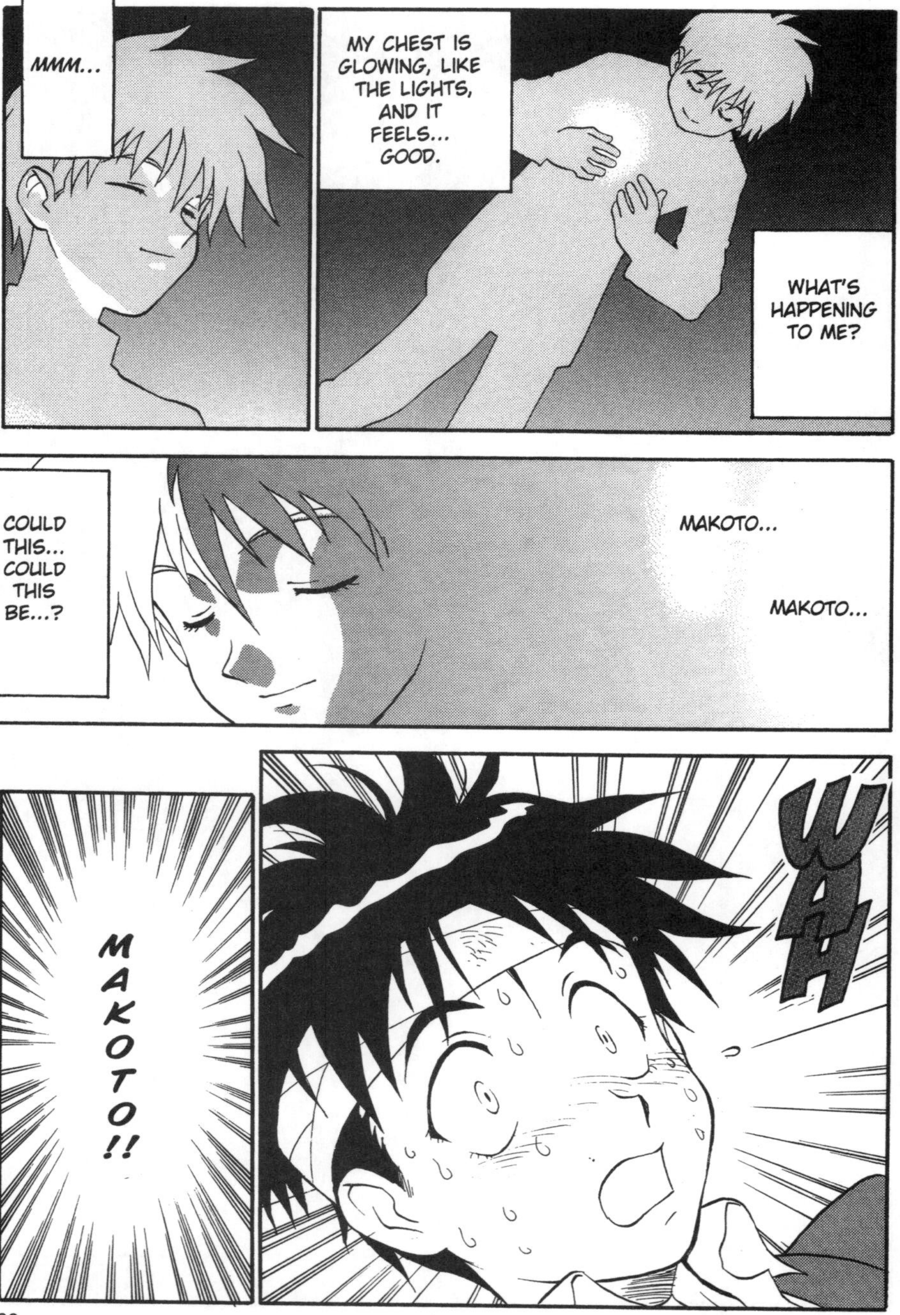
MMM...
MY CHEST IS GLOWING, LIKE THE LIGHTS, AND IT FEELS... GOOD.
WHAT'S HAPPENING TO ME?
COULD THIS... COULD THIS BE...?
MAKOTO...
MAKOTO...
MAKOTO!!
WAH

NA-NAMI?

ALIELLE?

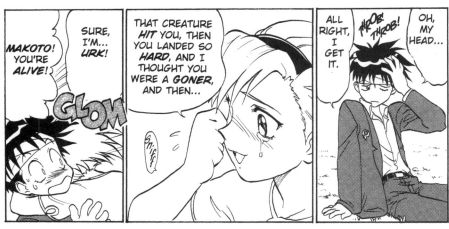

MAKOTO! YOU'RE ALIVE!

SURE, I'M... URK!

GLOM

THAT CREATURE *HIT* YOU, THEN YOU LANDED SO *HARD*, AND I THOUGHT YOU WERE A *GONER*, AND THEN...

snf...

ALL RIGHT, I GET IT.

THROB THROB!

OH, MY HEAD...

WAIT! THE *PRINCESS!* IS SHE...?

GONE, MAKOTO. THE *DEMON GODS* TOOK HER.

AND I COULDN'T *STOP* THEM!

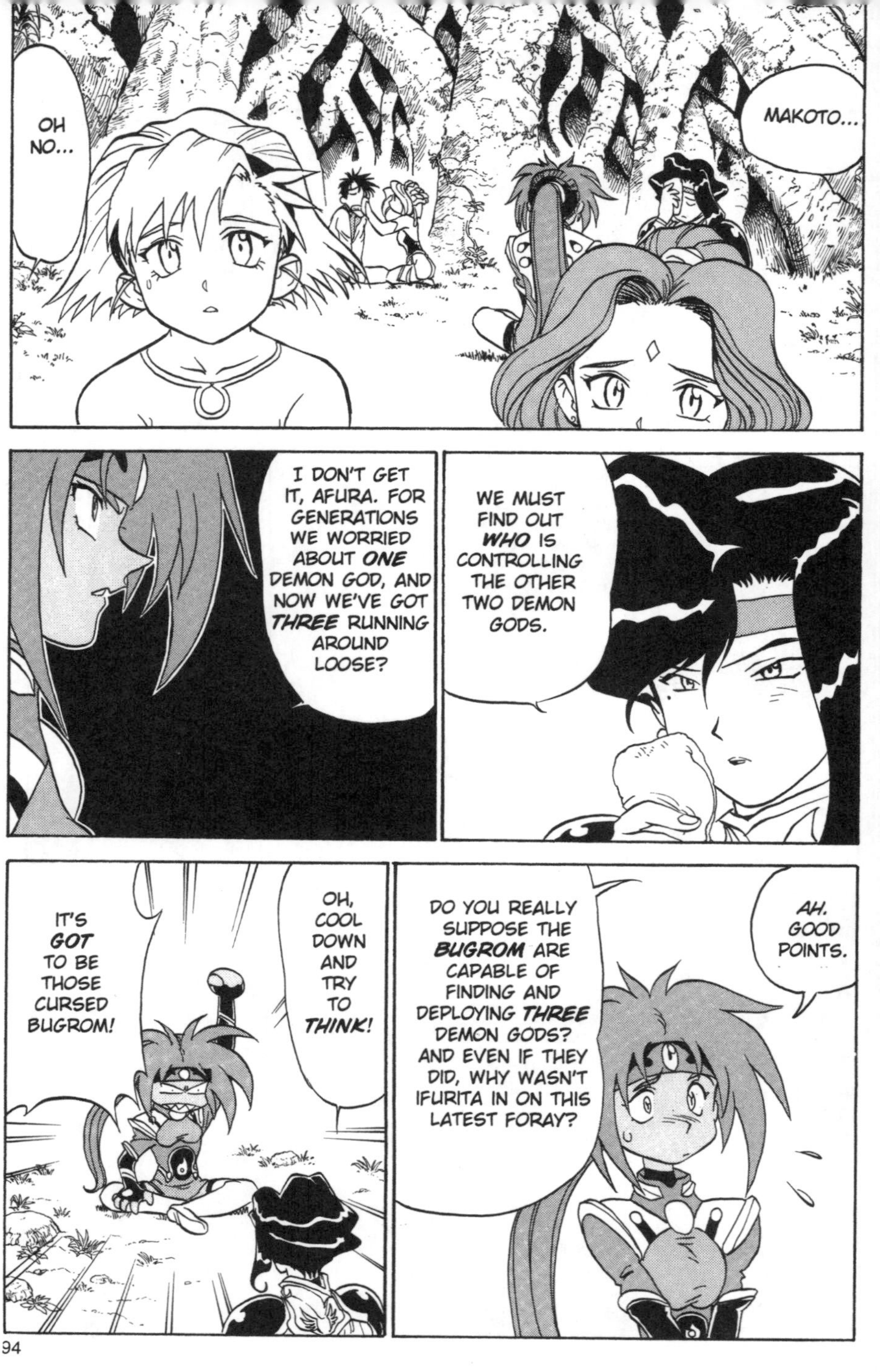

OH NO...
MAKOTO...
I DON'T GET IT, AFURA. FOR GENERATIONS WE WORRIED ABOUT ONE DEMON GOD, AND NOW WE'VE GOT THREE RUNNING AROUND LOOSE?
WE MUST FIND OUT WHO IS CONTROLLING THE OTHER TWO DEMON GODS.
IT'S GOT TO BE THOSE CURSED BUGROM!
OH, COOL DOWN AND TRY TO THINK!
DO YOU REALLY SUPPOSE THE BUGROM ARE CAPABLE OF FINDING AND DEPLOYING THREE DEMON GODS? AND EVEN IF THEY DID, WHY WASN'T IFURITA IN ON THIS LATEST FORAY?
AH. GOOD POINTS.

THEN WHO--?

SHAYLA SHAYLA, LET'S NOT JUMP TO ANY HASTY CONCLUSIONS.

SCRUNCH!

WE'LL GO BACK TO THE CASTLE AND THINK THIS SITUATION OVER.

LET'S MOVE OUT.

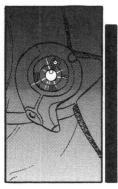

SHWO OOOMM

SO HE SURVIVED...

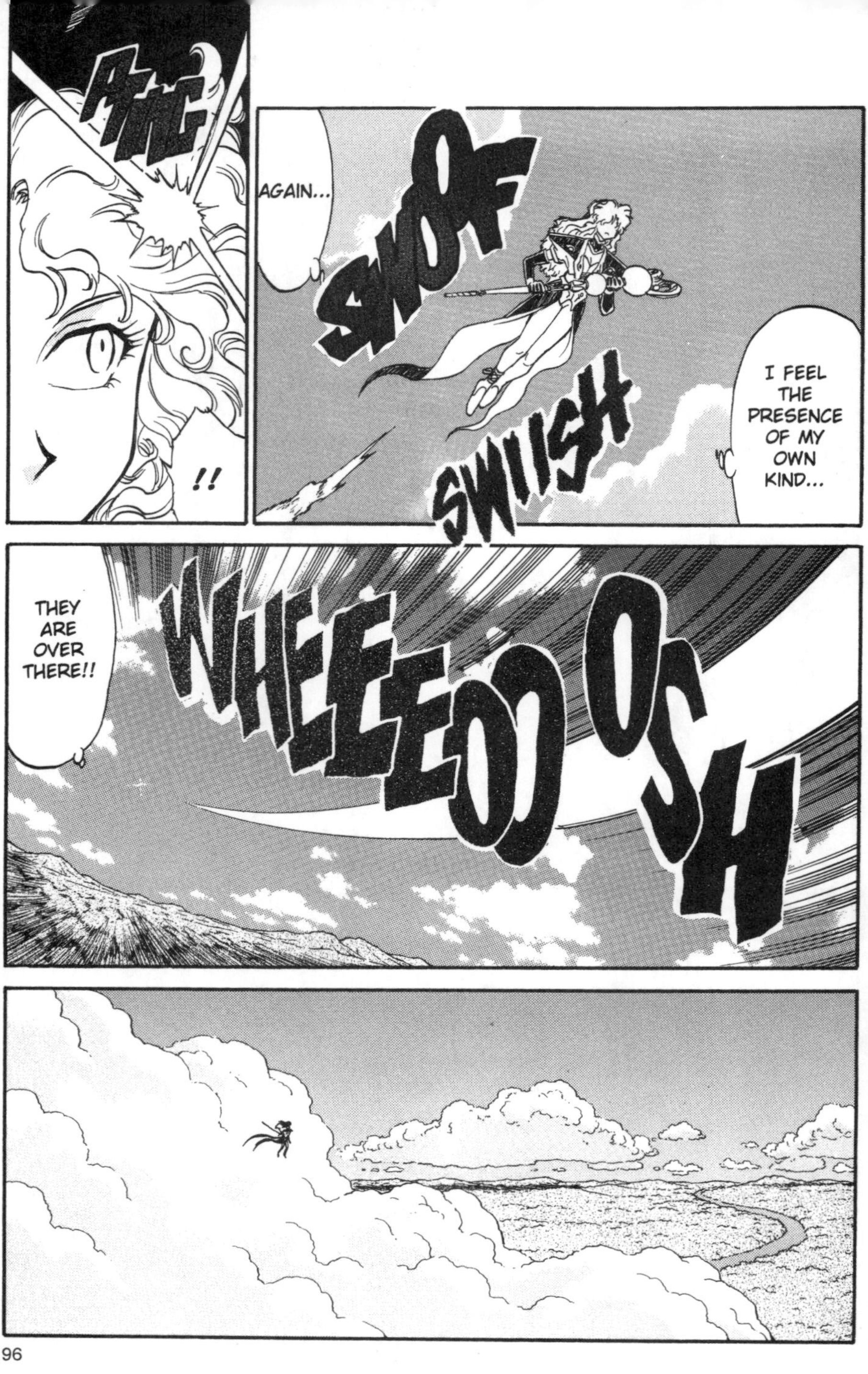
!!
AGAIN...
SWOOF
SWIISH
I FEEL THE PRESENCE OF MY OWN KIND...
THEY ARE OVER THERE!!
WHEEEOOOSH

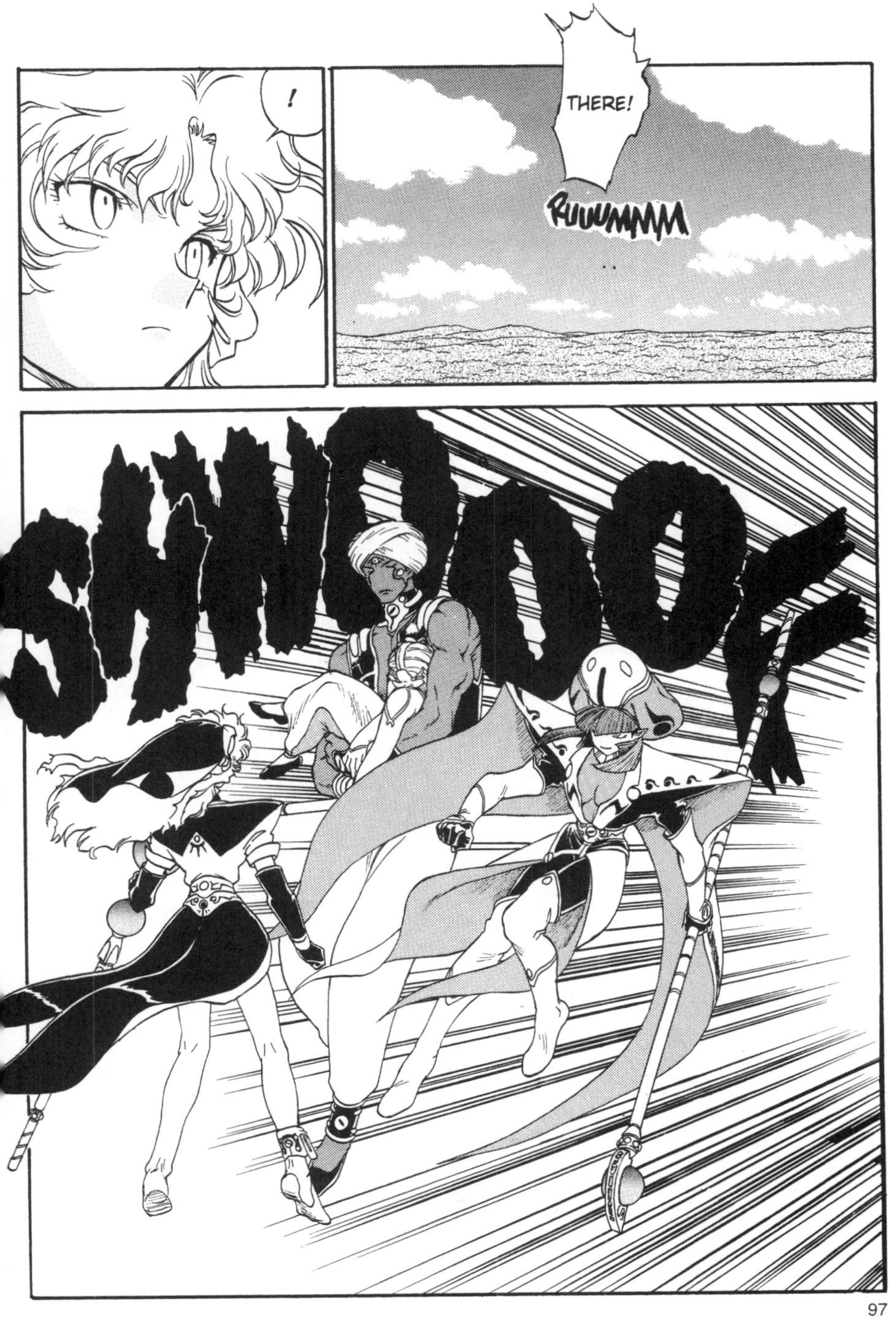
!
THERE!
RUUUMMMM
SHWOOOF

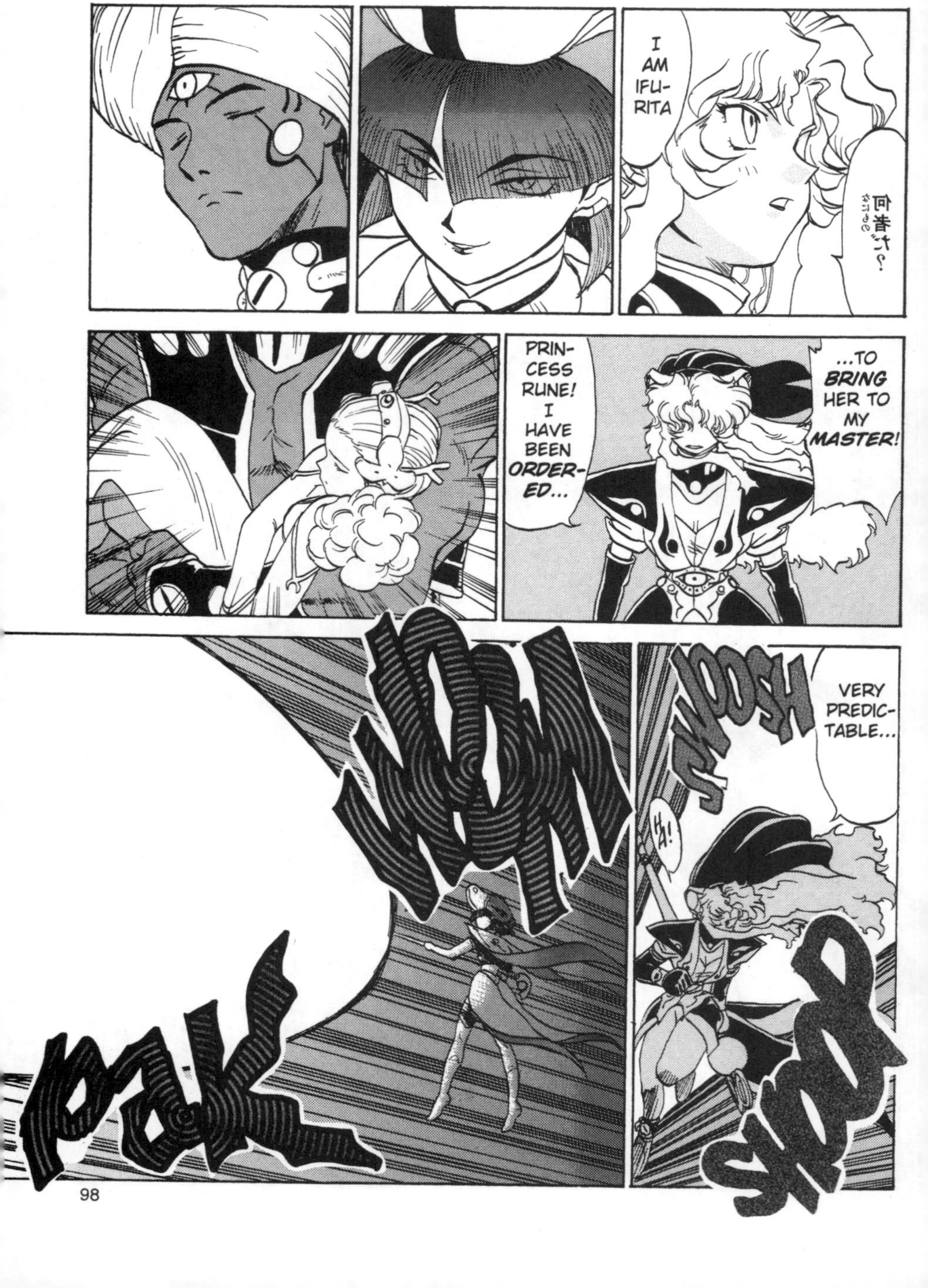

I AM IFURITA
何者だ？
PRINCESS RUNE! I HAVE BEEN ORDERED...
...TO BRING HER TO MY MASTER!
WOOM
KRAK
WOOSH
VERY PREDICTABLE...
HA!
SKREE

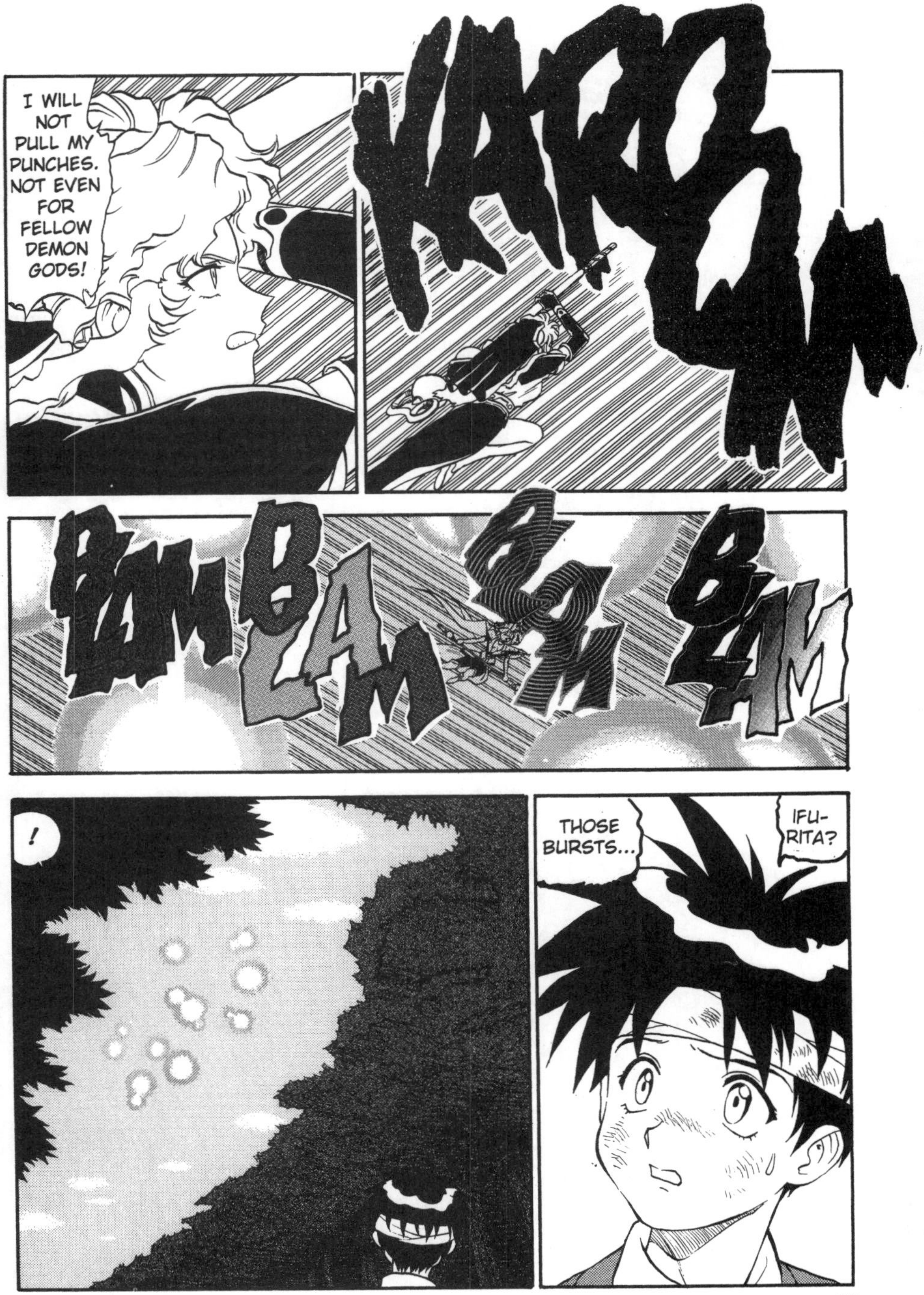
I WILL NOT PULL MY PUNCHES. NOT EVEN FOR FELLOW DEMON GODS!
BLAM
BLAM
BLAM
BLAM
!
THOSE BURSTS...
IFU-RITA?

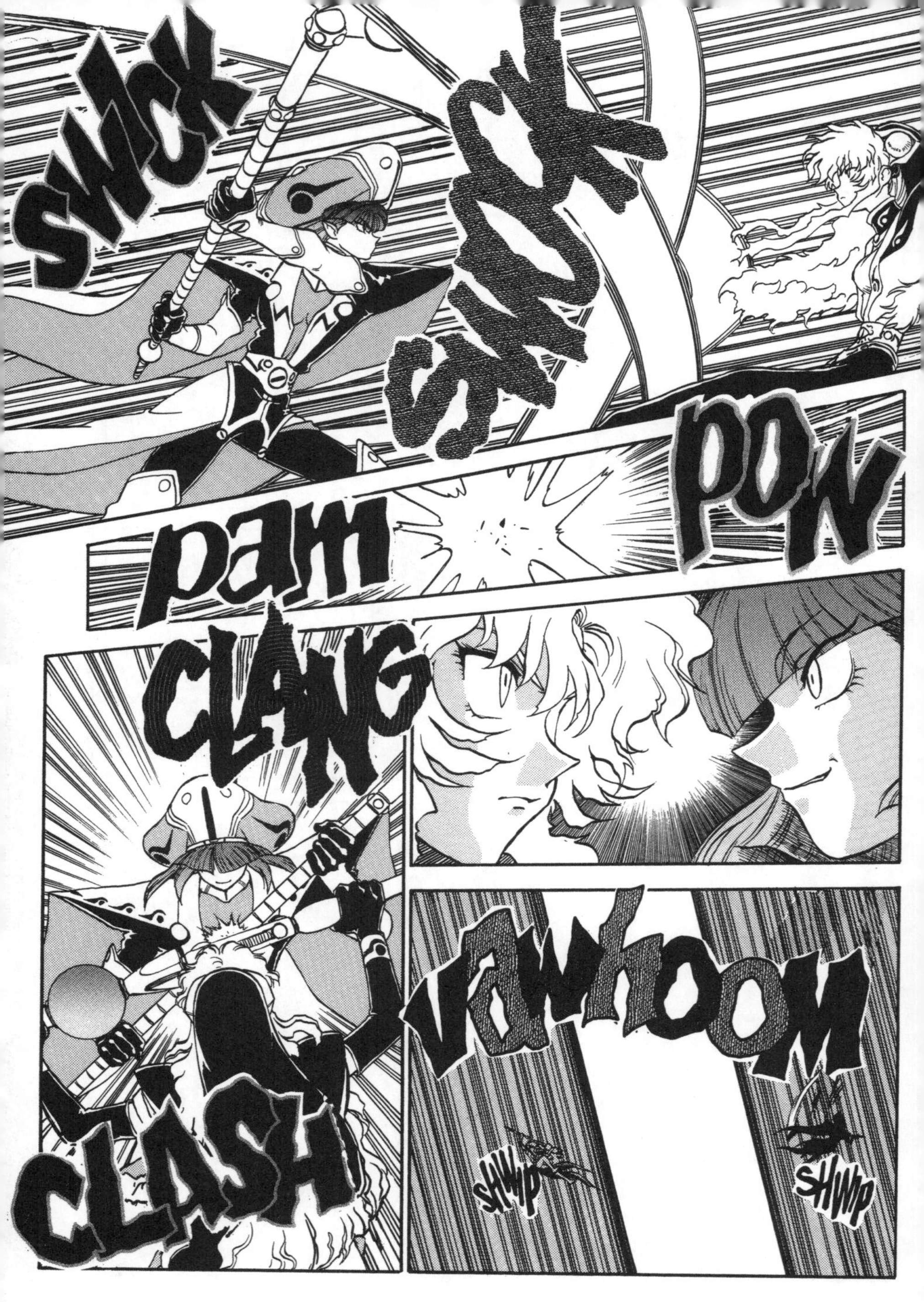
SWOCK
SWOCK
pam
POW
CLANG
CLASH
VAWHOOM
SHWIP
SHWIP

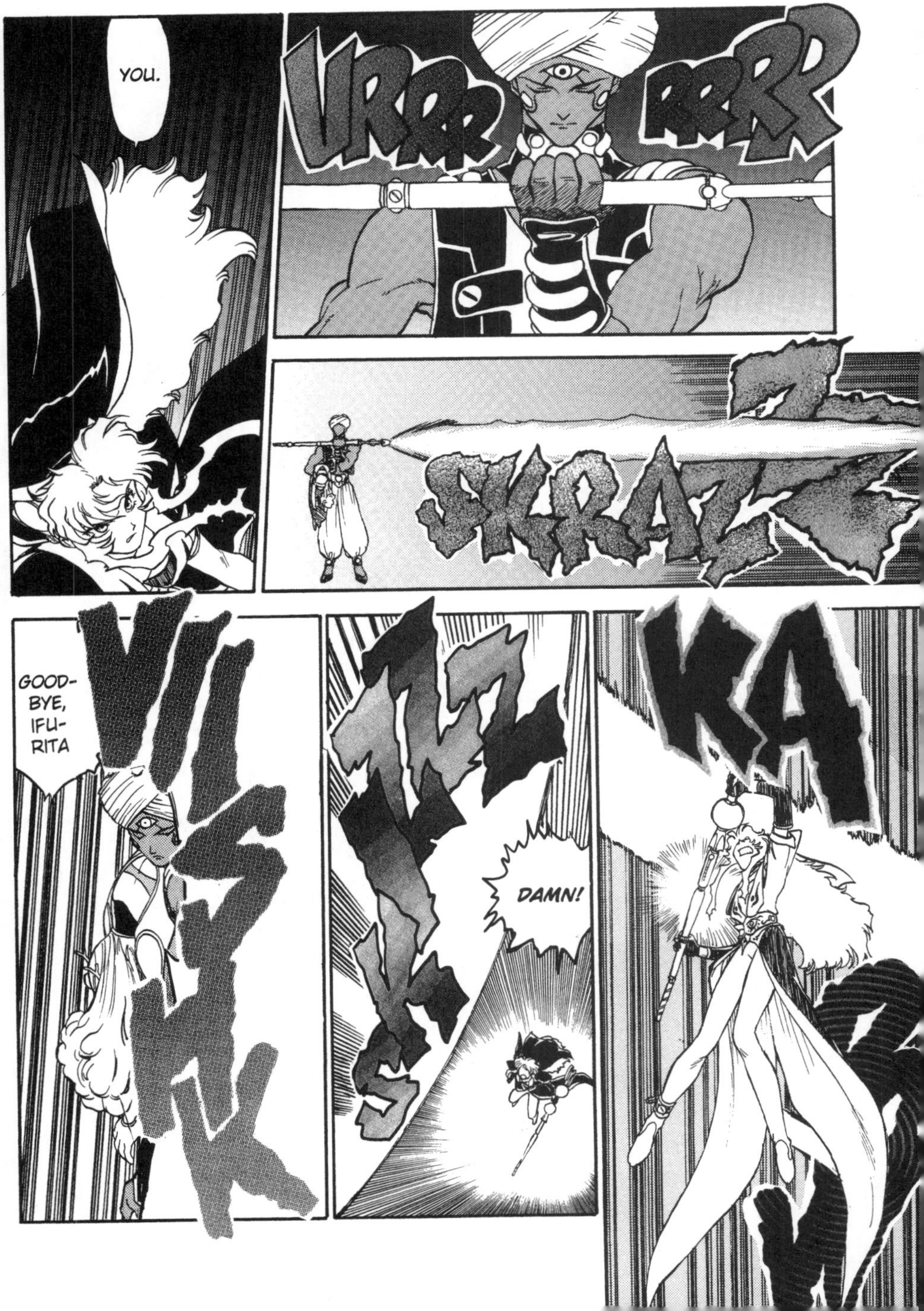
YOU.
URRR
RRRR
GOOD-BYE, IFU-RITA
DAMN!
KA

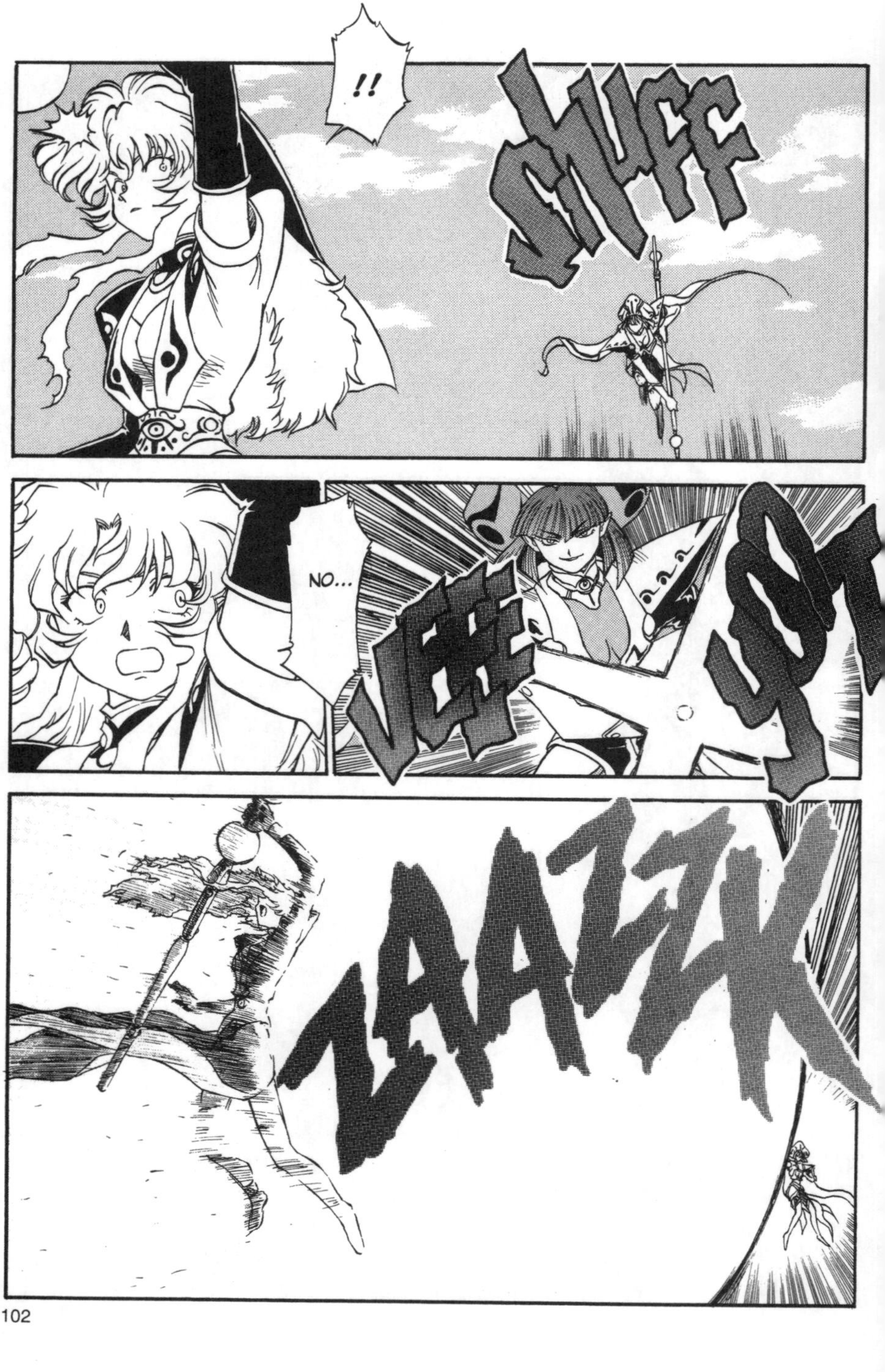
!!
SHUFF
NO...
VEEE

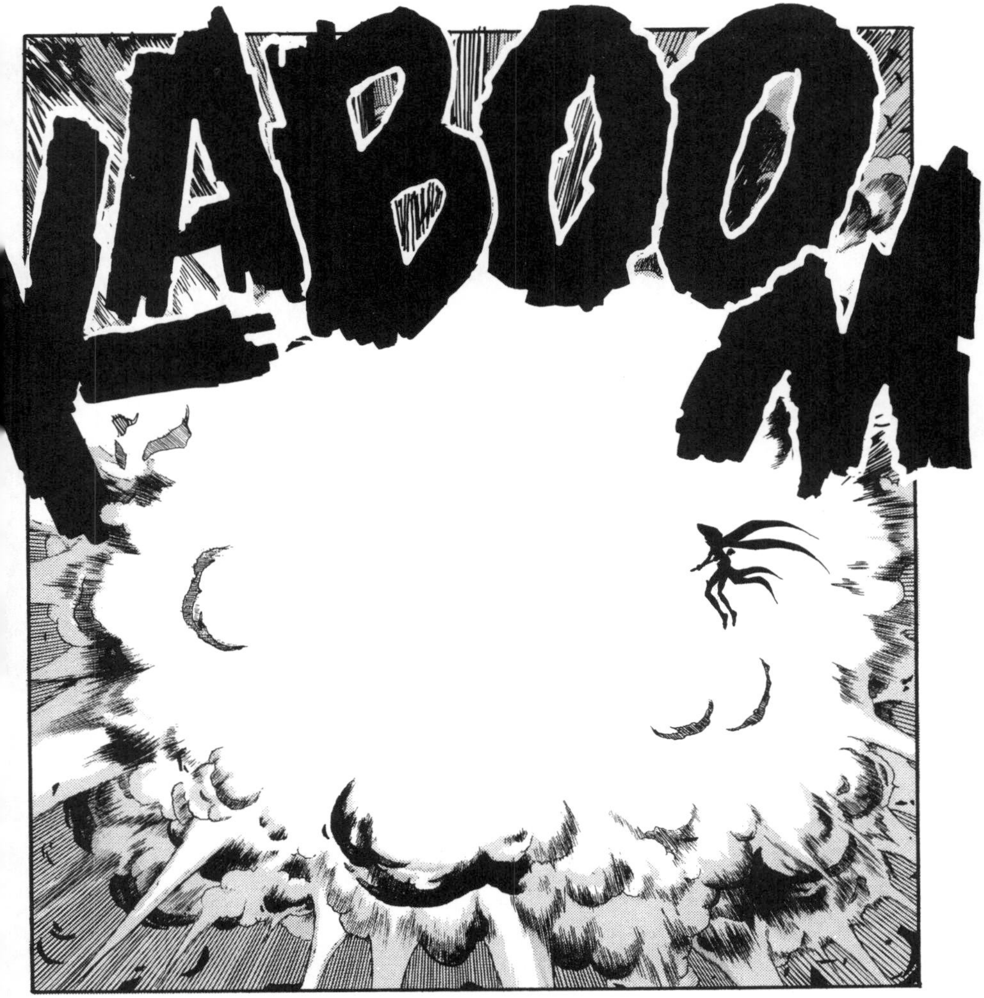
KABOOM

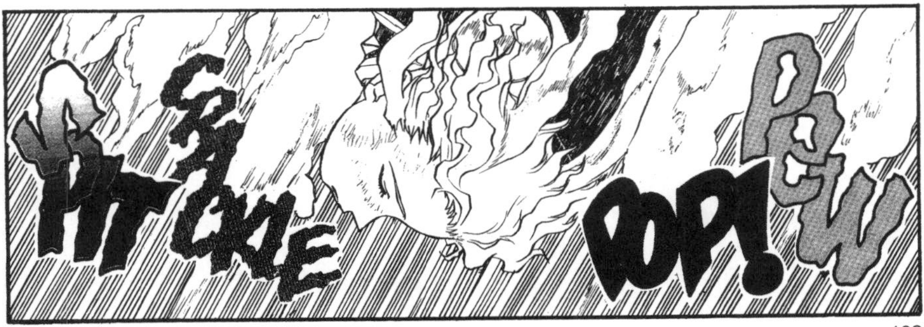
SPIT
CRACKLE
POP!
PEW

ALL SIGNIFICANT OPPOSITION HAS BEEN ELIMINATED.
WE MAY NOW PROCEED UNIMPEDED.

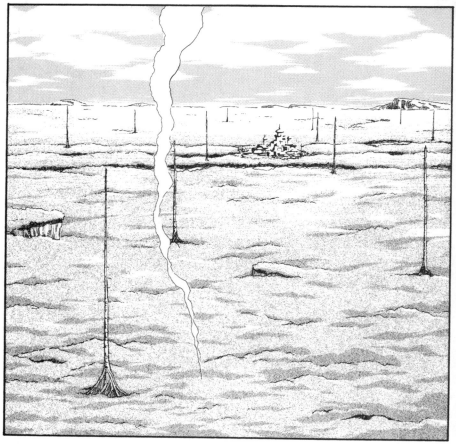

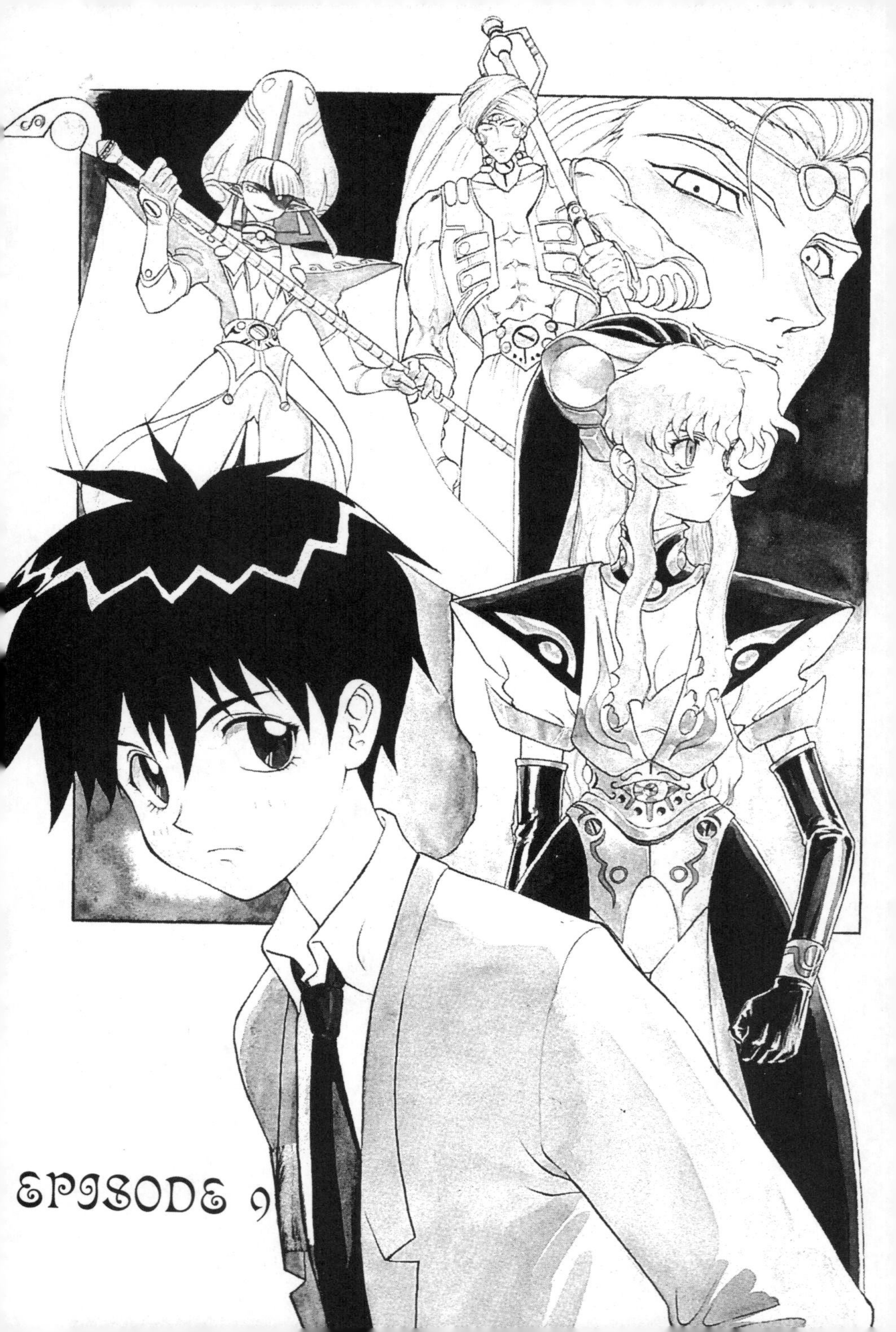
EPISODE 9

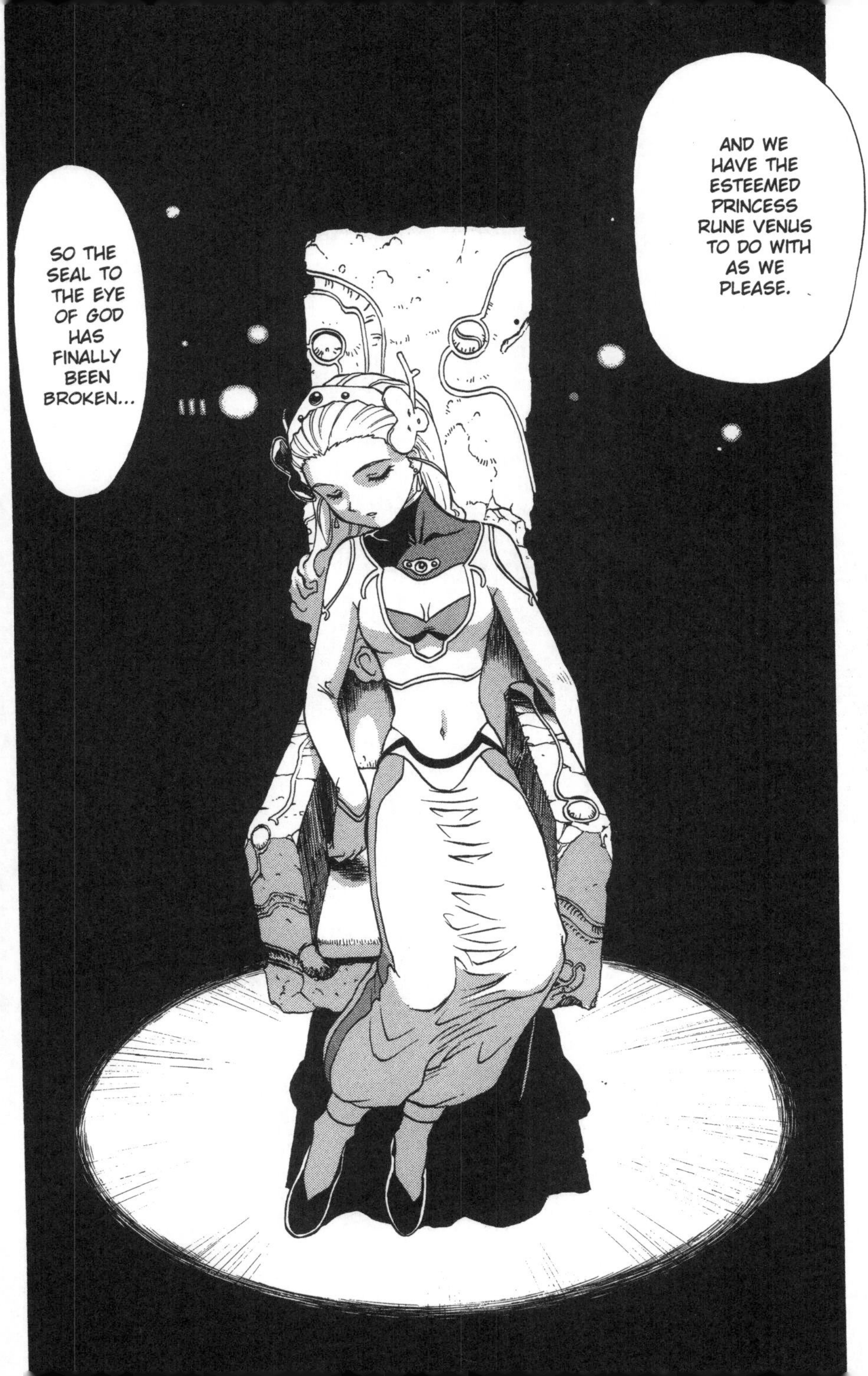
SO THE SEAL TO THE EYE OF GOD HAS FINALLY BEEN BROKEN...
AND WE HAVE THE ESTEEMED PRINCESS RUNE VENUS TO DO WITH AS WE PLEASE.

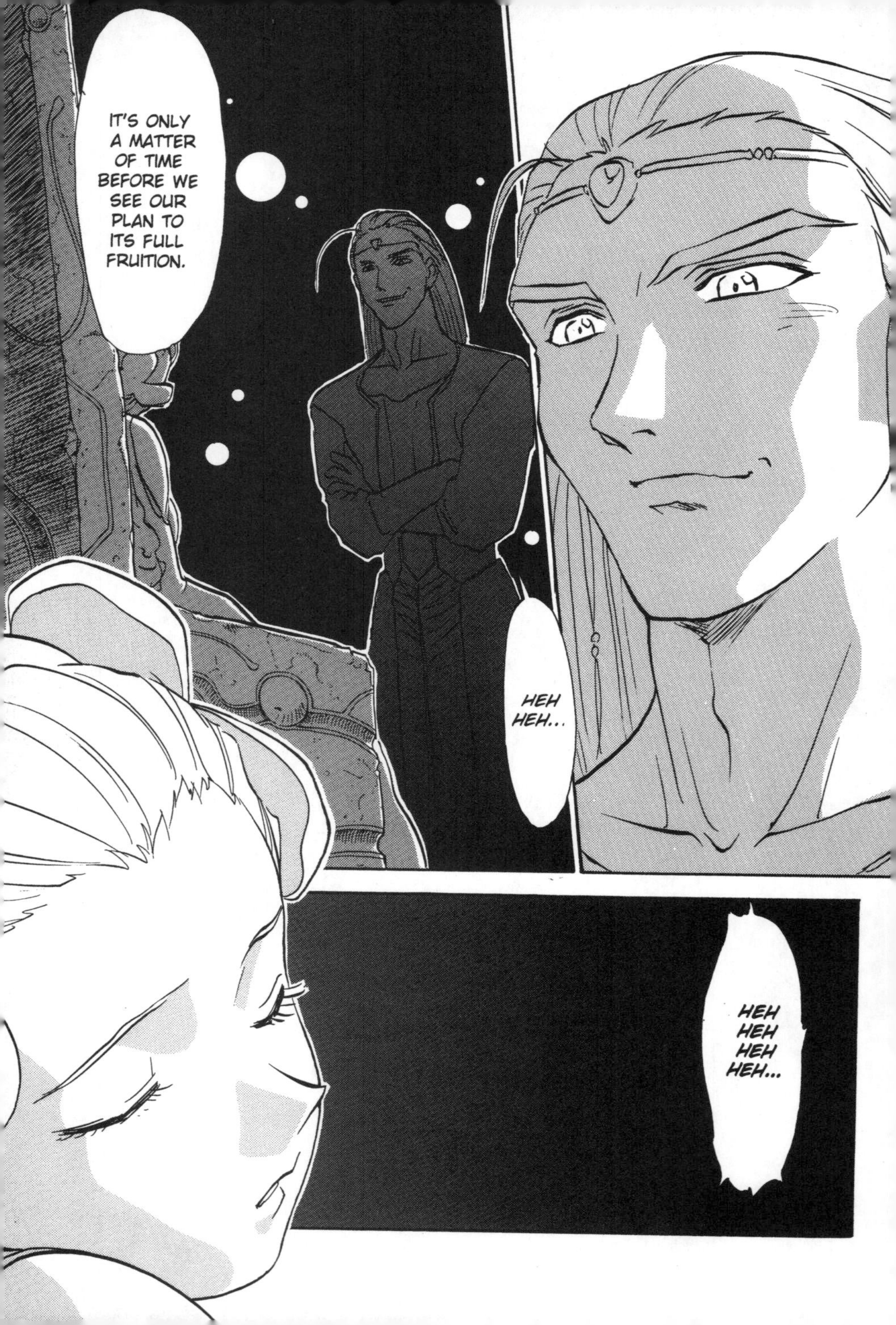
IT'S ONLY A MATTER OF TIME BEFORE WE SEE OUR PLAN TO ITS FULL FRUITION.
HEH HEH...
HEH HEH HEH HEH...

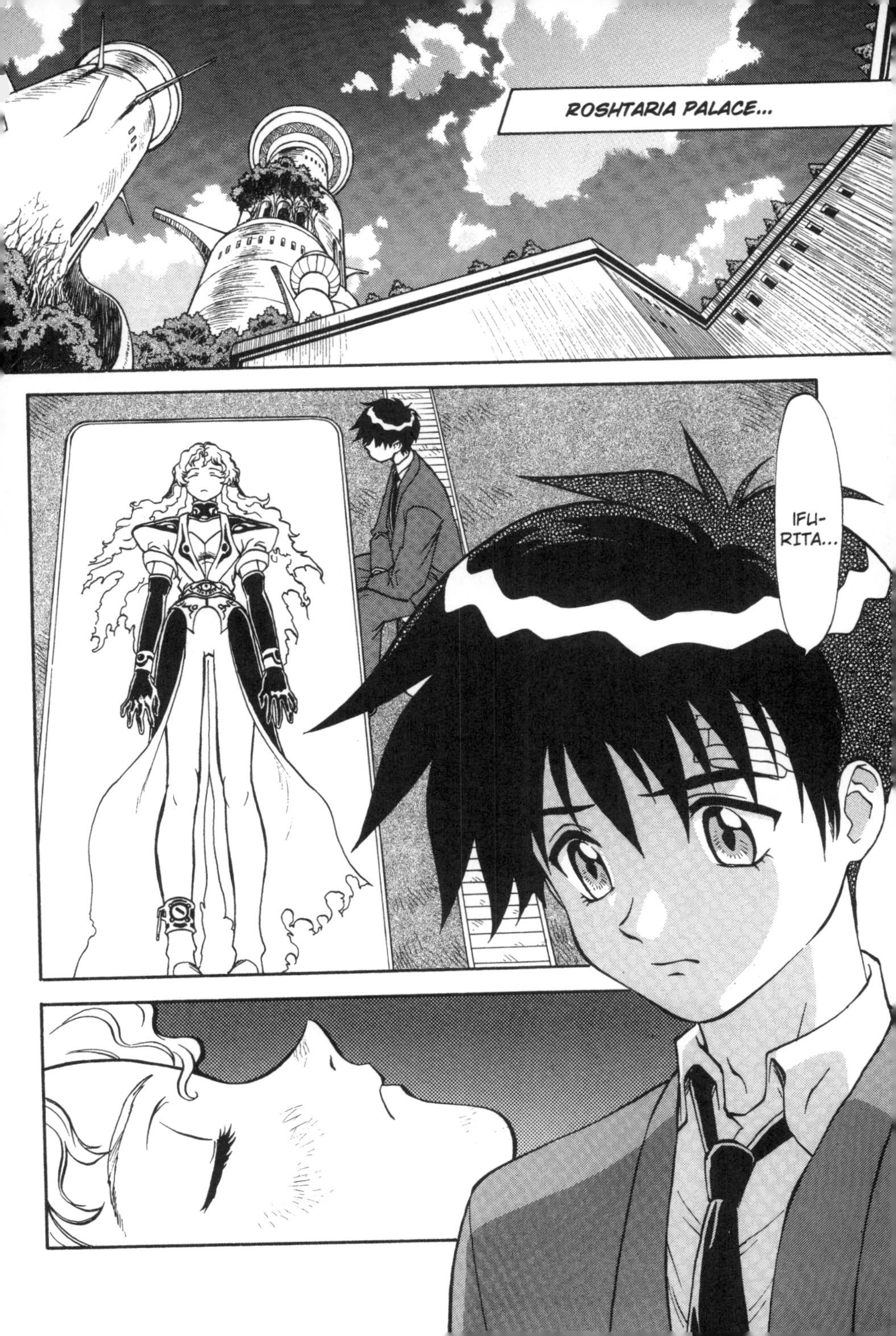
ROSHTARIA PALACE...
IFU-RITA...

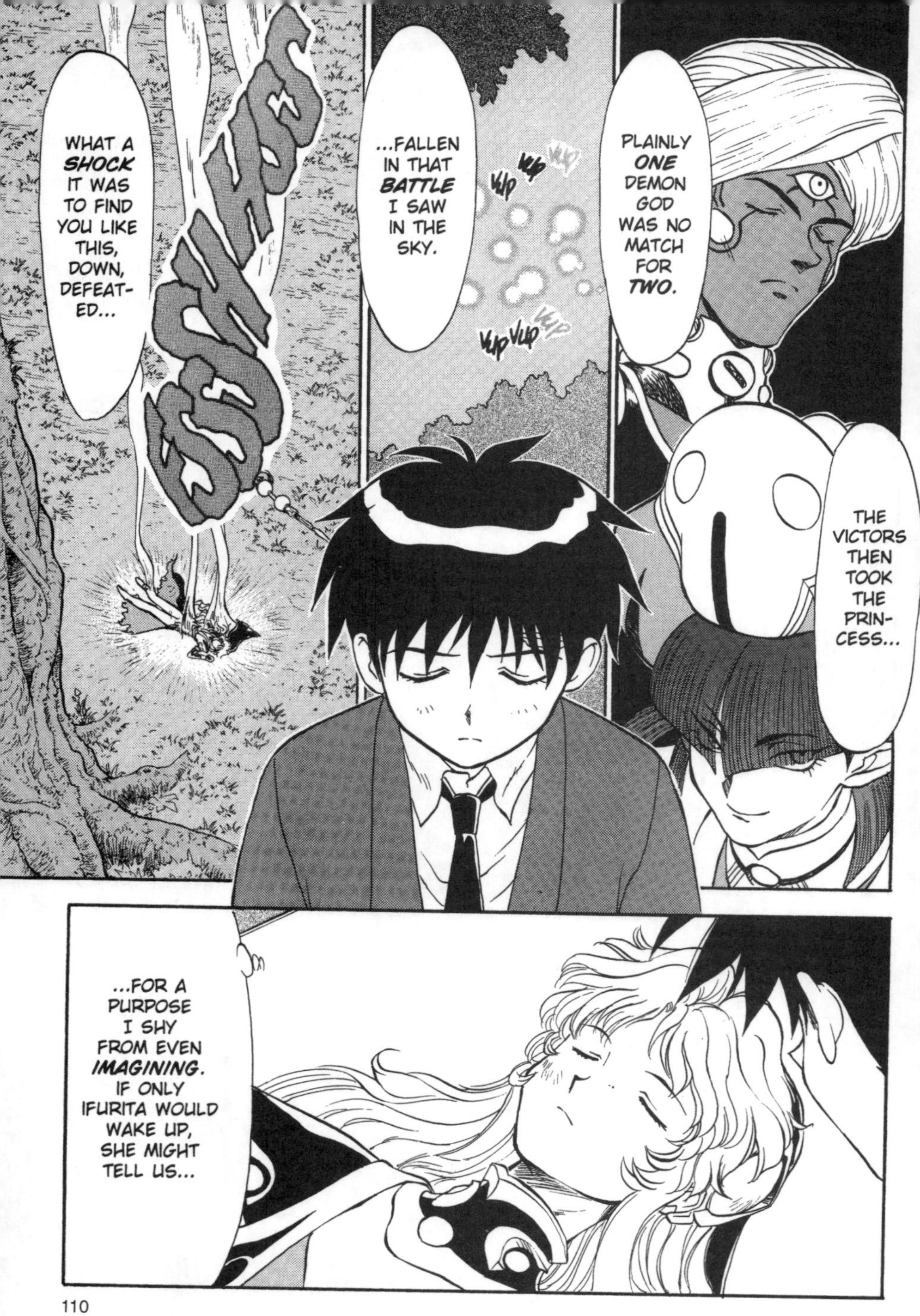
WHAT A SHOCK IT WAS TO FIND YOU LIKE THIS, DOWN, DEFEAT-ED...
...FALLEN IN THAT BATTLE I SAW IN THE SKY.
VUP VUP VUP
VUP VUP VUP
PLAINLY ONE DEMON GOD WAS NO MATCH FOR TWO.
THE VICTORS THEN TOOK THE PRIN-CESS...
...FOR A PURPOSE I SHY FROM EVEN IMAGINING. IF ONLY IFURITA WOULD WAKE UP, SHE MIGHT TELL US...

CLUMP CLUMP

HOW'S THE PATIENT, MAKOTO? ANY CHANGE?

HOW DID THINGS GO WITH THE ALLIANCE COUNCIL?

I'M AFRAID NOT.

SIGH... PRETTY MUCH AS USUAL.

THE OTHER NATIONS CONCLUDED THAT *EVERYTHING'S* FLORISTICA'S FAULT.

111

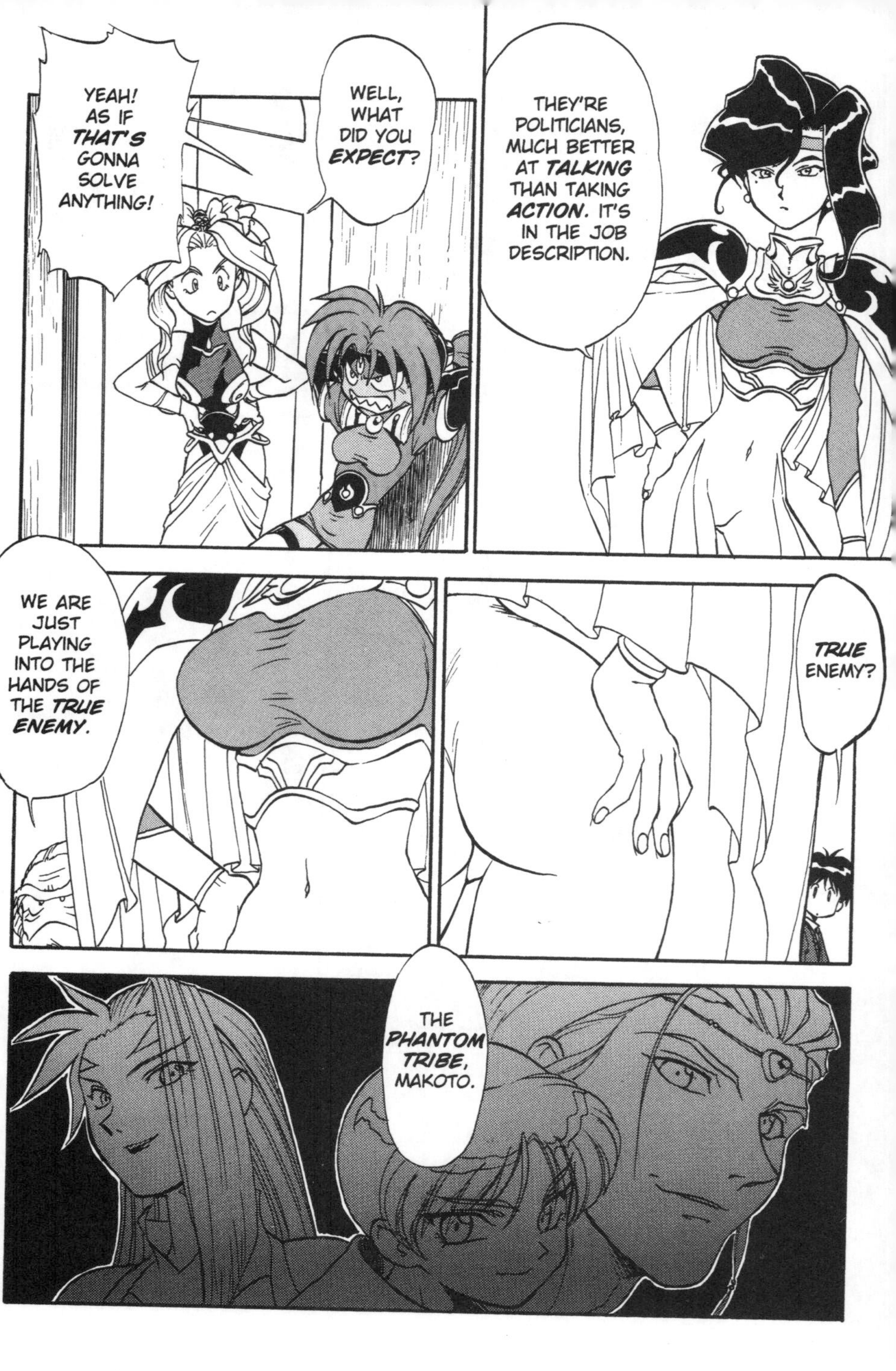
YEAH! AS IF *THAT'S* GONNA SOLVE ANYTHING!
WELL, WHAT DID YOU *EXPECT*?
THEY'RE POLITICIANS, MUCH BETTER AT *TALKING* THAN TAKING *ACTION*. IT'S IN THE JOB DESCRIPTION.
WE ARE JUST PLAYING INTO THE HANDS OF THE *TRUE ENEMY*.
TRUE ENEMY?
THE *PHANTOM TRIBE*, MAKOTO.

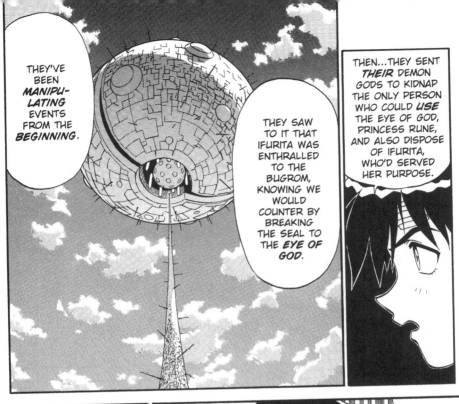

THEY'VE BEEN *MANIPU-LATING* EVENTS FROM THE *BEGINNING*.

THEY SAW TO IT THAT IFURITA WAS ENTHRALLED TO THE BUGROM, KNOWING WE WOULD COUNTER BY BREAKING THE SEAL TO THE *EYE OF GOD*.

THEN...THEY SENT *THEIR* DEMON GODS TO KIDNAP THE ONLY PERSON WHO COULD *USE* THE EYE OF GOD, PRINCESS RUNE, AND ALSO DISPOSE OF IFURITA, WHO'D SERVED HER PURPOSE.

YES, ALL SO *THEY* MAY GAIN CONTROL OF THE EYE.

TIME IS TOO SHORT TO HUNT THESE ILLUSIONISTS DOWN, BUT WE *KNOW* WHERE THEY WILL *STRIKE*: AT THE *STAIRWELL TO HEAVEN!*

IF THEY CAPTURE *THAT*, THE EYE OF GOD IS *THEIRS!*

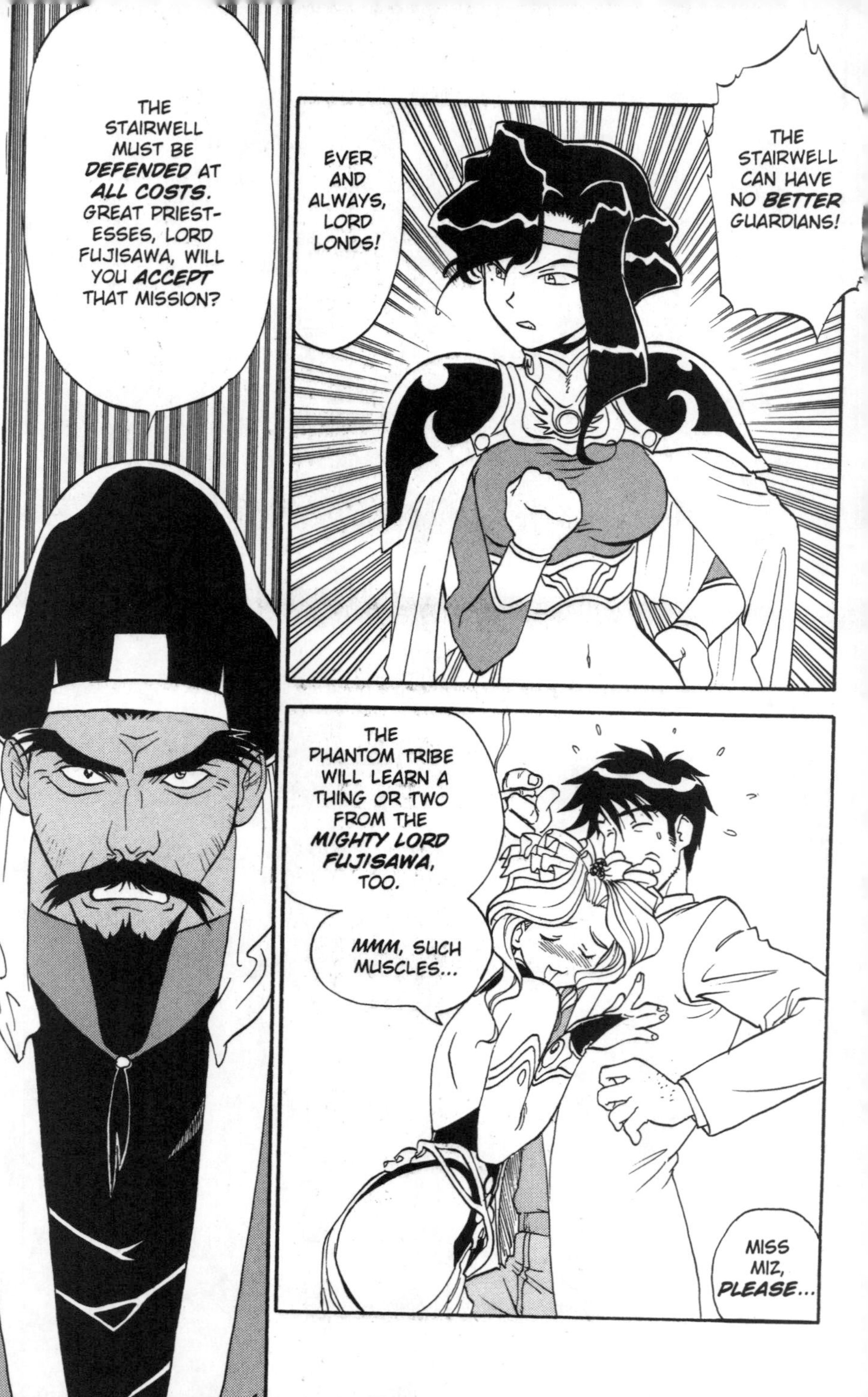
THE STAIRWELL MUST BE DEFENDED AT ALL COSTS. GREAT PRIEST-ESSES, LORD FUJISAWA, WILL YOU ACCEPT THAT MISSION?
EVER AND ALWAYS, LORD LONDS!
THE STAIRWELL CAN HAVE NO BETTER GUARDIANS!
THE PHANTOM TRIBE WILL LEARN A THING OR TWO FROM THE MIGHTY LORD FUJISAWA, TOO.
MMM, SUCH MUSCLES...
MISS MIZ, PLEASE...

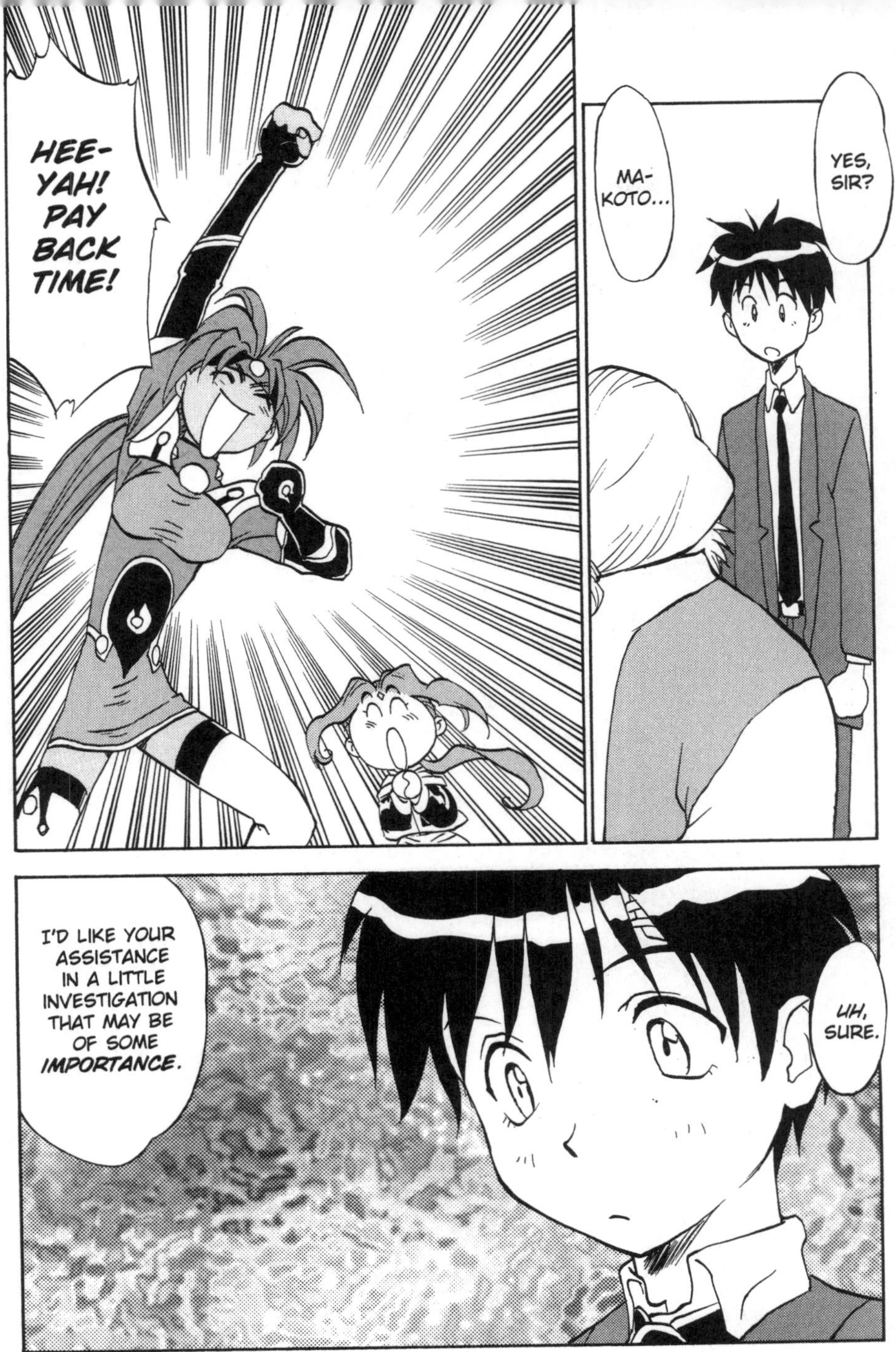
HEE-YAH! PAY BACK TIME!
MA-KOTO...
YES, SIR?
I'D LIKE YOUR ASSISTANCE IN A LITTLE INVESTIGATION THAT MAY BE OF SOME *IMPORTANCE*.
UH, SURE.

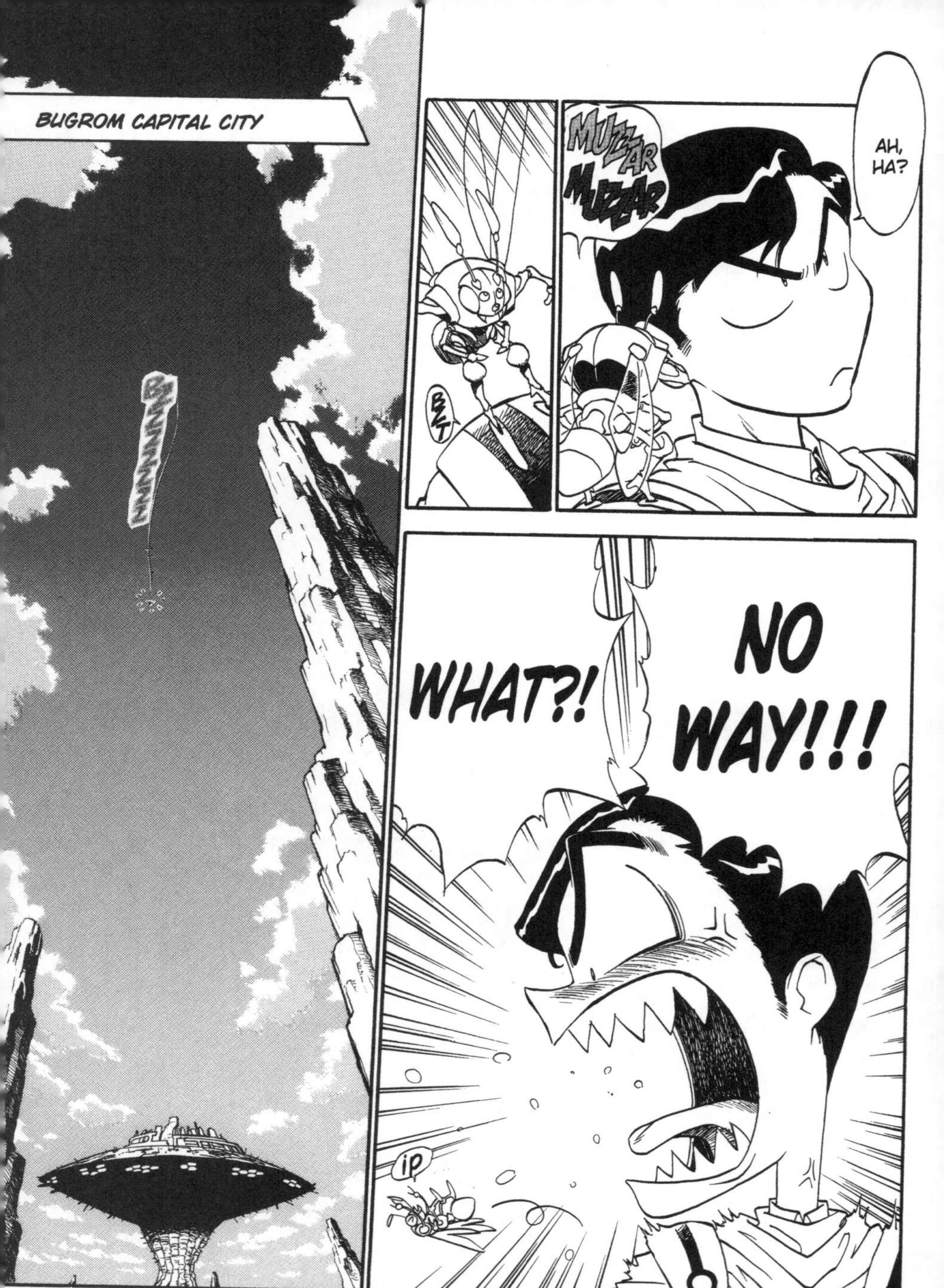
BUGROM CAPITAL CITY
BZT
MUZZAR MUZZAR
AH, HA?
WHAT?!
NO WAY!!!
ip

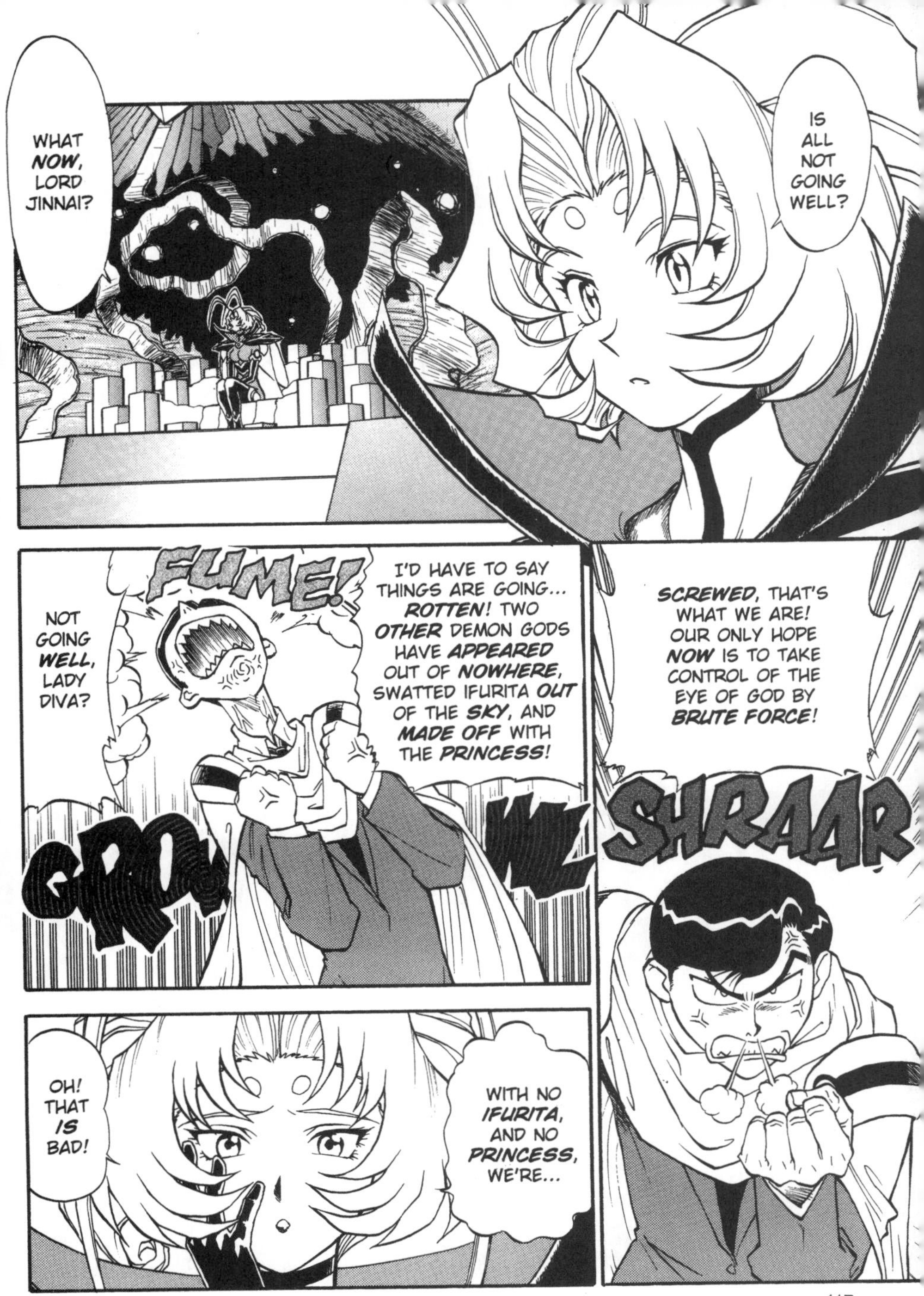
WHAT NOW, LORD JINNAI?
IS ALL NOT GOING WELL?
FUME!
NOT GOING WELL, LADY DIVA?
I'D HAVE TO SAY THINGS ARE GOING... ROTTEN! TWO OTHER DEMON GODS HAVE APPEARED OUT OF NOWHERE, SWATTED IFURITA OUT OF THE SKY, AND MADE OFF WITH THE PRINCESS!
GROWL
OH! THAT IS BAD!
WITH NO IFURITA, AND NO PRINCESS, WE'RE...
SCREWED, THAT'S WHAT WE ARE! OUR ONLY HOPE NOW IS TO TAKE CONTROL OF THE EYE OF GOD BY BRUTE FORCE!
SHRAAR

BUGROM ASSE- MBLE! WE MARCH IMMED- IATELY!

AND TO DO *THAT*, WE MUST *FIRST* CAPTURE THE *STAIRWELL* TO *HEAVEN*!

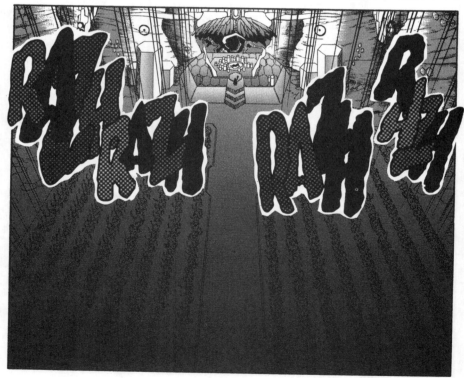

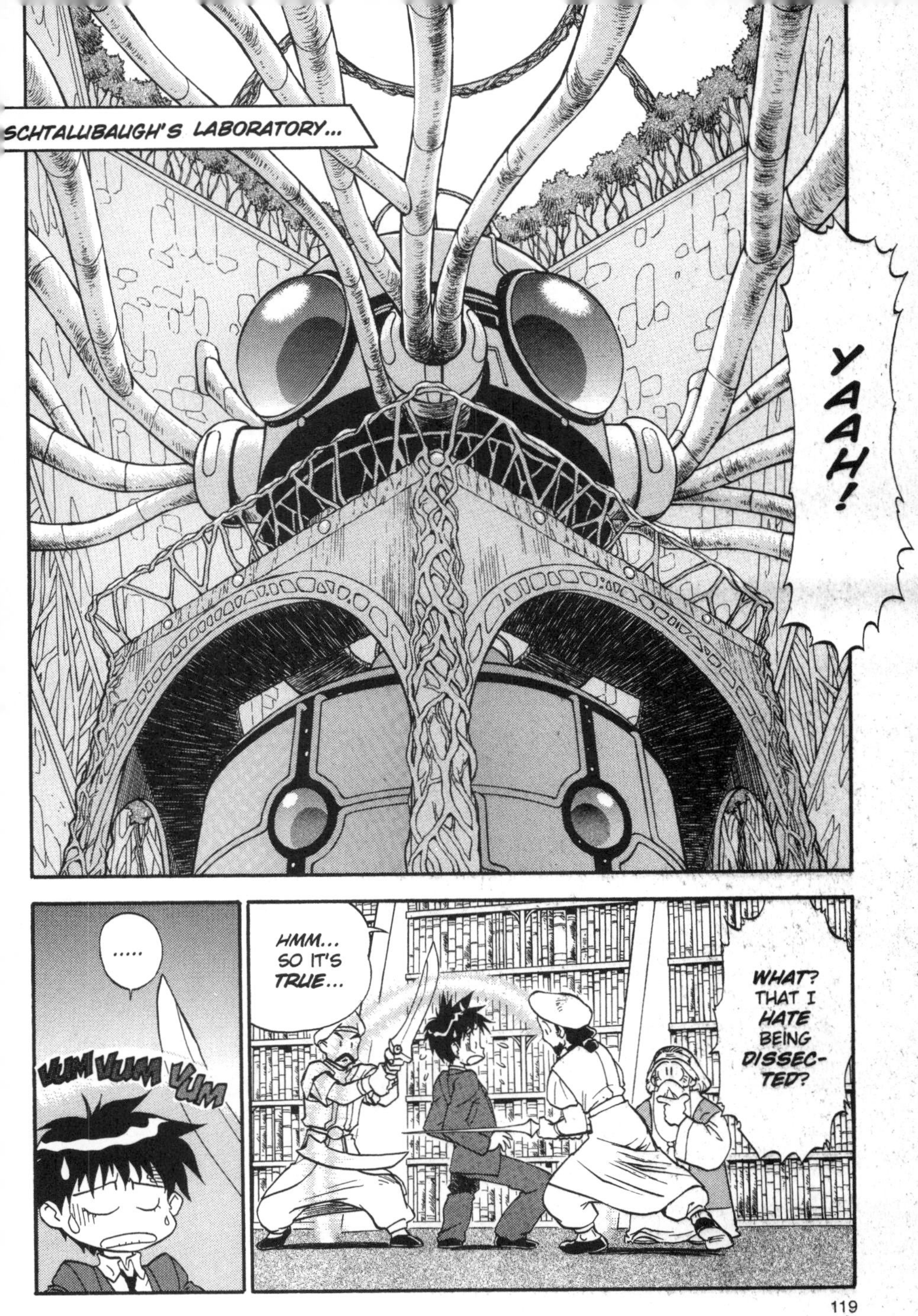
SCHTALUBAUGH'S LABORATORY...
YAAH!
.....
VUM VUM VUM VUM
HMM... SO IT'S TRUE...
WHAT? THAT I HATE BEING DISSECTED?

SORRY, MY BOY. WE'VE SO LITTLE TIME, AND I *HAD* TO BE SURE...

...THAT THE *ROYAL AMULET* WAS INDEED THE *SOURCE* OF YOUR *PROTECTIVE FORCE FIELD*.

IT IS AN ANCIENT TALISMAN, IN LEGEND SAID TO BESTOW REMARKABLE GIFTS ON CERTAIN DESCENDANTS OF THE ROYAL LINE. NO SUCH GIFTS HAVE MANIFESTED IN GENERATIONS, BUT...

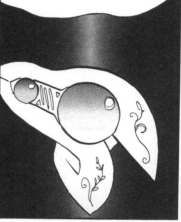

...YOUR *ALIEN NATURE* SOMEHOW *TRIGGERED* ONE OF THEM.

DUN-DUN-DUN-DUN!!

THE PROTECTION ISN'T PERFECT, AS WE'VE SEEN. YOU MUST BE FOCUSED ON YOUR OWN SURVIVAL FOR IT TO WORK.

AS FOR THESE VISIONS YOU HAD WHEN YOU WERE UNCONSCIOUS--I HAVE A THEORY...

I BELIEVE WHAT YOU SAW IS SOME KIND OF NETWORK OF EXTRA-PHYSICAL ENERGIES CREATED BY THE ANCIENT EL-HAZARD CIVILIZATION. IT IS GROUNDED IN THE SUBSTRATES OF OUR WORLD.

IT'S PURPOSE, AND WHAT USE IT MAY BE TO YOU, WE WILL HAVE TO DISCOVER.

OKAY, PROFES--SOR, BUT...

...WHAT ABOUT IFURITA? SHE'S *PART* OF THIS SOMEHOW...

I KNOW...

...AND I'M *SORRY.*

IT'S OUT OF MY HANDS. SHE'S TO BE *DISMANTLED* TOMORROW, BY ALLIANCE *EDICT.* THEY SAY THAT *NOW* IS OUR *CHANCE*, WHILE SHE IS NON-FUNCTIONAL...

IT'S UNDERSTANDABLE THAT THEY'D WANT TO BE RID OF AT LEAST *ONE* DEMON GOD, AND CAN'T SEE WHAT COULD BE *LOST.* IF ONLY SHE WASN'T LOCKED INTO *OBEYING* THAT *MADMAN*, JINNAI...

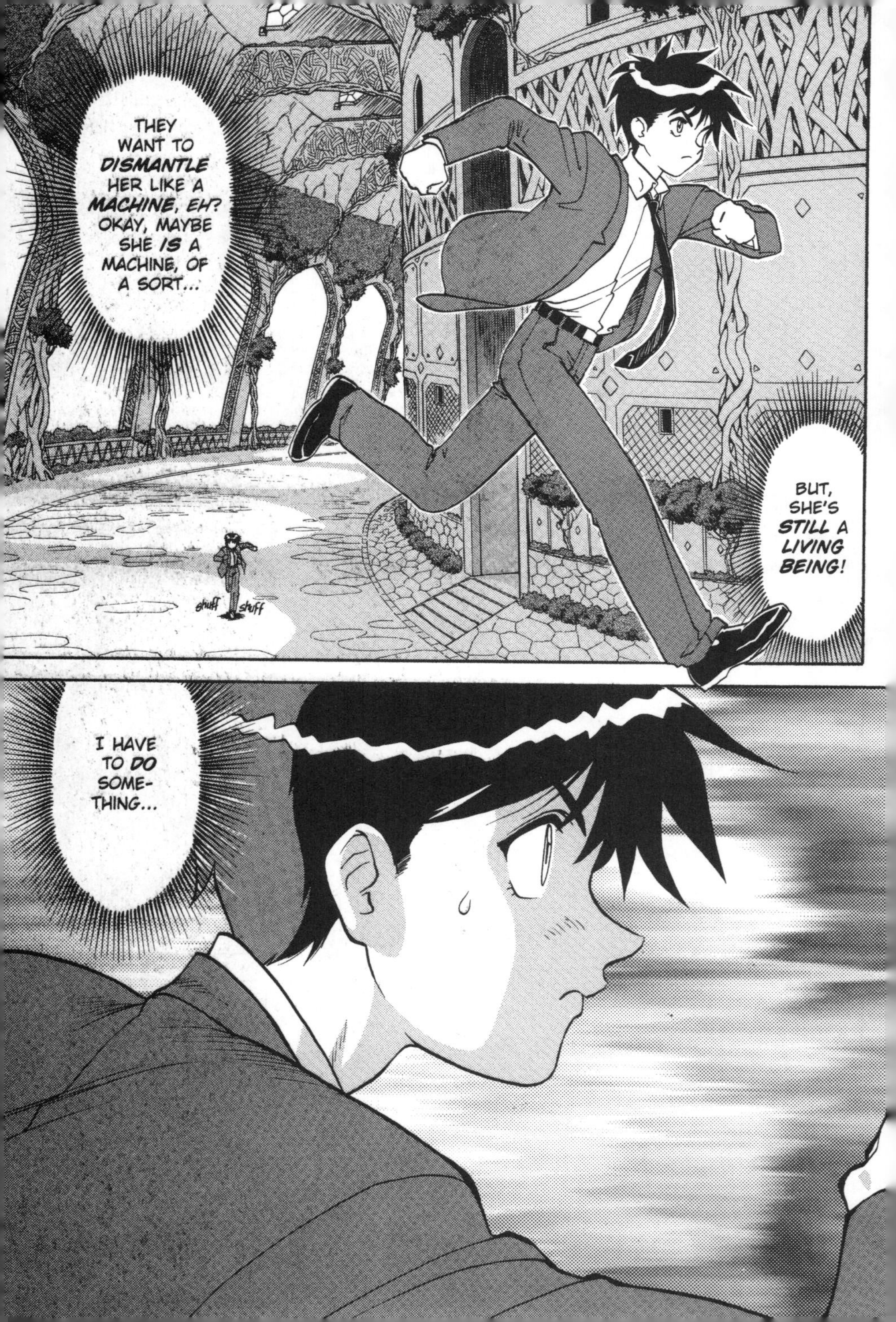

THEY WANT TO DISMANTLE HER LIKE A MACHINE, EH? OKAY, MAYBE SHE IS A MACHINE, OF A SORT...
shuff shuff
BUT, SHE'S STILL A LIVING BEING!
I HAVE TO DO SOME-THING...

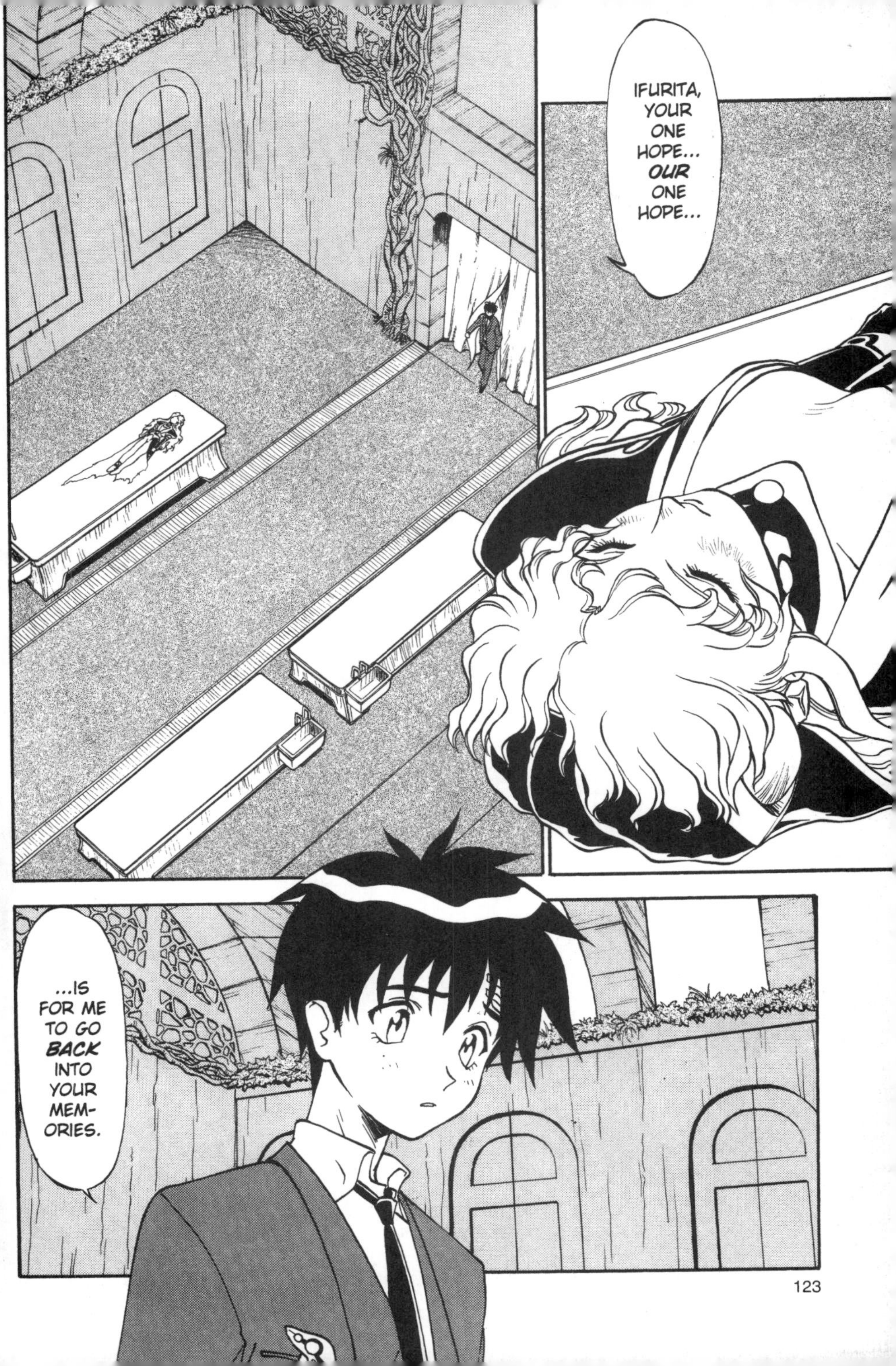
IFURITA, YOUR ONE HOPE... **OUR** ONE HOPE...
...IS FOR ME TO GO **BACK** INTO YOUR MEM-ORIES.

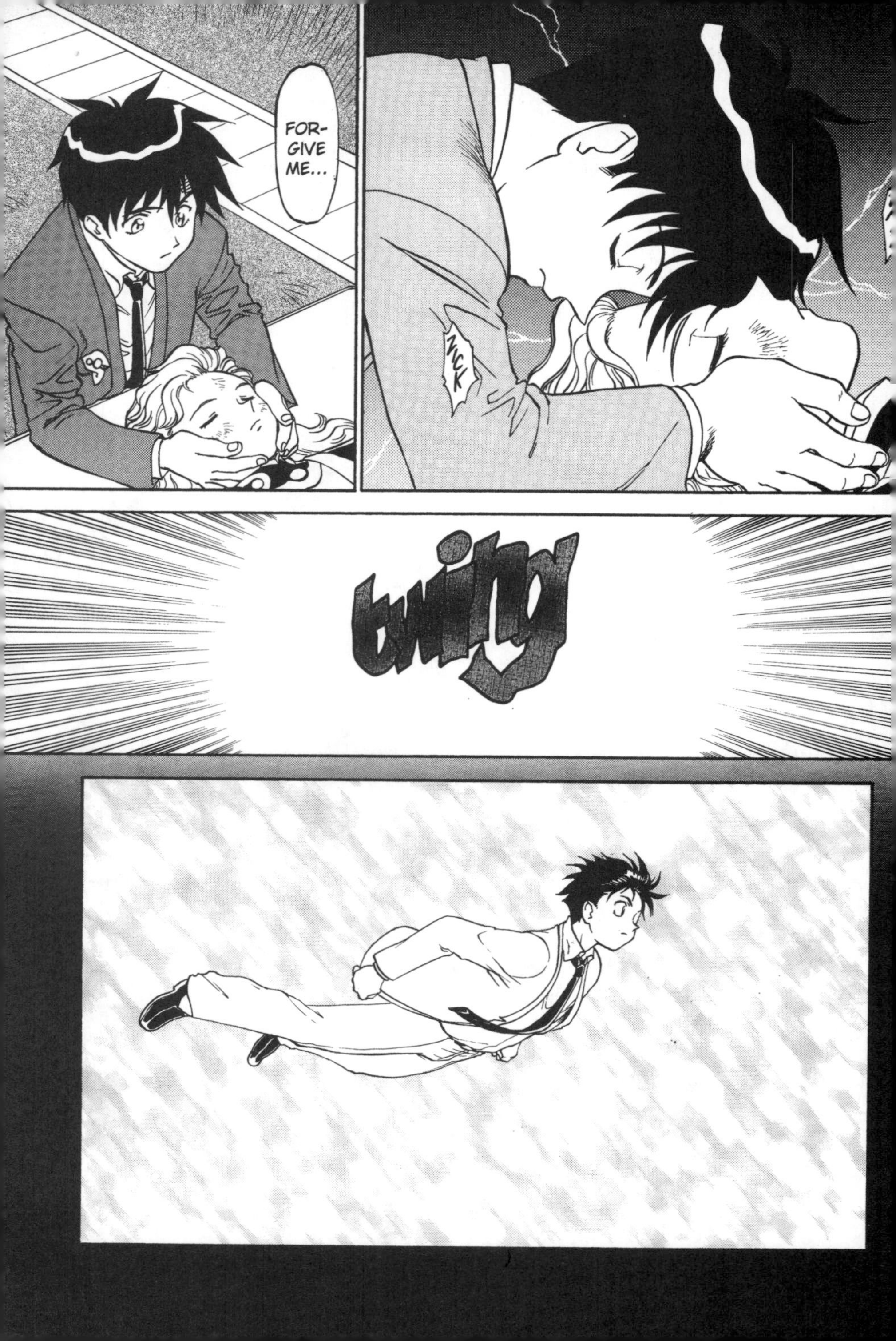
FOR-GIVE ME...
ZICK
twing

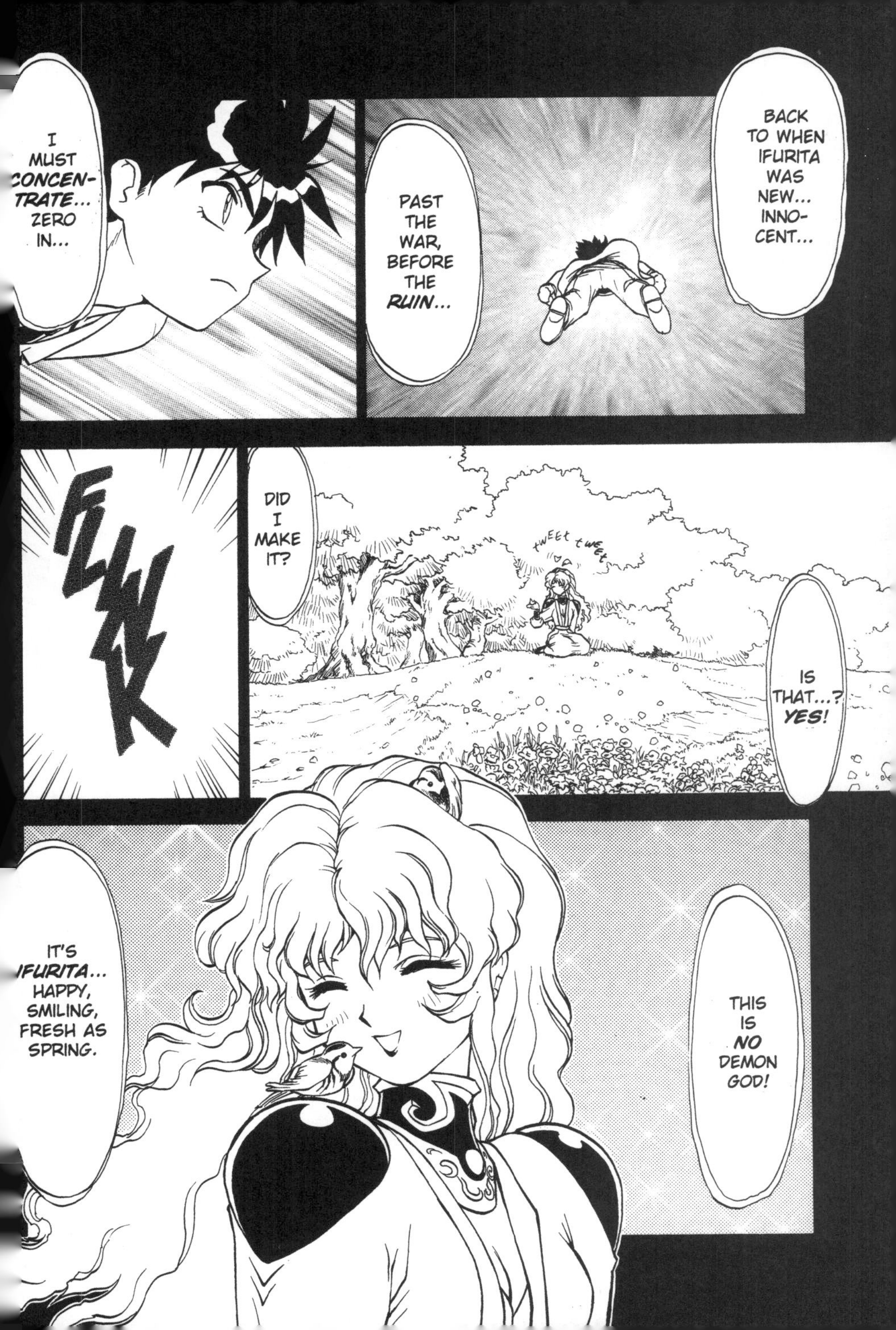
I MUST CONCENTRATE... ZERO IN...
PAST THE WAR, BEFORE THE RUIN...
BACK TO WHEN IFURITA WAS NEW... INNOCENT...
FLWNK
DID I MAKE IT?
TWEET TWEET
IS THAT...? YES!
IT'S IFURITA... HAPPY, SMILING, FRESH AS SPRING.
THIS IS NO DEMON GOD!

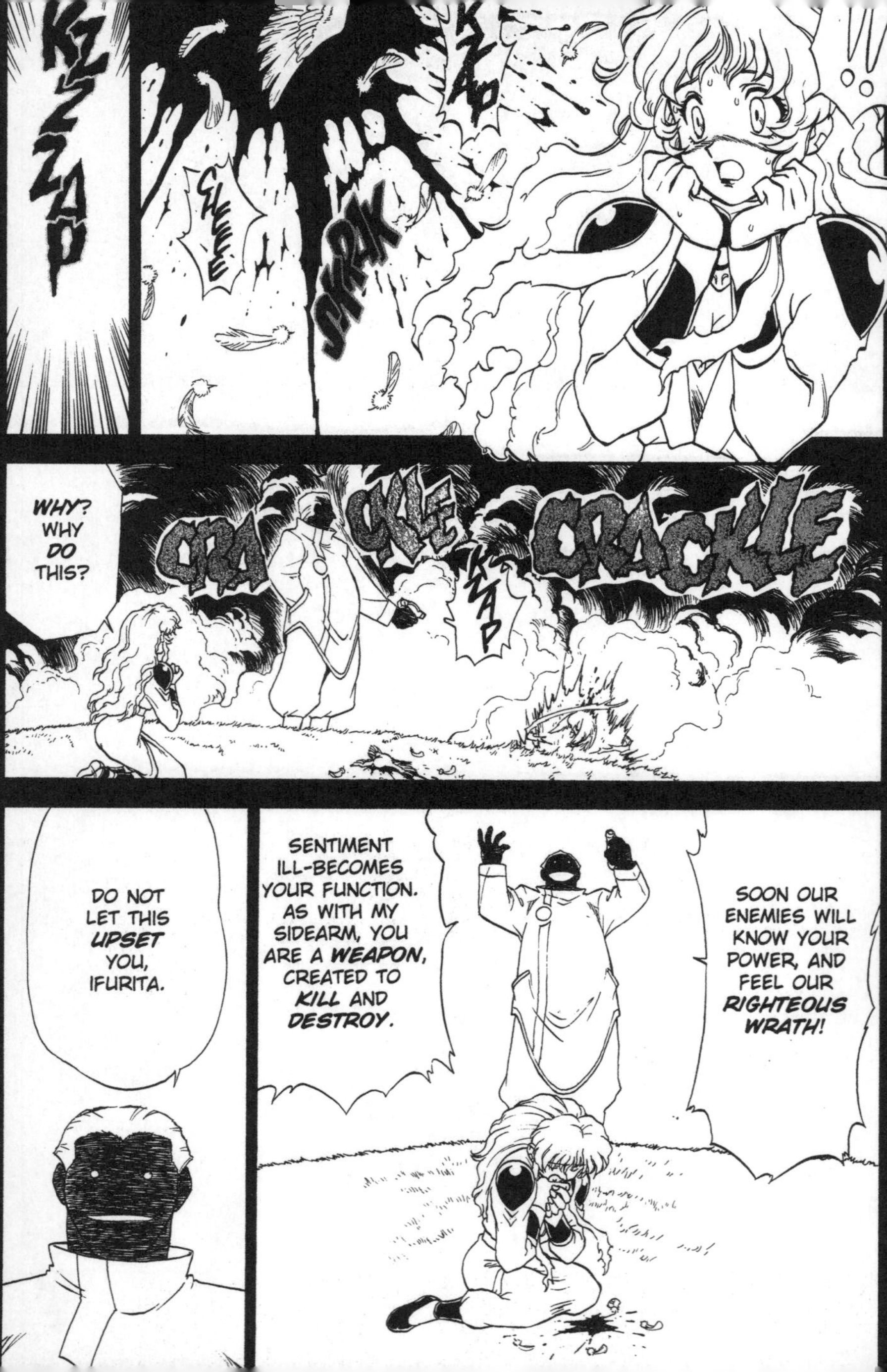

KZZZAP
CHEEEE
SPRAK
KZAP
!!
WHY? WHY DO THIS?
CRACKLE
KZAP
CRACKLE
DO NOT LET THIS UPSET YOU, IFURITA.
SENTIMENT ILL-BECOMES YOUR FUNCTION. AS WITH MY SIDEARM, YOU ARE A WEAPON, CREATED TO KILL AND DESTROY.
SOON OUR ENEMIES WILL KNOW YOUR POWER, AND FEEL OUR RIGHTEOUS WRATH!

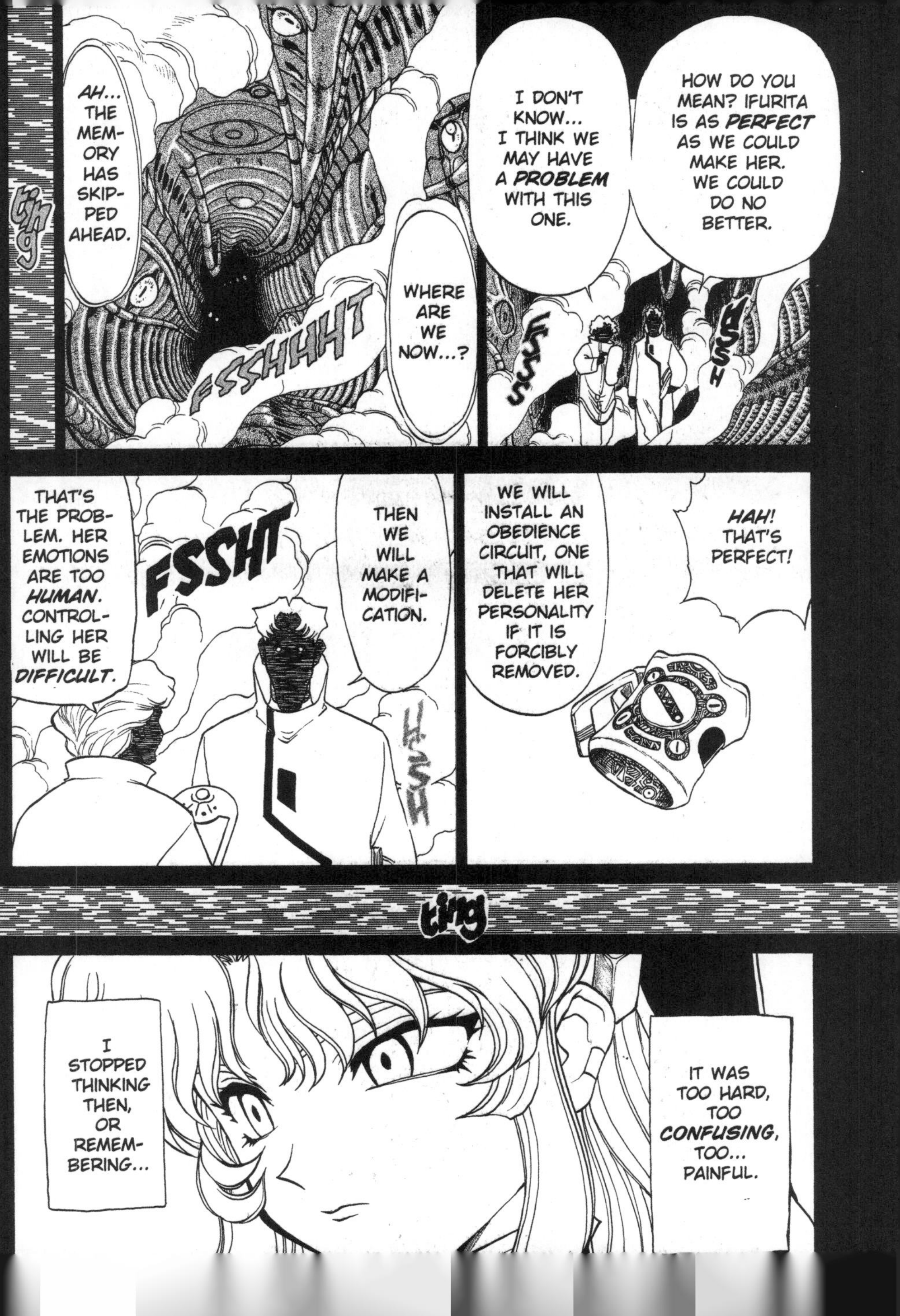
AH... THE MEMORY HAS SKIPPED AHEAD.
ting
FSSHHHT
WHERE ARE WE NOW...?
I DON'T KNOW... I THINK WE MAY HAVE A **PROBLEM** WITH THIS ONE.
HOW DO YOU MEAN? IFURITA IS AS **PERFECT** AS WE COULD MAKE HER. WE COULD DO NO BETTER.
THAT'S THE PROBLEM. HER EMOTIONS ARE TOO **HUMAN**. CONTROLLING HER WILL BE **DIFFICULT**.
FSSHT
THEN WE WILL MAKE A MODIFICATION.
WE WILL INSTALL AN OBEDIENCE CIRCUIT, ONE THAT WILL DELETE HER PERSONALITY IF IT IS FORCIBLY REMOVED.
HAH! THAT'S PERFECT!
ting!
I STOPPED THINKING THEN, OR REMEMBERING...
IT WAS TOO HARD, TOO **CONFUSING**, TOO... PAINFUL.

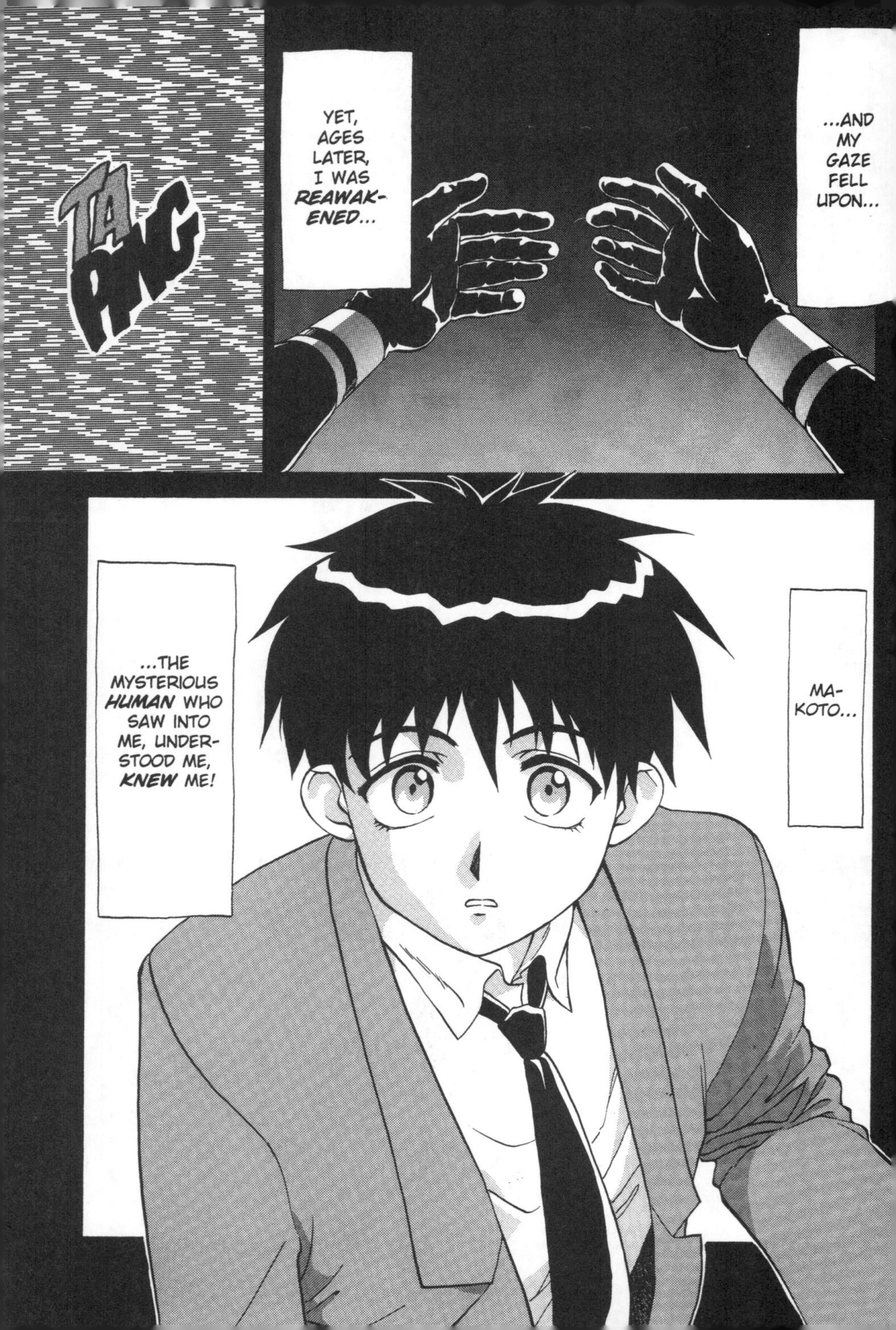
TA PING
YET, AGES LATER, I WAS REAWAKENED...
...AND MY GAZE FELL UPON...
...THE MYSTERIOUS HUMAN WHO SAW INTO ME, UNDERSTOOD ME, KNEW ME!
MAKOTO...

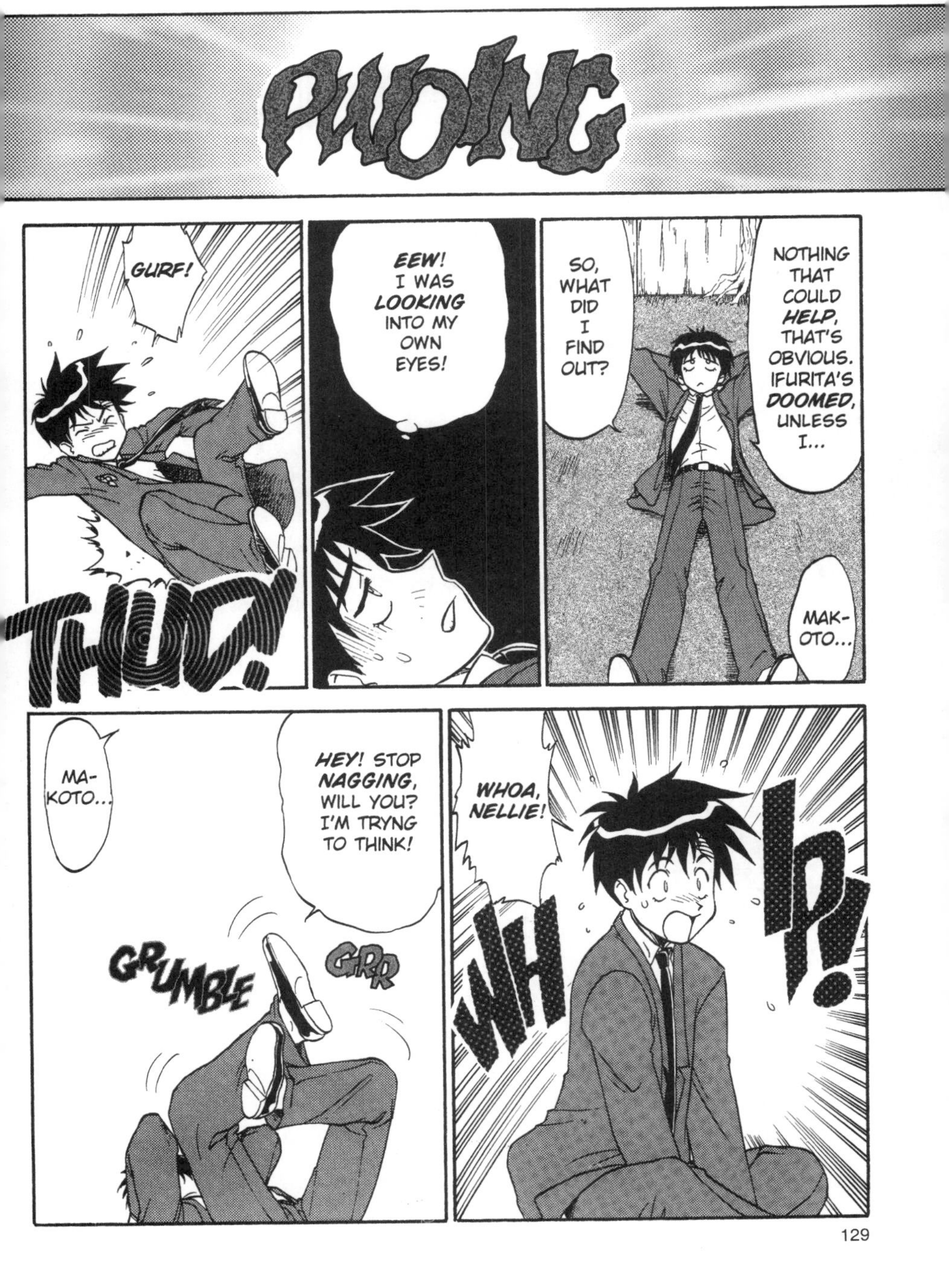
PWOING
GURF!
THUD!
EEW! I WAS LOOKING INTO MY OWN EYES!
SO, WHAT DID I FIND OUT?
NOTHING THAT COULD HELP, THAT'S OBVIOUS. IFURITA'S DOOMED, UNLESS I...
MAK-OTO...
MA-KOTO...
HEY! STOP NAGGING, WILL YOU? I'M TRYNG TO THINK!
GRUMBLE
GRR
WHOA, NELLIE!
WHUP!!

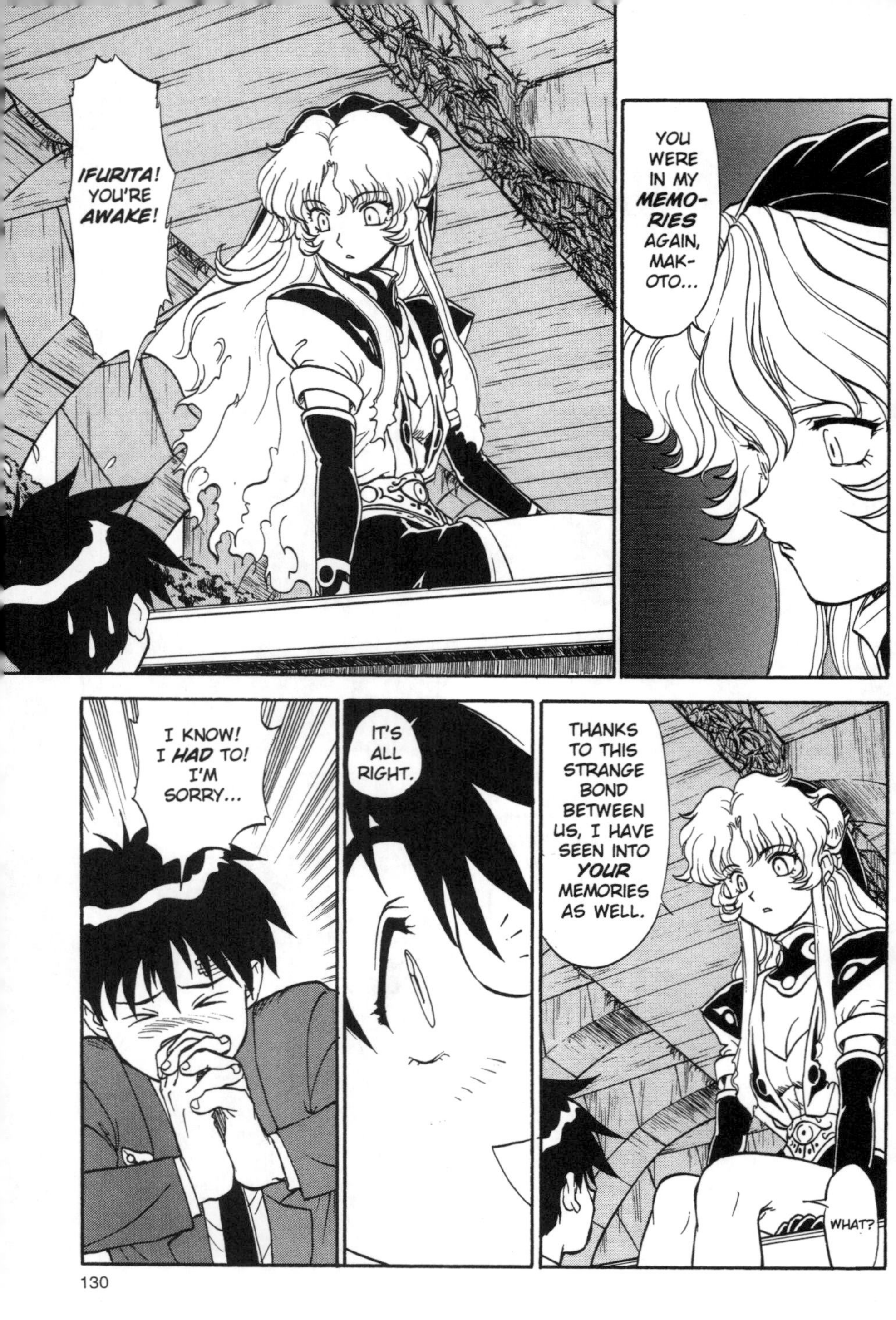
IFURITA! YOU'RE AWAKE!
YOU WERE IN MY MEMORIES AGAIN, MAKOTO...
I KNOW! I HAD TO! I'M SORRY...
IT'S ALL RIGHT.
THANKS TO THIS STRANGE BOND BETWEEN US, I HAVE SEEN INTO YOUR MEMORIES AS WELL.
WHAT?

I WIT-NESSED OUR INEXPLICABLE MEETING IN YOUR WORLD...

...AN EXPERIENCE YOU'D HAVE **NO** REASON TO QUESTION.

BUT KNOW THIS: THE GIRL YOU MET MAY **NOT** HAVE BEEN **ME**.

HUH?

BUT IT **WAS**...

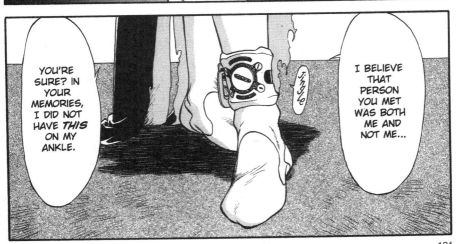

YOU'RE SURE? IN YOUR MEMORIES, I DID NOT HAVE **THIS** ON MY ANKLE.

jingle

I BELIEVE THAT PERSON YOU MET WAS BOTH ME AND NOT ME...

131

I... DON'T KNOW WHAT TO SAY...

MA-KOTO...

...DON'T MISTAKE WHAT HAS HAP-PENED HERE.

I AM STILL WHA I AM.

!!

NO! YOU *CAN'T* GO BACK TO *JINNAI!*

I CER-TAINLY *WON'T.*

trip-FALL

NOT UNTIL I HAVE THE PRIN-CESS...

...AND *CRACK* SOME FELLOW DEMON GOD *HEADS!*

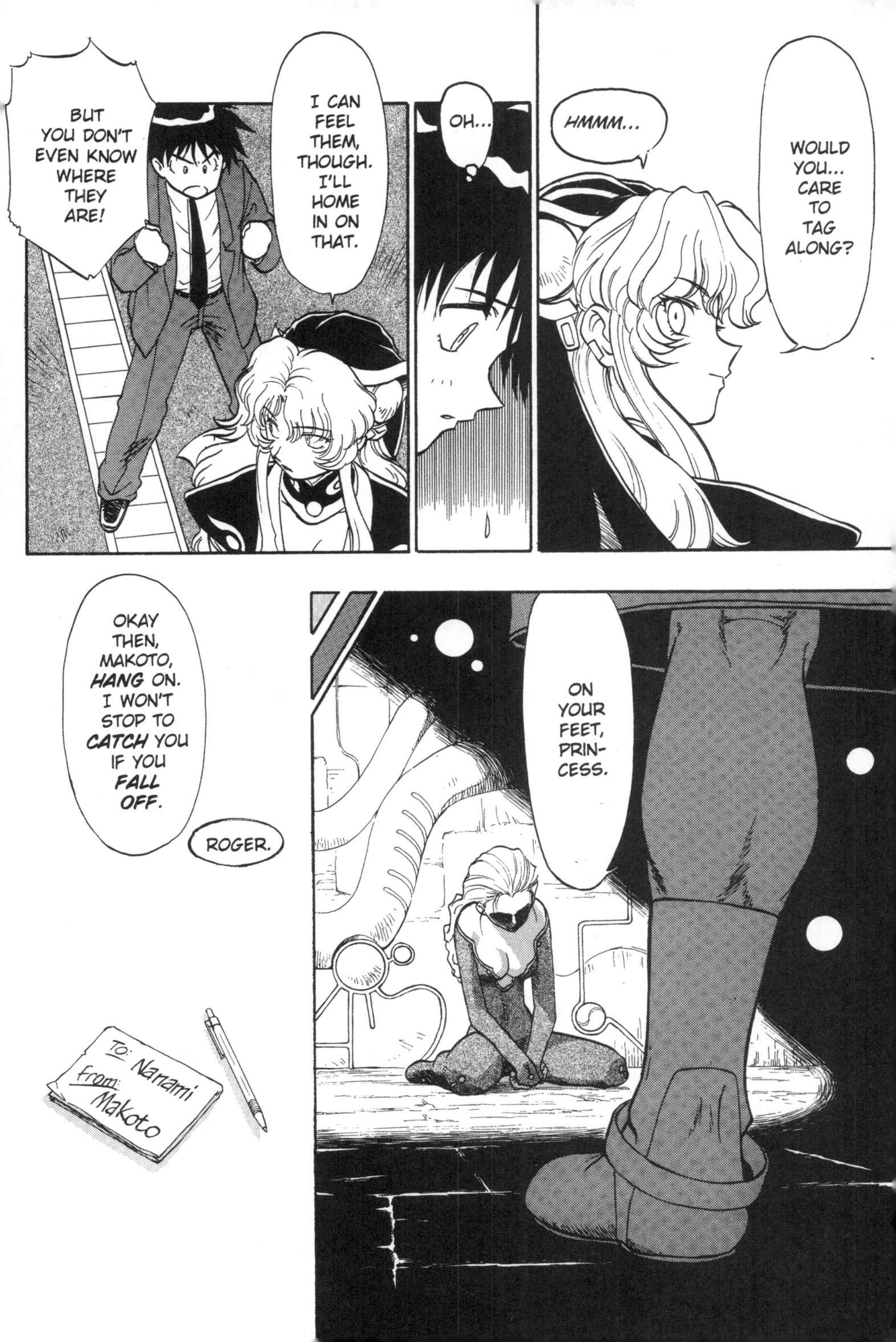
BUT YOU DON'T EVEN KNOW WHERE THEY ARE!
I CAN FEEL THEM, THOUGH. I'LL HOME IN ON THAT.
OH...
HMMM...
WOULD YOU... CARE TO TAG ALONG?
OKAY THEN, MAKOTO, HANG ON. I WON'T STOP TO CATCH YOU IF YOU FALL OFF.
ROGER.
To: Nanami
From: Makoto
ON YOUR FEET, PRIN-CESS.

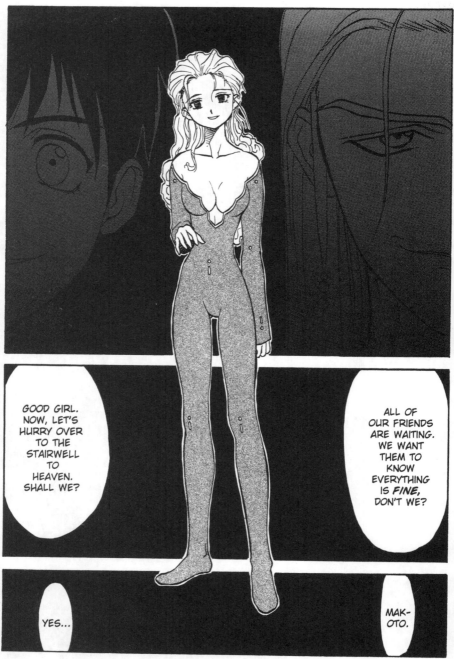

GOOD GIRL. NOW, LET'S HURRY OVER TO THE STAIRWELL TO HEAVEN. SHALL WE?

ALL OF OUR FRIENDS ARE WAITING. WE WANT THEM TO KNOW EVERYTHING IS *FINE*, DON'T WE?

YES...

MAK-OTO.

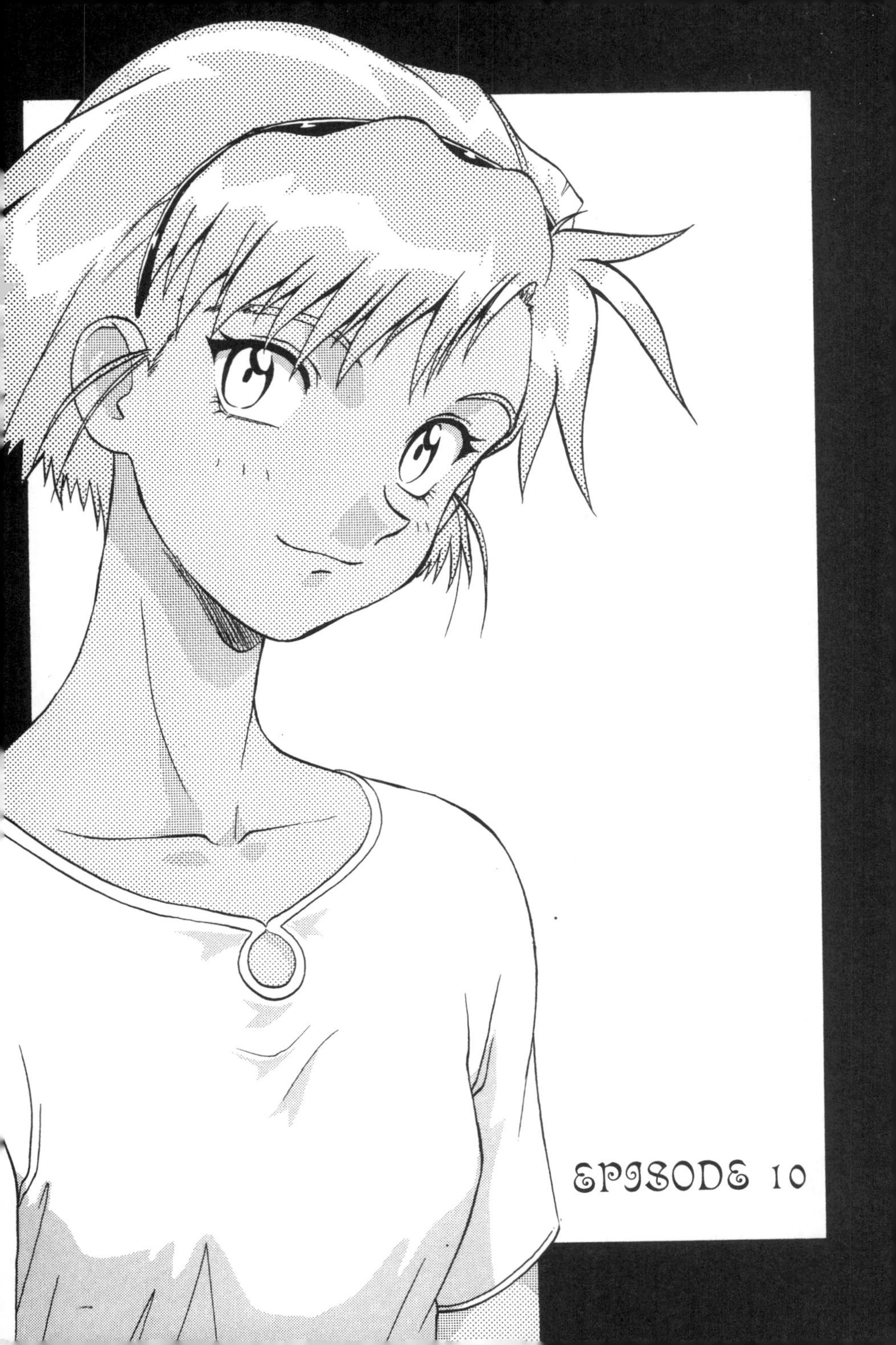

EPISODE 10

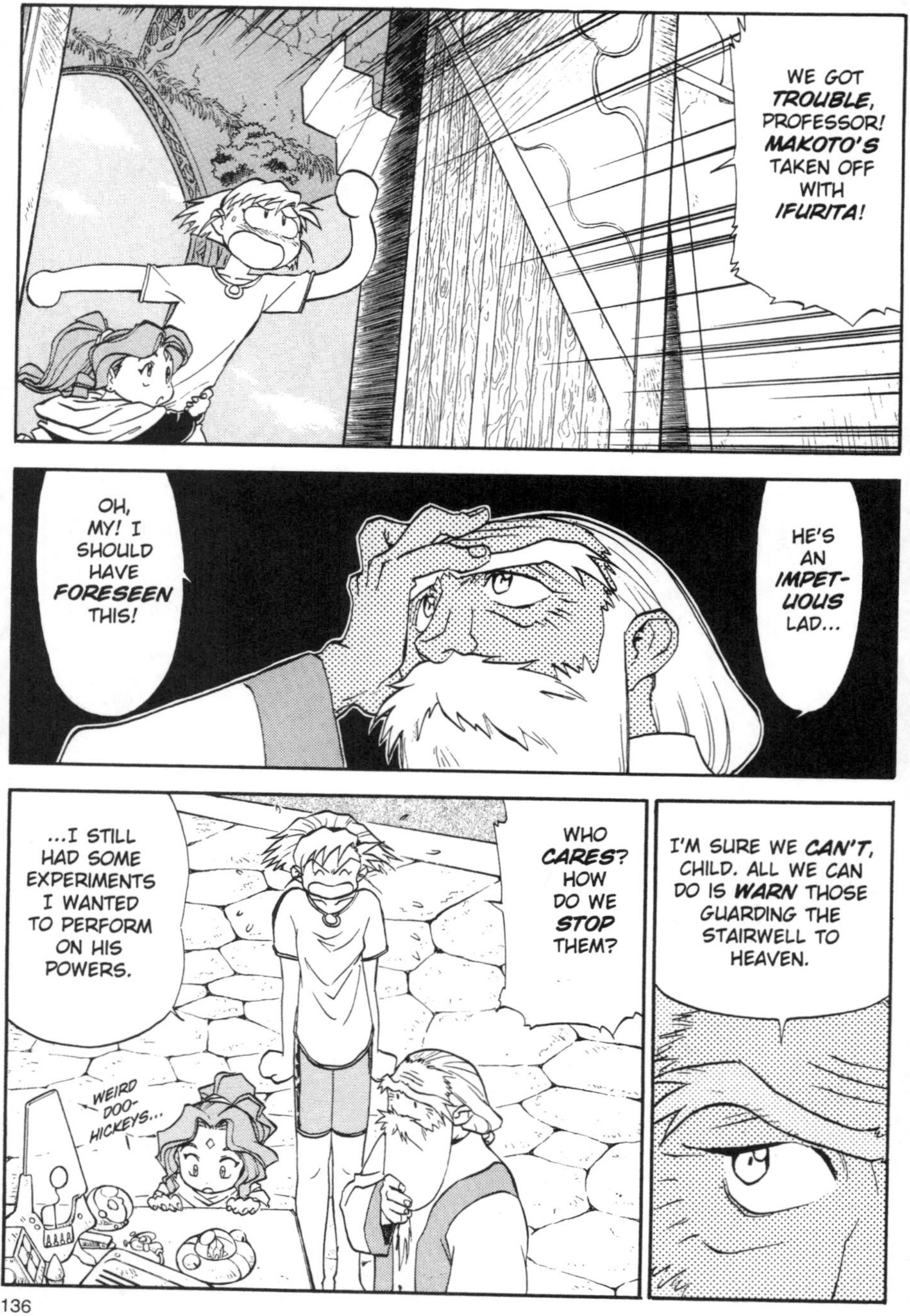
WE GOT TROUBLE, PROFESSOR! MAKOTO'S TAKEN OFF WITH IFURITA!
OH, MY! I SHOULD HAVE FORESEEN THIS!
HE'S AN IMPETUOUS LAD...
...I STILL HAD SOME EXPERIMENTS I WANTED TO PERFORM ON HIS POWERS.
WEIRD DOO-HICKEYS...
WHO CARES? HOW DO WE STOP THEM?
I'M SURE WE CAN'T, CHILD. ALL WE CAN DO IS WARN THOSE GUARDING THE STAIRWELL TO HEAVEN.

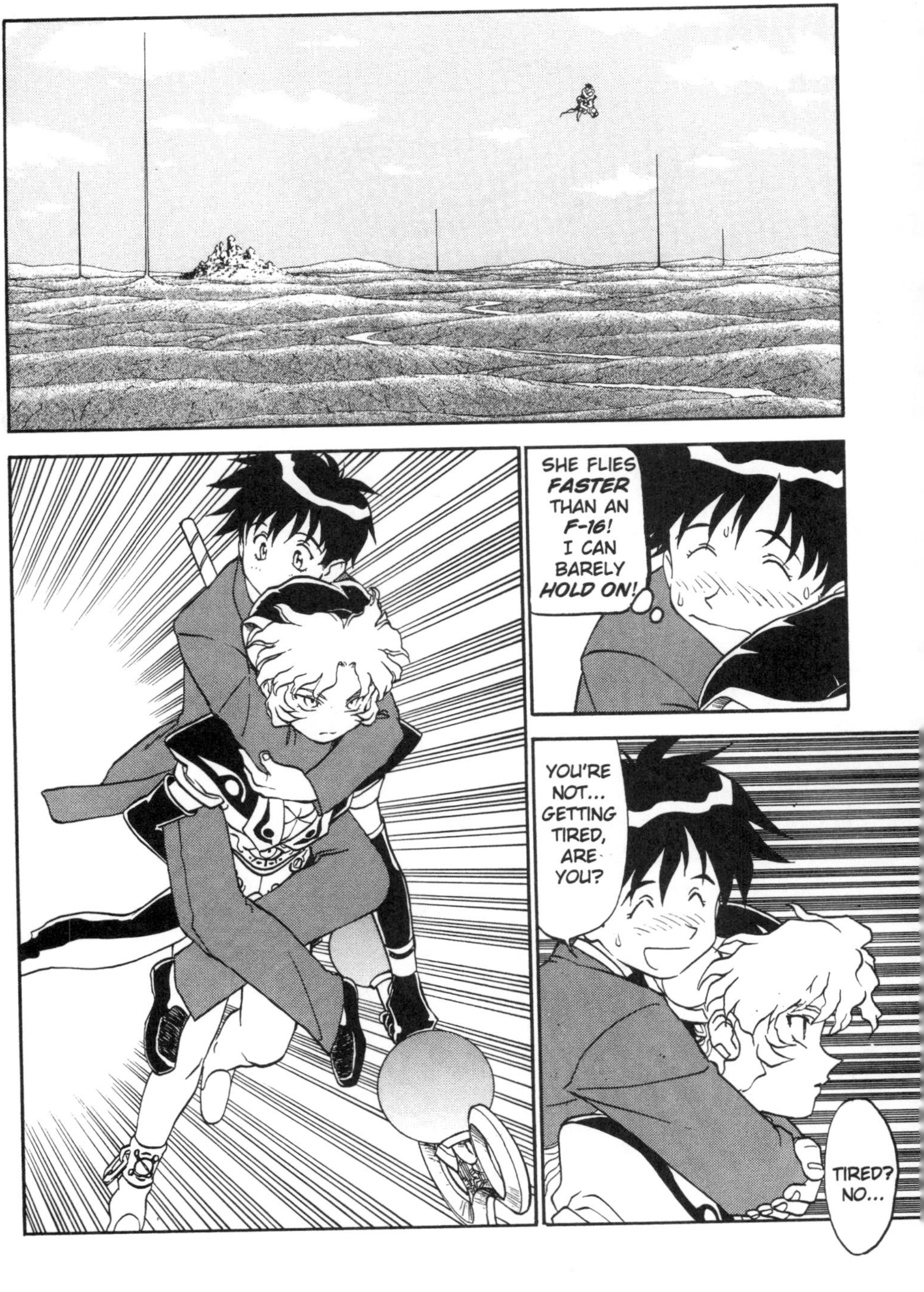
SHE FLIES FASTER THAN AN F-16! I CAN BARELY HOLD ON!
YOU'RE NOT... GETTING TIRED, ARE YOU?
TIRED? NO...

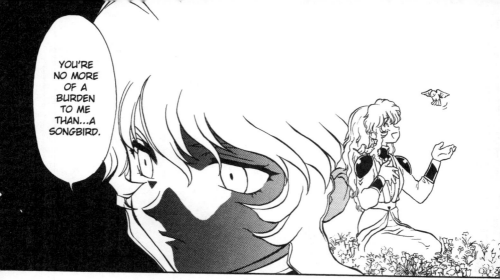

YOU'RE NO MORE OF A BURDEN TO ME THAN...A SONGBIRD.

.....

I KNEW I WAS RIGHT, IFURITA. I *KNEW* YOU WEREN'T A DEMON.

OR A WEAPON. YOU'RE FAR *MORE*!

YOU'RE *HUMAN*, WITH A *SOUL* AND A *HEART*!

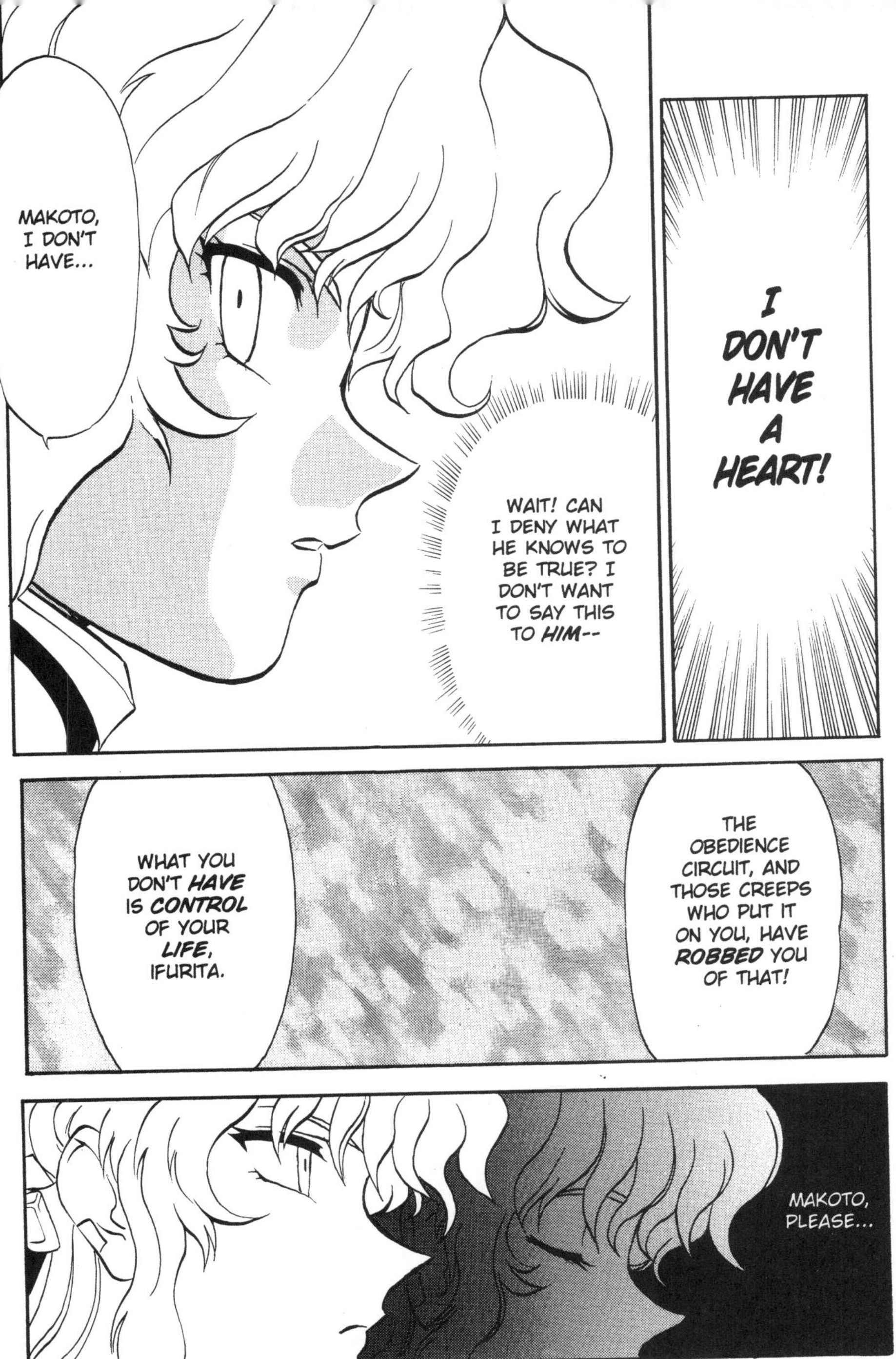
MAKOTO, I DON'T HAVE...
WAIT! CAN I DENY WHAT HE KNOWS TO BE TRUE? I DON'T WANT TO SAY THIS TO HIM--
I DON'T HAVE A HEART!
WHAT YOU DON'T HAVE IS CONTROL OF YOUR LIFE, IFURITA.
THE OBEDIENCE CIRCUIT, AND THOSE CREEPS WHO PUT IT ON YOU, HAVE ROBBED YOU OF THAT!
MAKOTO, PLEASE...

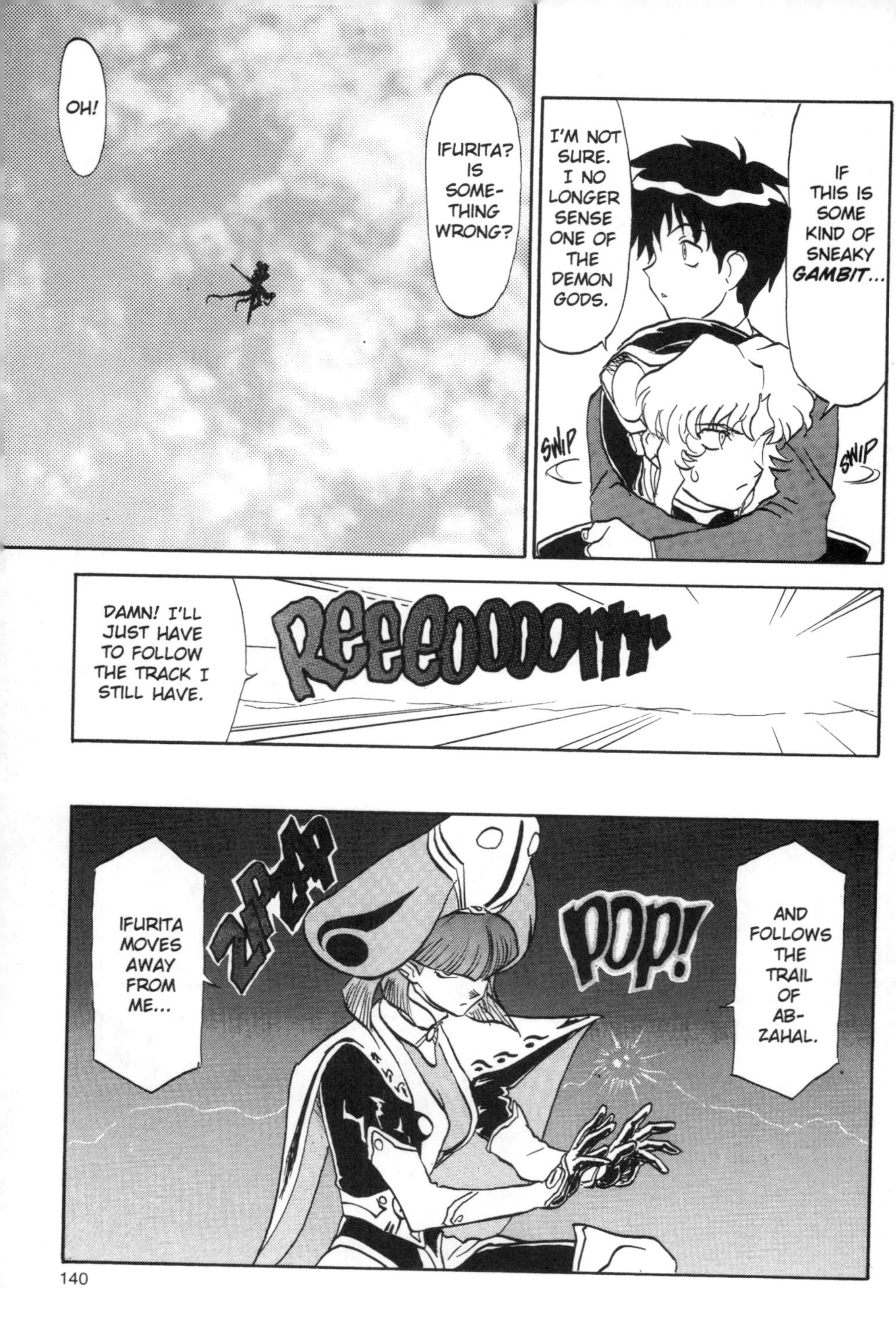
OH!
IFURITA? IS SOME-THING WRONG?
I'M NOT SURE. I NO LONGER SENSE ONE OF THE DEMON GODS.
IF THIS IS SOME KIND OF SNEAKY **GAMBIT**...
SWIP
SWIP
DAMN! I'LL JUST HAVE TO FOLLOW THE TRACK I STILL HAVE.
REEEOOOOM
IFURITA MOVES AWAY FROM ME...
ZZAP
POP!
AND FOLLOWS THE TRAIL OF AB-ZAHAL.

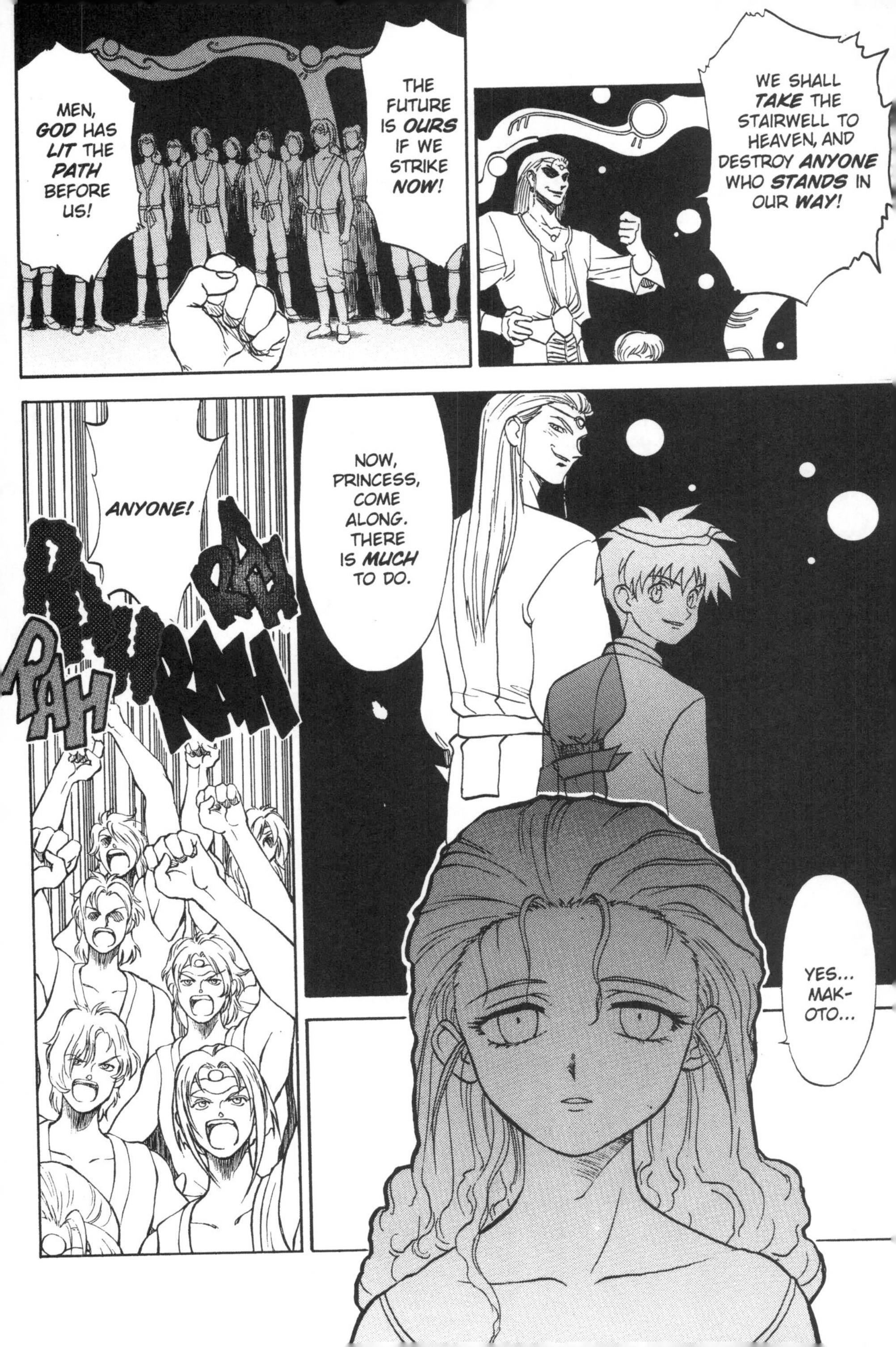
MEN, GOD HAS LIT THE PATH BEFORE US!
THE FUTURE IS OURS IF WE STRIKE NOW!
WE SHALL TAKE THE STAIRWELL TO HEAVEN, AND DESTROY ANYONE WHO STANDS IN OUR WAY!
ANYONE!
RAH RAH
PAH RAH
NOW, PRINCESS, COME ALONG. THERE IS MUCH TO DO.
YES... MAK-OTO...

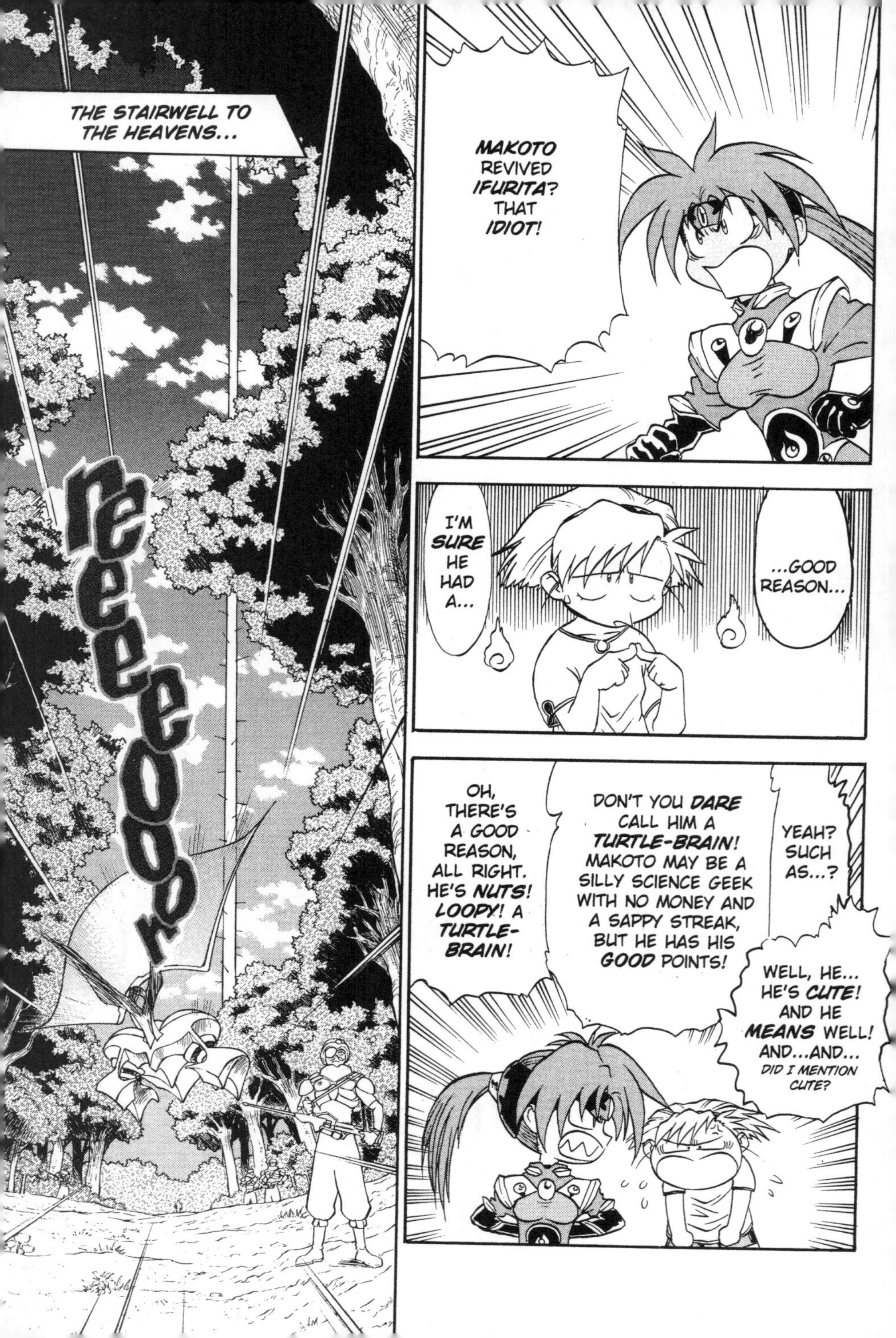
THE STAIRWELL TO THE HEAVENS...
reeeeooor
MAKOTO REVIVED IFURITA? THAT IDIOT!
I'M SURE HE HAD A...
...GOOD REASON...
OH, THERE'S A GOOD REASON, ALL RIGHT. HE'S NUTS! LOOPY! A TURTLE-BRAIN!
DON'T YOU DARE CALL HIM A TURTLE-BRAIN! MAKOTO MAY BE A SILLY SCIENCE GEEK WITH NO MONEY AND A SAPPY STREAK, BUT HE HAS HIS GOOD POINTS!
YEAH? SUCH AS...?
WELL, HE... HE'S CUTE! AND HE MEANS WELL! AND...AND... DID I MENTION CUTE?

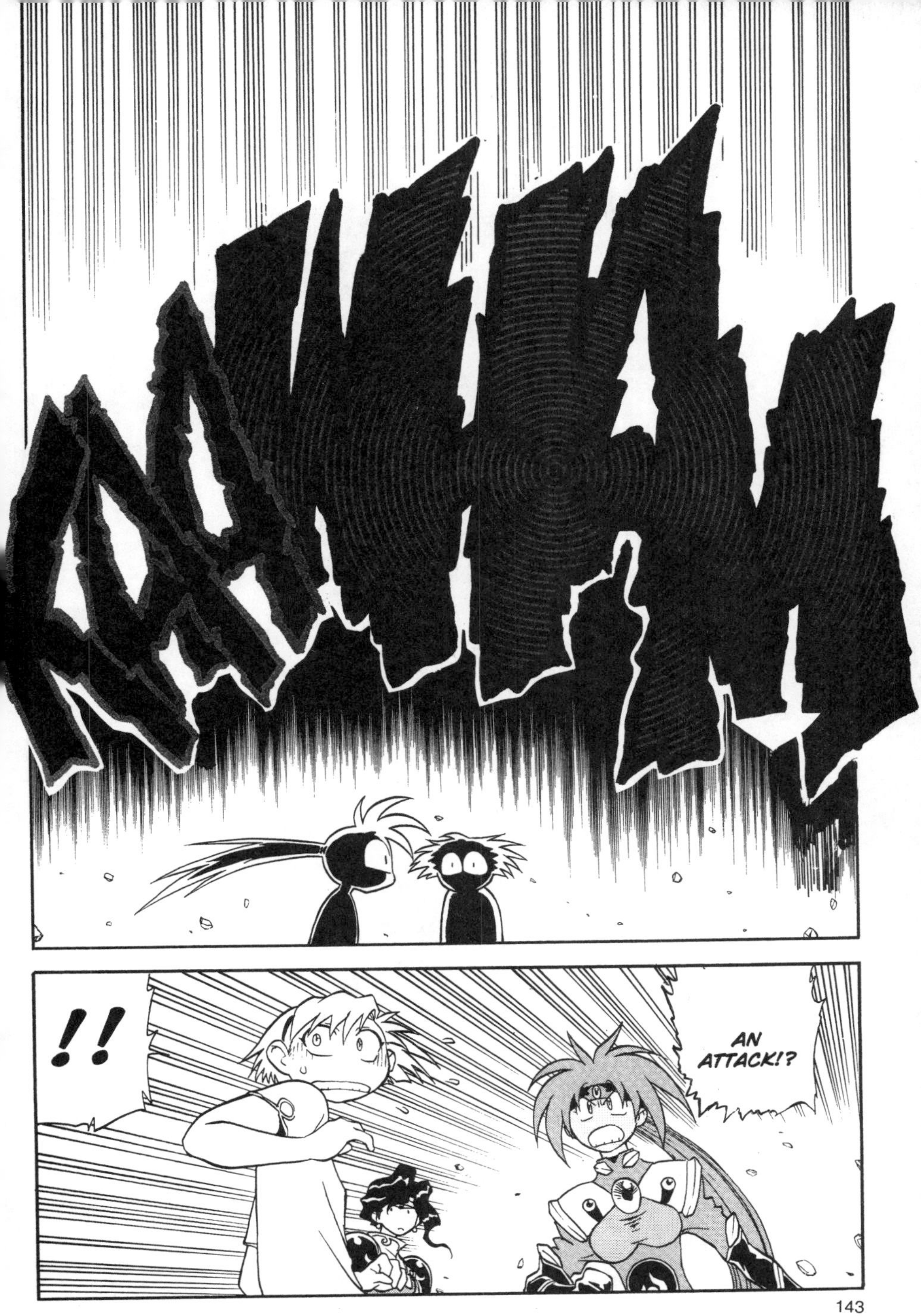
!!
AN ATTACK!?

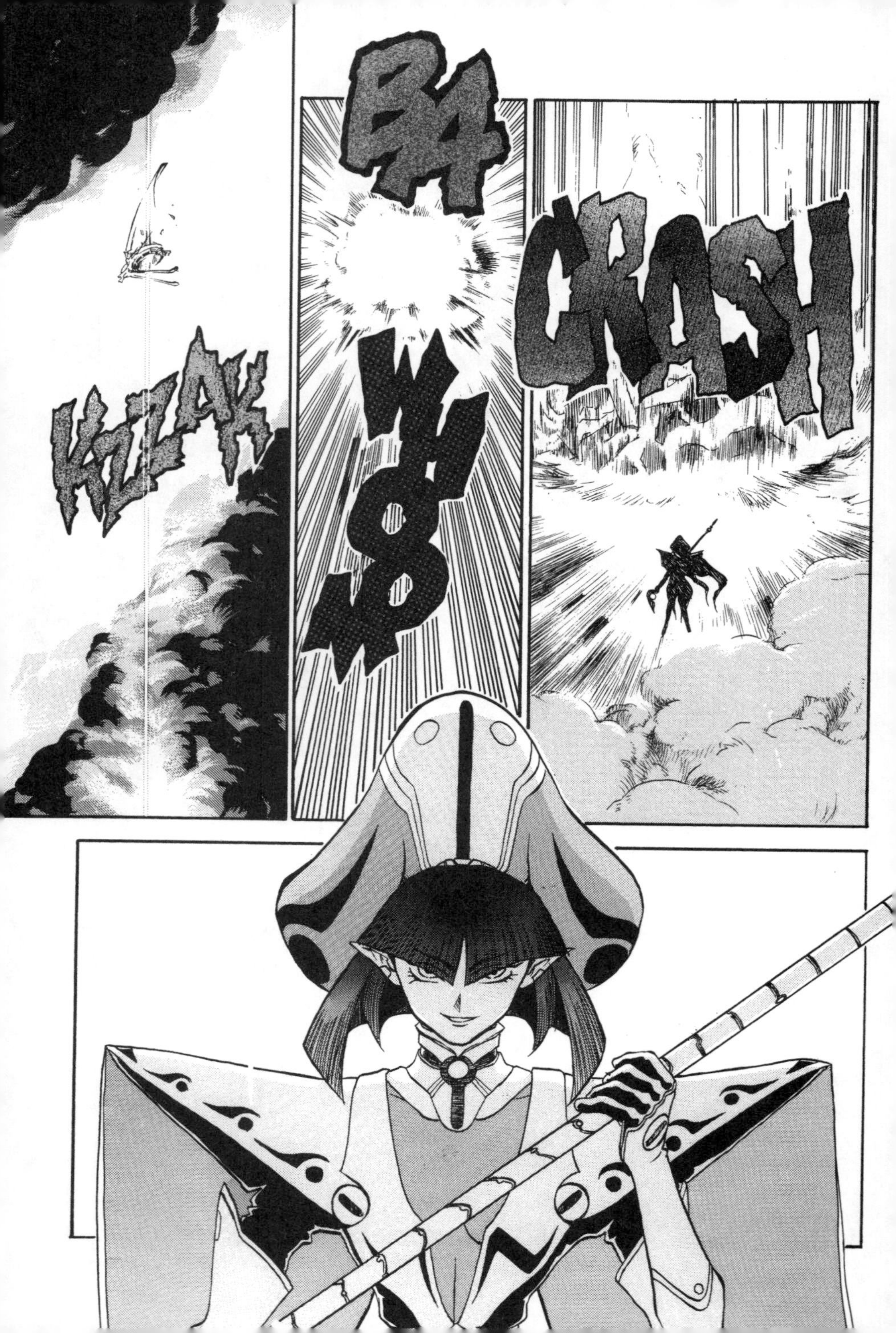
KZZAK
BA
WHOOSH
CRASH

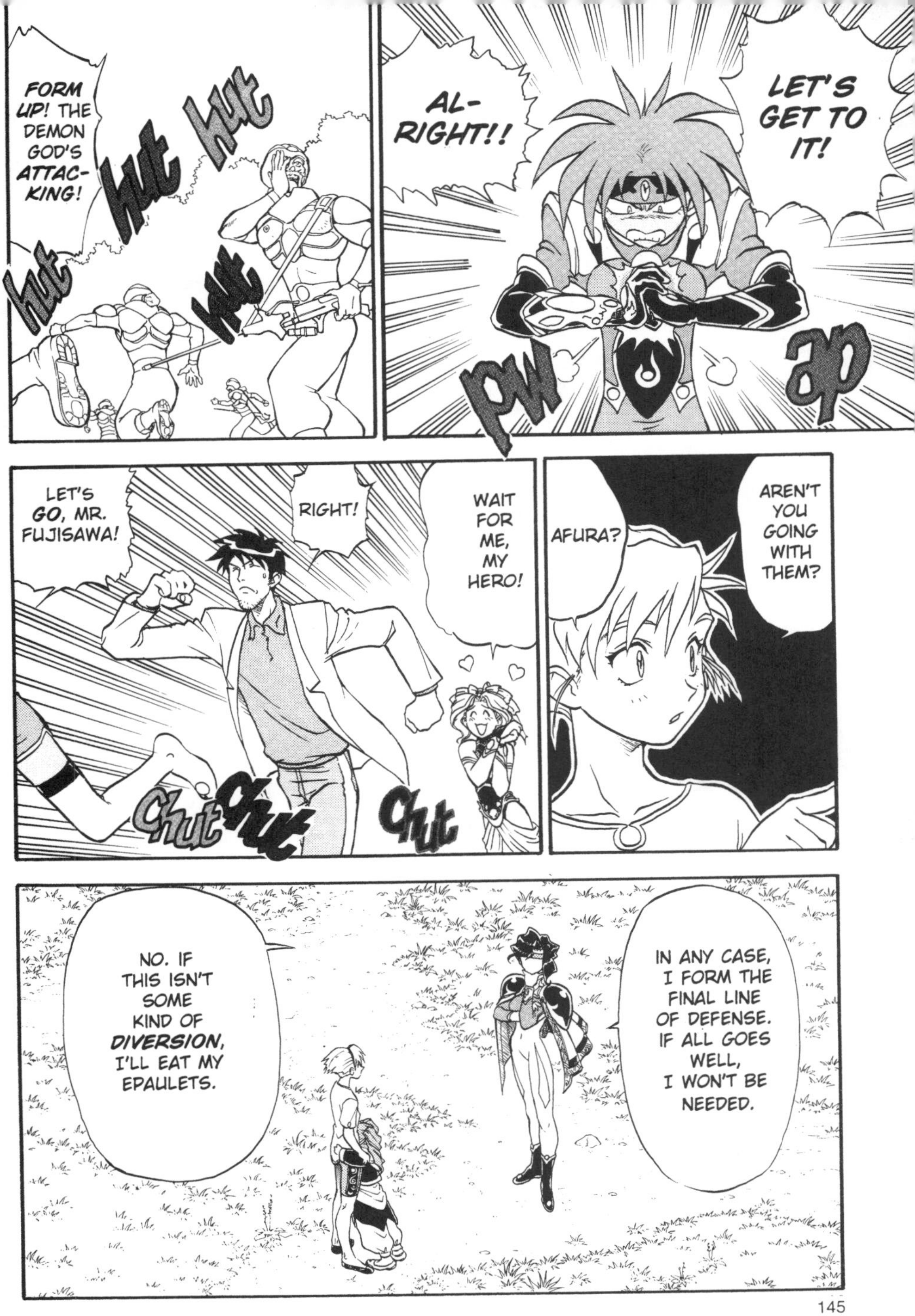
FORM UP! THE DEMON GOD'S ATTAC-KING!
hut hut hut
hut
hut
AL-RIGHT!!
LET'S GET TO IT!
pw ap
LET'S GO, MR. FUJISAWA!
RIGHT!
WAIT FOR ME, MY HERO!
Chut Chut Chut
AFURA?
AREN'T YOU GOING WITH THEM?
NO. IF THIS ISN'T SOME KIND OF DIVERSION, I'LL EAT MY EPAULETS.
IN ANY CASE, I FORM THE FINAL LINE OF DEFENSE. IF ALL GOES WELL, I WON'T BE NEEDED.

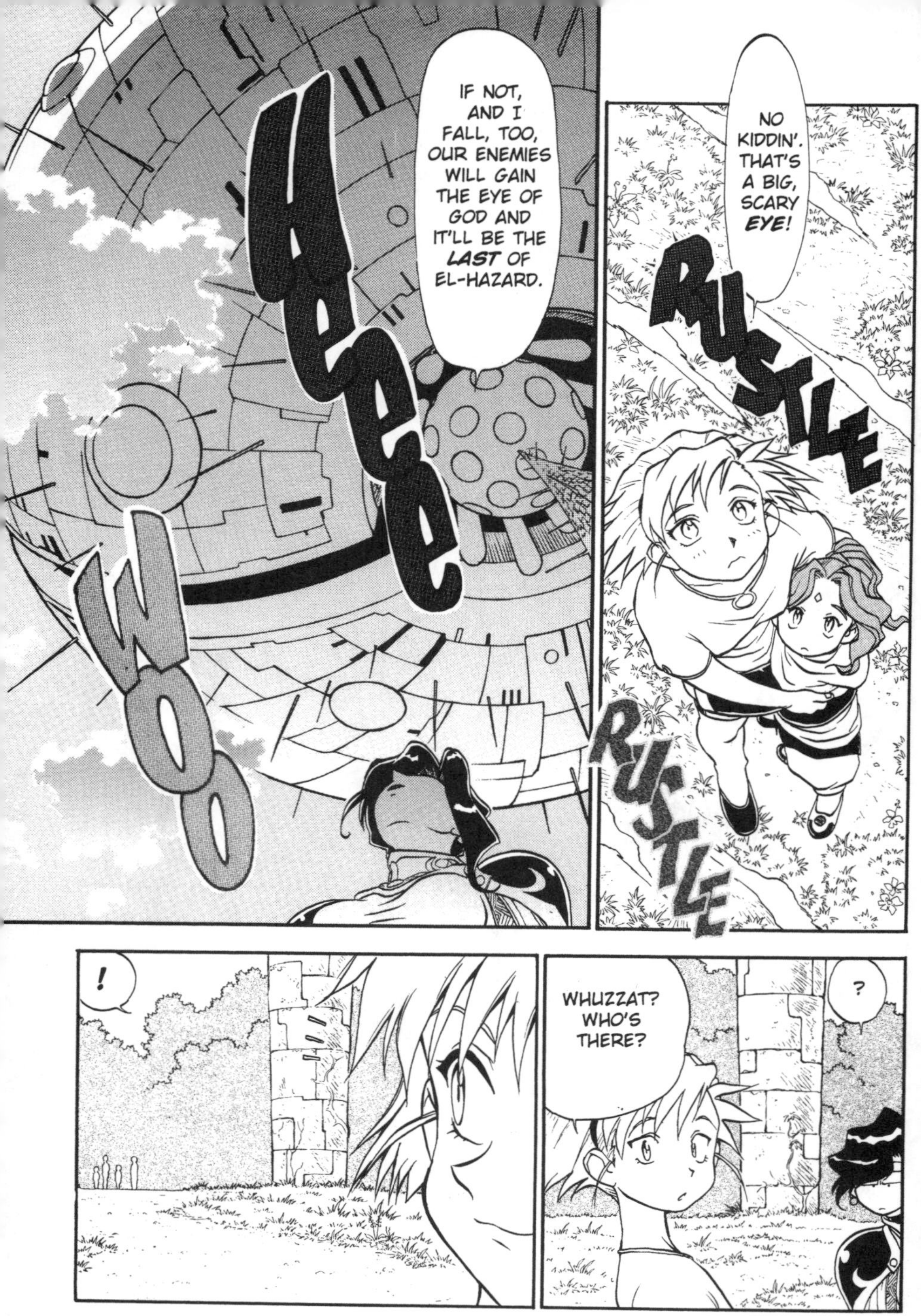
IF NOT, AND I FALL, TOO, OUR ENEMIES WILL GAIN THE EYE OF GOD AND IT'LL BE THE LAST OF EL-HAZARD.
Heeeee
WOOO
NO KIDDIN'. THAT'S A BIG, SCARY EYE!
RUSTLE
RUSTLE
!
WHUZZAT? WHO'S THERE?
?

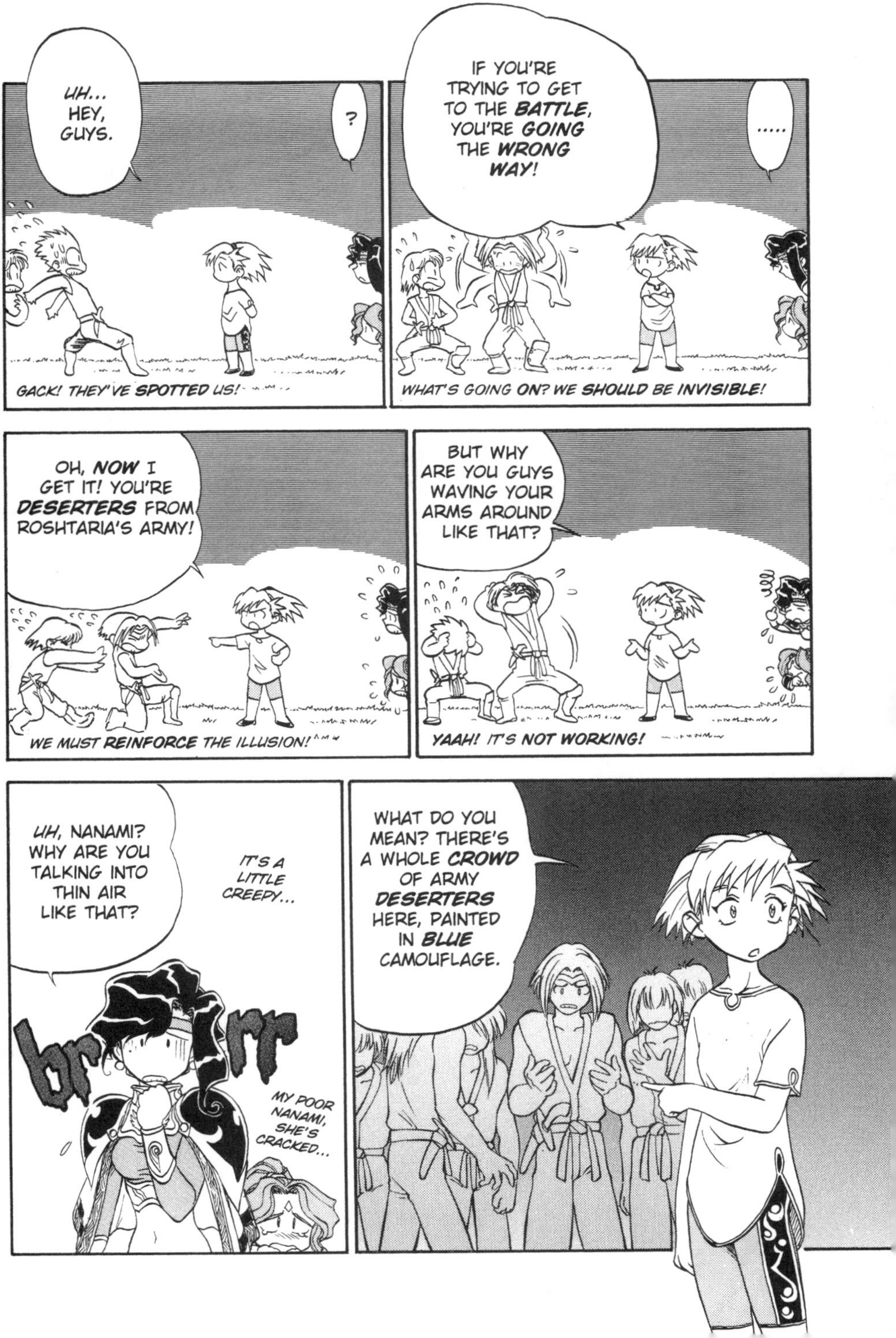
UH... HEY, GUYS.
?
GACK! THEY'VE SPOTTED US!
IF YOU'RE TRYING TO GET TO THE BATTLE, YOU'RE GOING THE WRONG WAY!
.....
WHAT'S GOING ON? WE SHOULD BE INVISIBLE!
OH, NOW I GET IT! YOU'RE DESERTERS FROM ROSHTARIA'S ARMY!
WE MUST REINFORCE THE ILLUSION!
BUT WHY ARE YOU GUYS WAVING YOUR ARMS AROUND LIKE THAT?
YAAH! IT'S NOT WORKING!
UH, NANAMI? WHY ARE YOU TALKING INTO THIN AIR LIKE THAT?
IT'S A LITTLE CREEPY...
MY POOR NANAMI, SHE'S CRACKED...
WHAT DO YOU MEAN? THERE'S A WHOLE CROWD OF ARMY DESERTERS HERE, PAINTED IN BLUE CAMOUFLAGE.

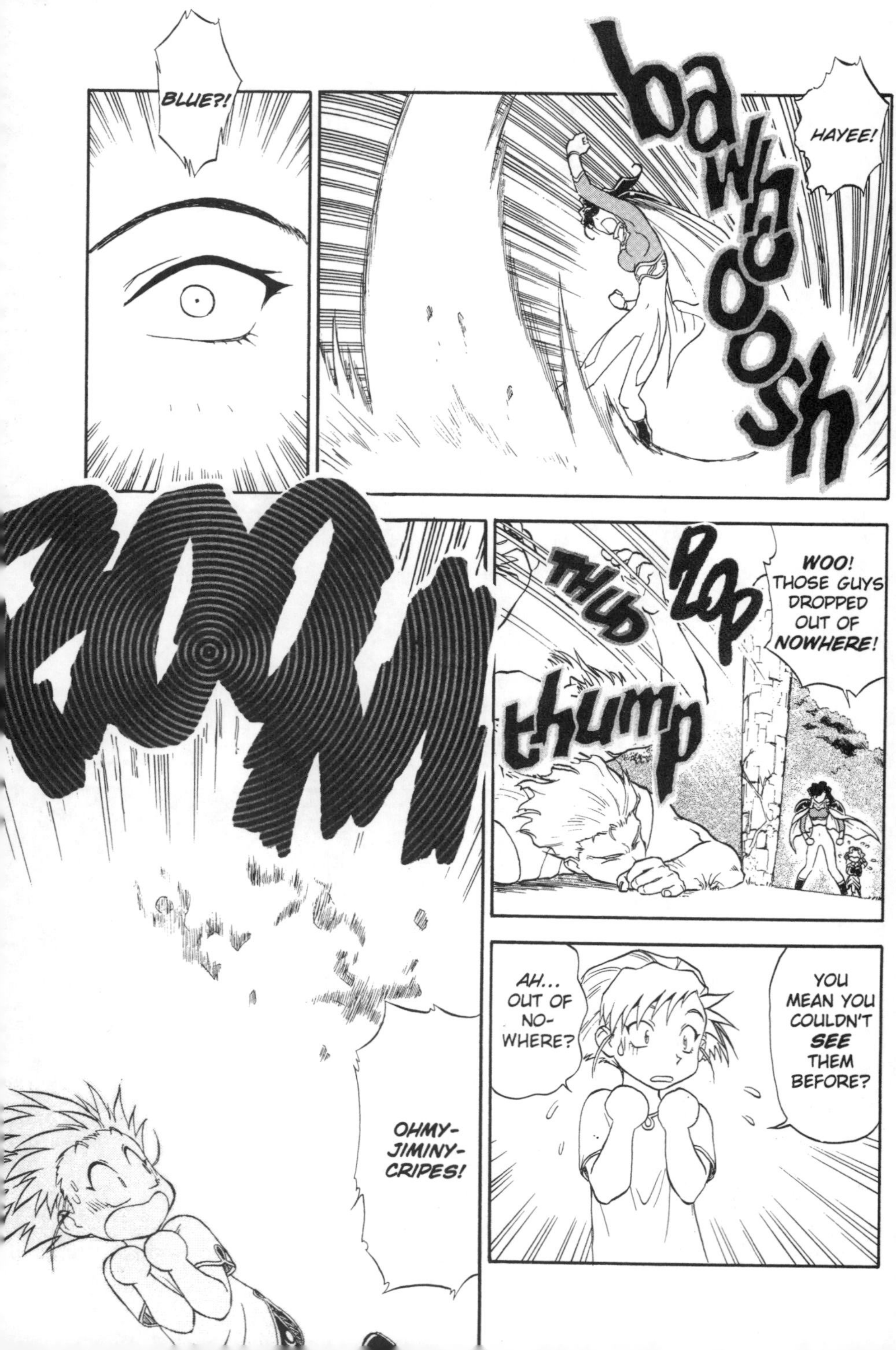
BLUE?!
HAYEE!
bawhaoosh
ZOOM
OHMY-JIMINY-CRIPES!
THUD
PLOP
thump
WOO! THOSE GUYS DROPPED OUT OF *NOWHERE!*
AH... OUT OF NO-WHERE?
YOU MEAN YOU COULDN'T *SEE* THEM BEFORE?

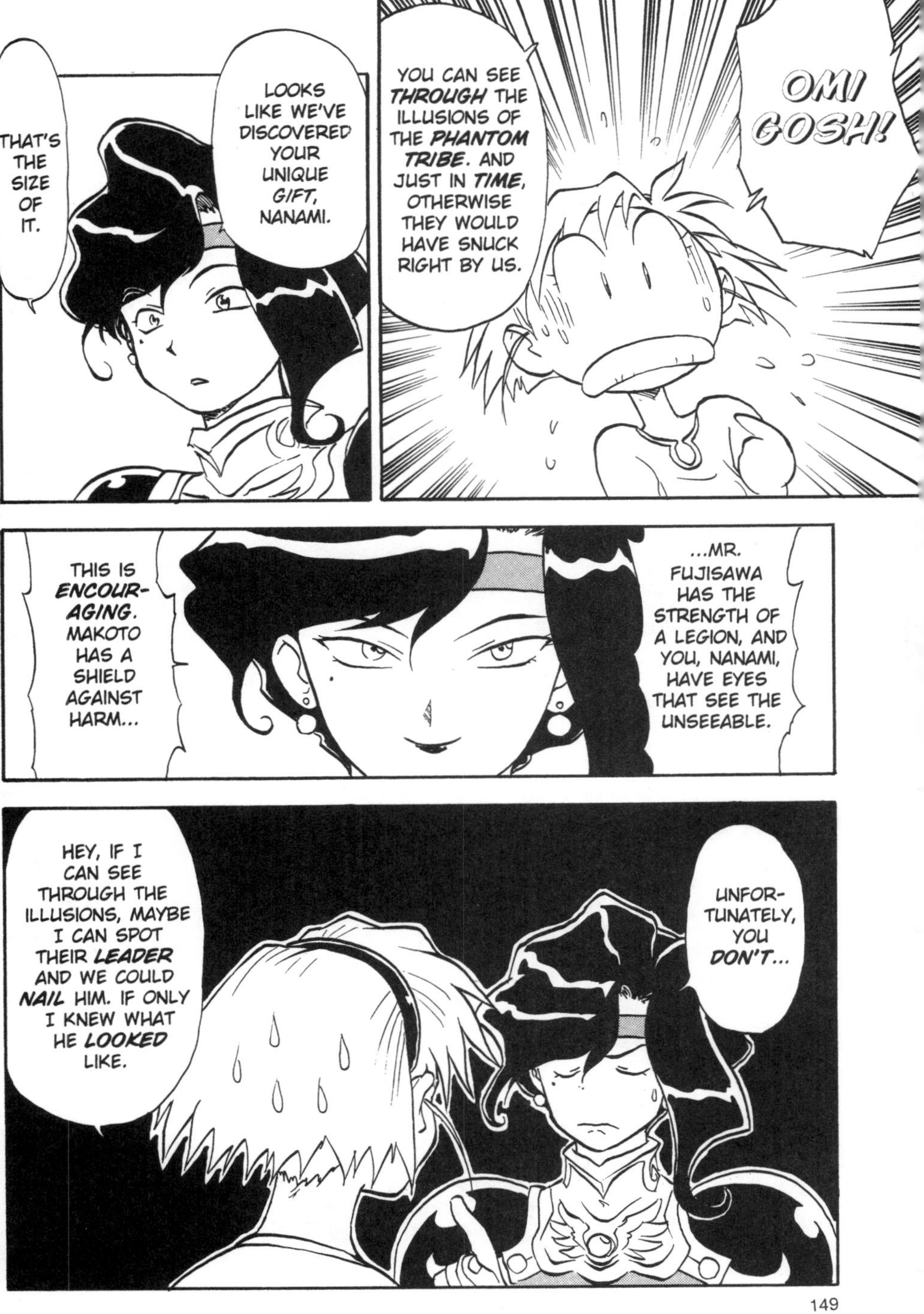
THAT'S THE SIZE OF IT.
LOOKS LIKE WE'VE DISCOVERED YOUR UNIQUE GIFT, NANAMI.
YOU CAN SEE THROUGH THE ILLUSIONS OF THE PHANTOM TRIBE. AND JUST IN TIME, OTHERWISE THEY WOULD HAVE SNUCK RIGHT BY US.
OMI GOSH!
THIS IS ENCOURAGING. MAKOTO HAS A SHIELD AGAINST HARM...
...MR. FUJISAWA HAS THE STRENGTH OF A LEGION, AND YOU, NANAMI, HAVE EYES THAT SEE THE UNSEEABLE.
HEY, IF I CAN SEE THROUGH THE ILLUSIONS, MAYBE I CAN SPOT THEIR LEADER AND WE COULD NAIL HIM. IF ONLY I KNEW WHAT HE LOOKED LIKE.
UNFORTUNATELY, YOU DON'T...

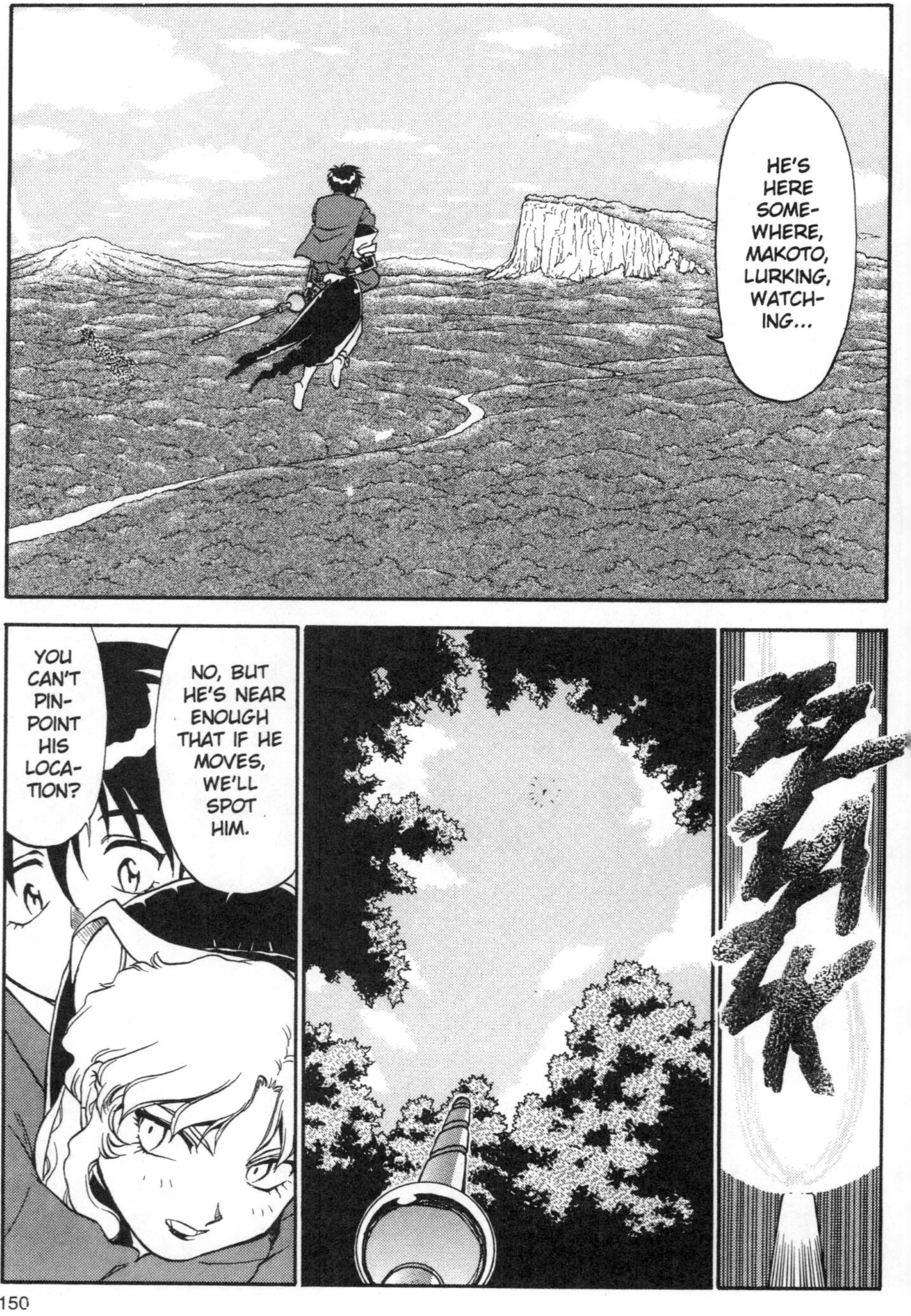
HE'S HERE SOMEWHERE, MAKOTO, LURKING, WATCHING...
YOU CAN'T PINPOINT HIS LOCATION?
NO, BUT HE'S NEAR ENOUGH THAT IF HE MOVES, WE'LL SPOT HIM.

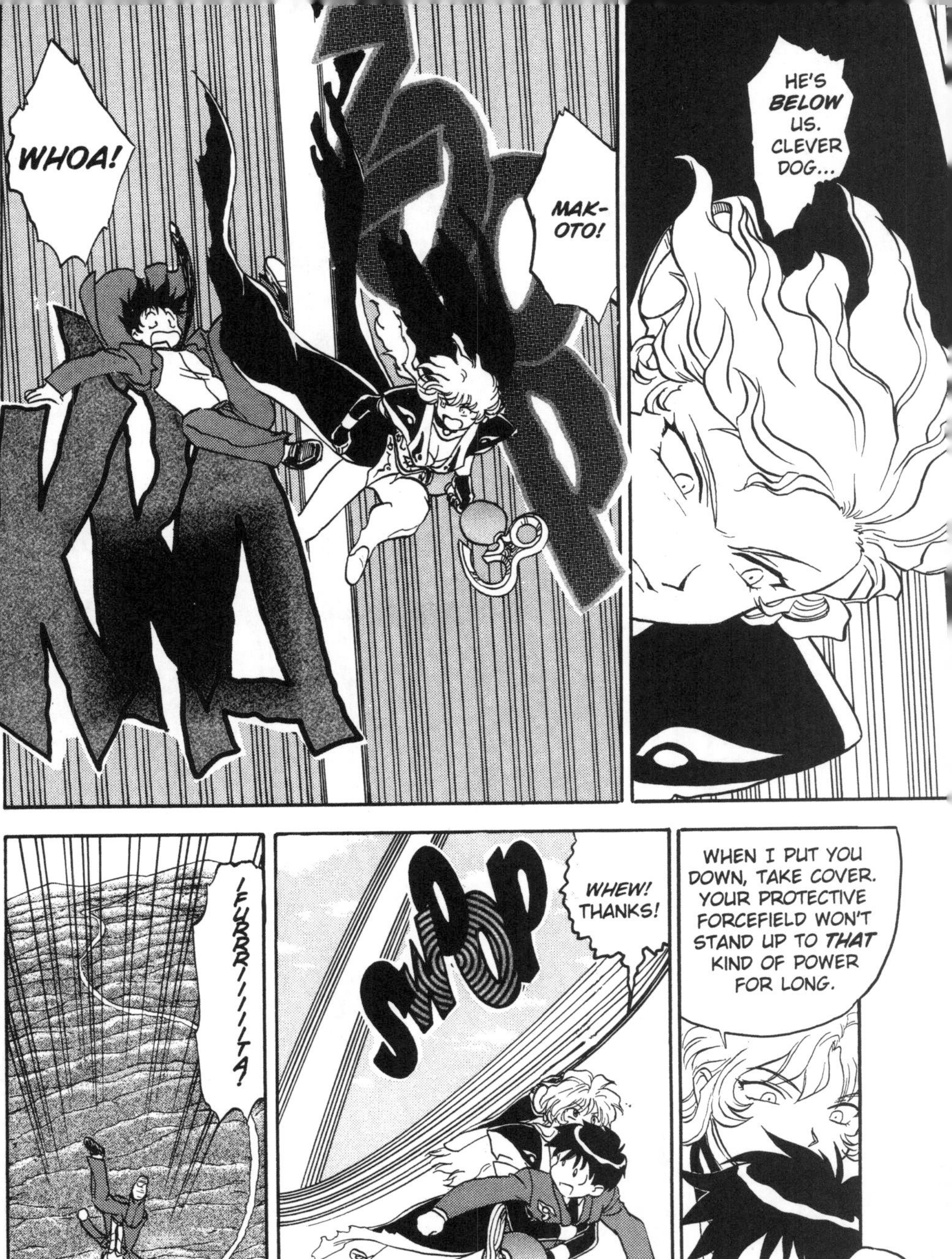
WHOA!
MAK-OTO!
HE'S *BELOW* US. CLEVER DOG...
FURRRIIIIITA!
SWOOP
WHEW! THANKS!
WHEN I PUT YOU DOWN, TAKE COVER. YOUR PROTECTIVE FORCEFIELD WON'T STAND UP TO *THAT* KIND OF POWER FOR LONG.
WHAT ABOUT *YOU*?

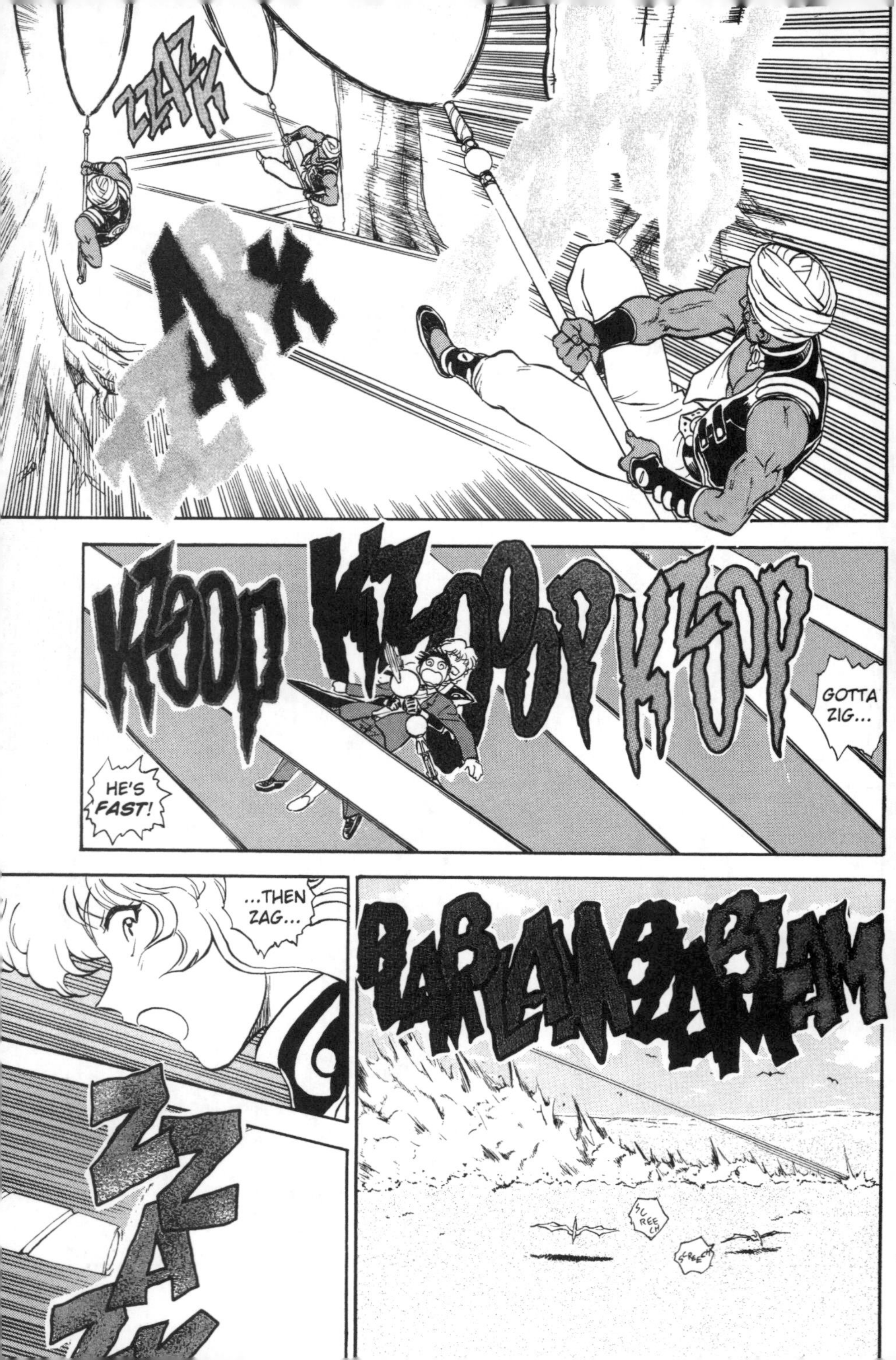
ZZAK
ZZAK
KZOOP KZOOP KZOOP KZOOP
GOTTA ZIG...
HE'S *FAST!*
...THEN ZAG...
BLAM BLAM BLAM BLAM
SCREECH
SCREECH

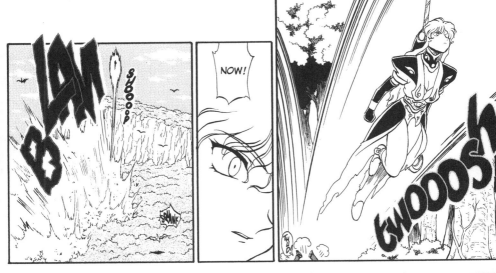

NOW!

SHOOOO

BLAM

SPRANK

tWOOOSh

SPROING

WATCH YOUR-SELF, IFU-RITA...

WEE EEE OOO

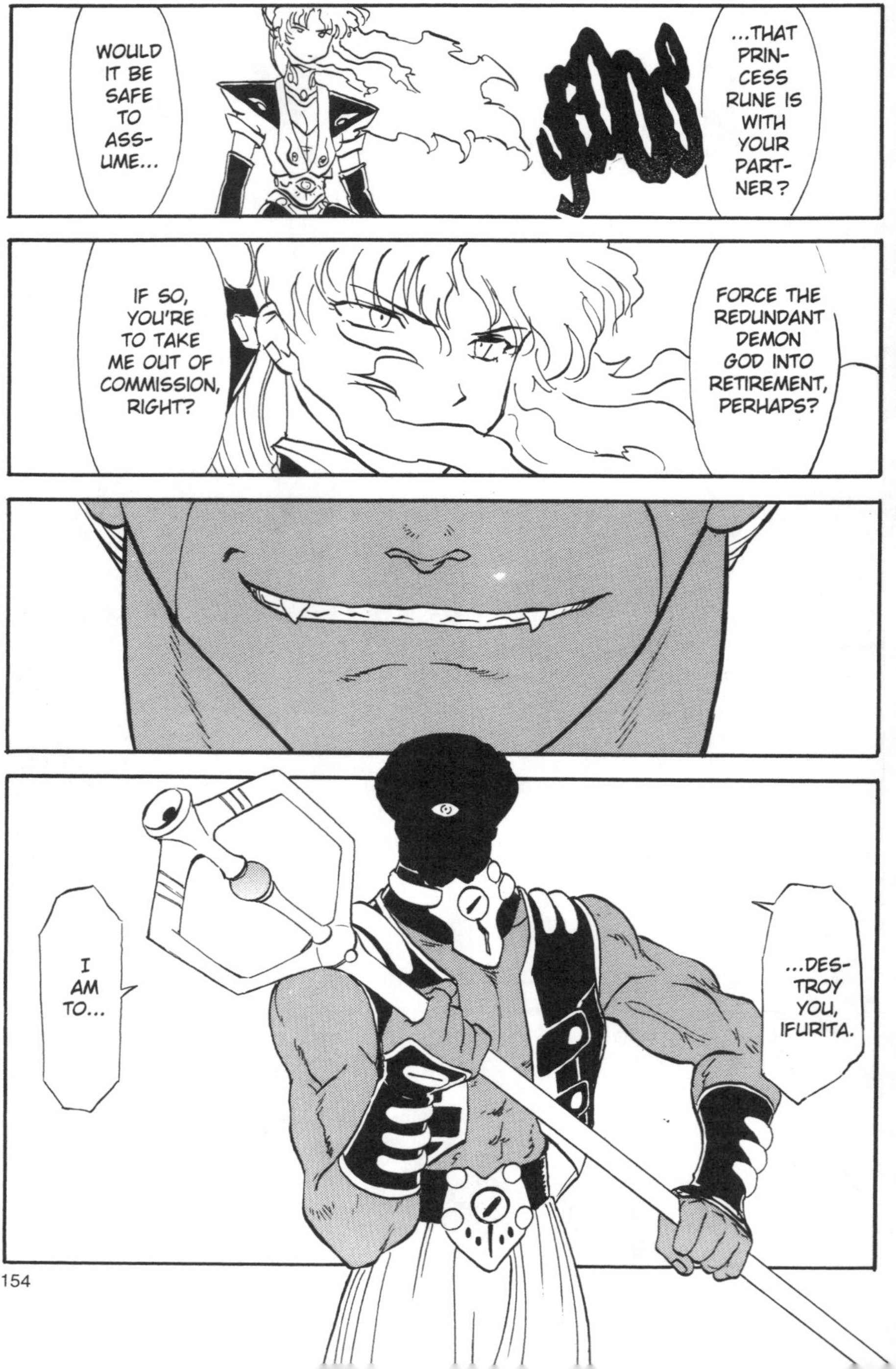
WOULD IT BE SAFE TO ASSUME...
...THAT PRINCESS RUNE IS WITH YOUR PARTNER?
IF SO, YOU'RE TO TAKE ME OUT OF COMMISSION, RIGHT?
FORCE THE REDUNDANT DEMON GOD INTO RETIREMENT, PERHAPS?
I AM TO...
...DESTROY YOU, IFURITA.

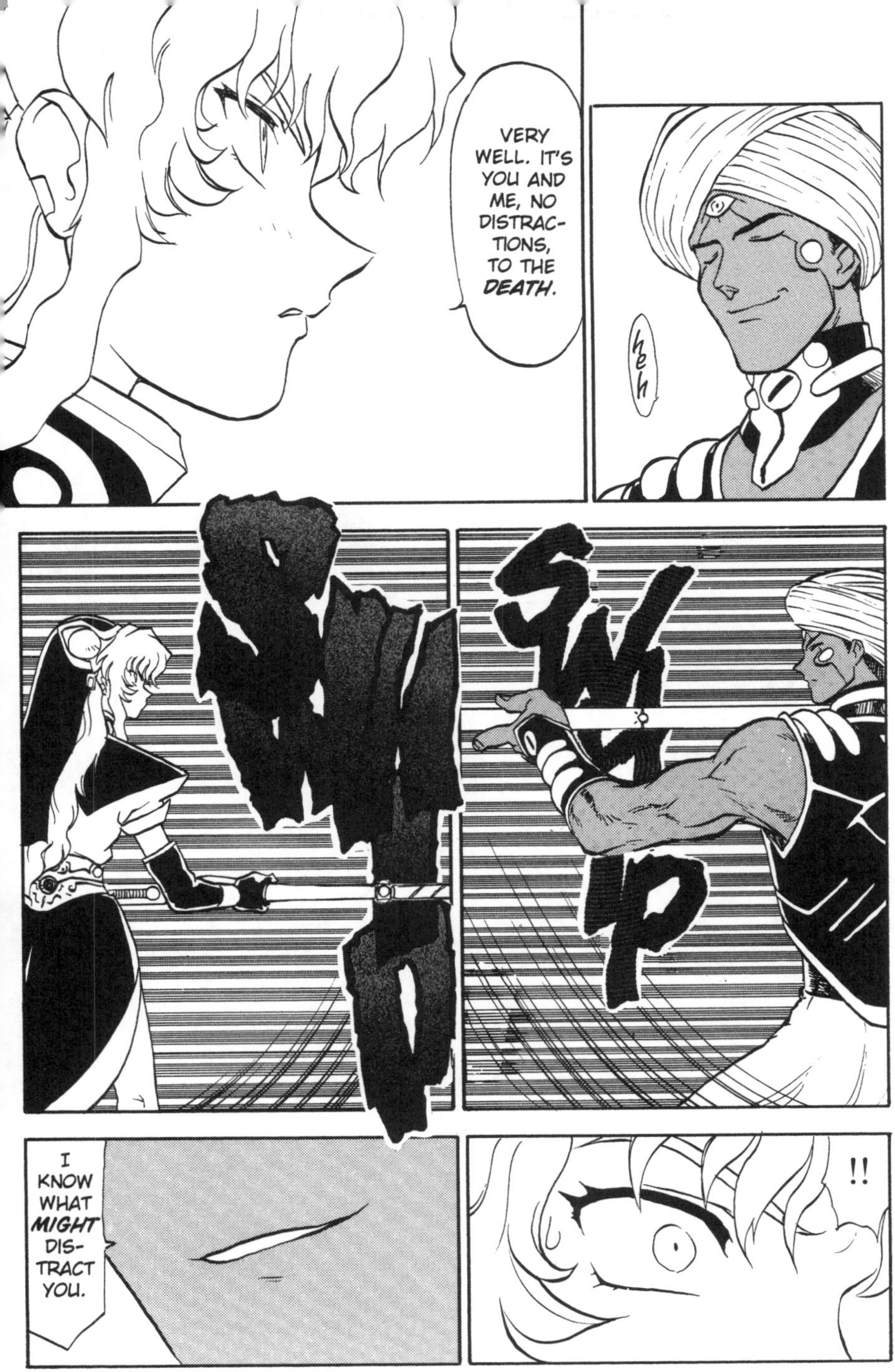
VERY WELL. IT'S YOU AND ME, NO DISTRACTIONS, TO THE *DEATH*.
heh
SWISH
SNAP
I KNOW WHAT *MIGHT* DISTRACT YOU.
!!

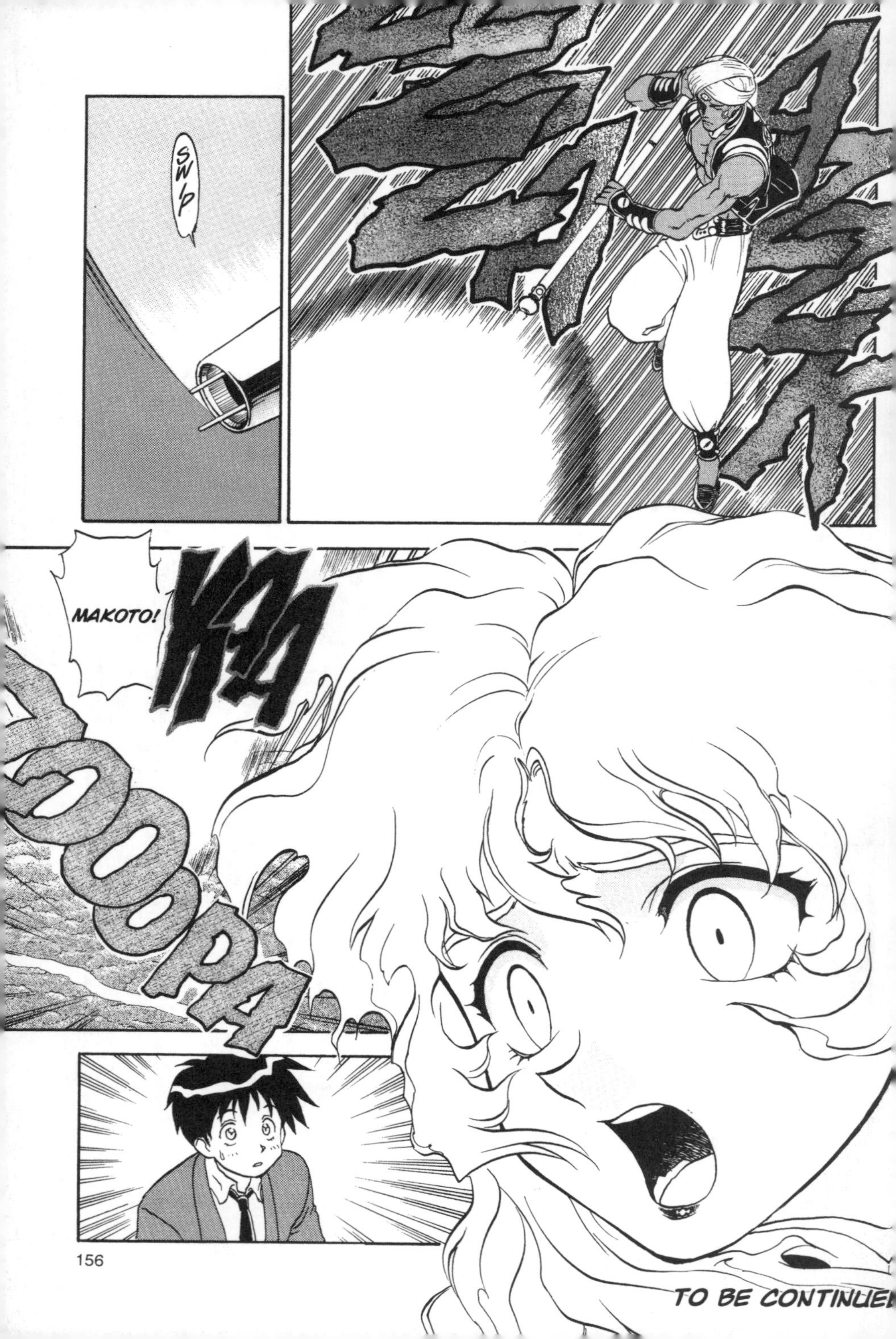
SWP
MAKOTO!
ZOOOPA

TO BE CONTINUED

PREVIEW

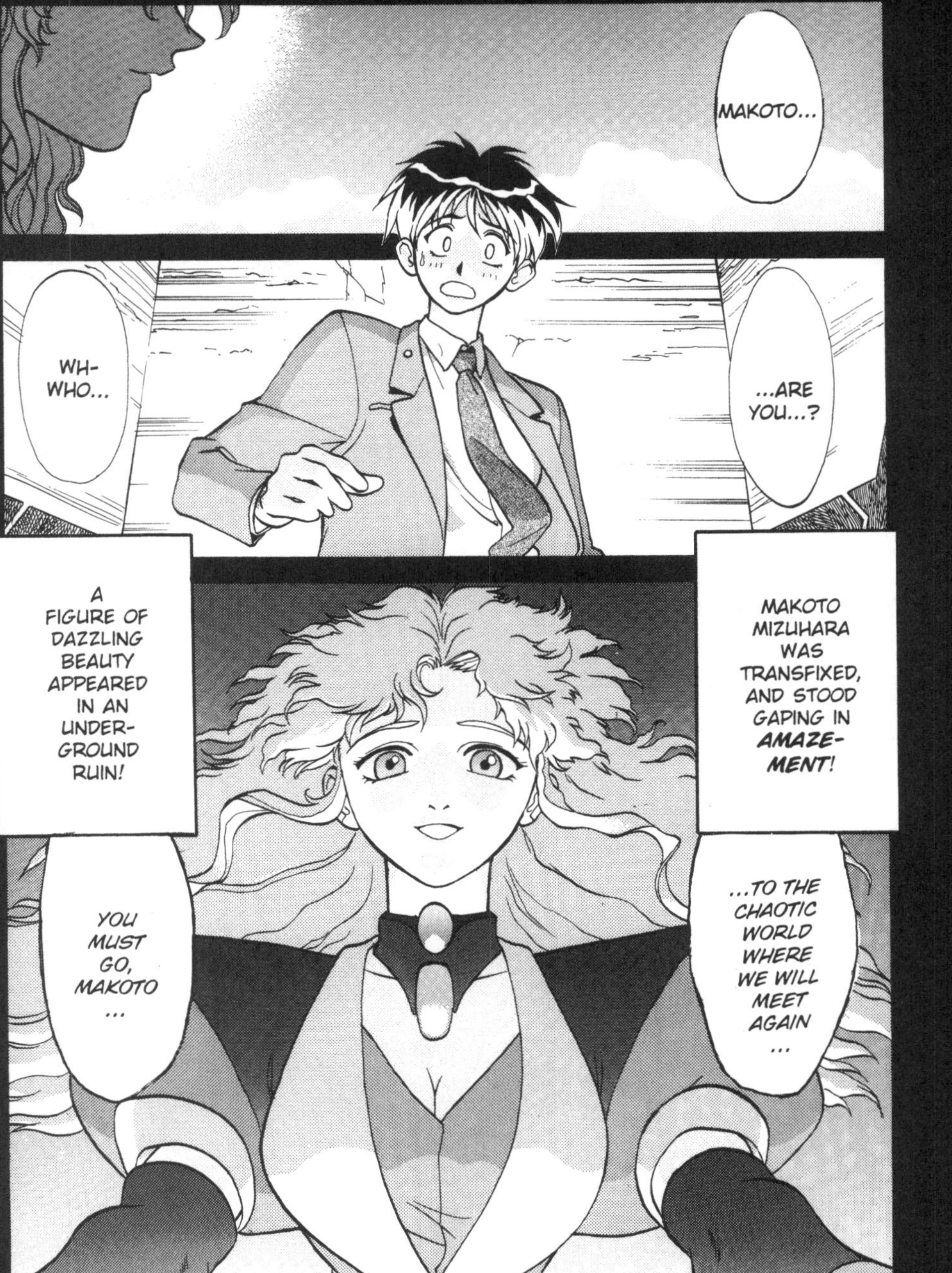
MAKOTO...
WH- WHO...
...ARE YOU...?
A FIGURE OF DAZZLING BEAUTY APPEARED IN AN UNDER-GROUND RUIN!
MAKOTO MIZUHARA WAS TRANSFIXED, AND STOOD GAPING IN ***AMAZE-MENT***!
YOU MUST GO, MAKOTO ...
...TO THE CHAOTIC WORLD WHERE WE WILL MEET AGAIN ...

THIS PREVIEW RAN IN THE NOVEMBER '95 ISSUE OF SHONEN CAPTAIN, PRECEDING EL-HAZARD'S SERIALIZATION.

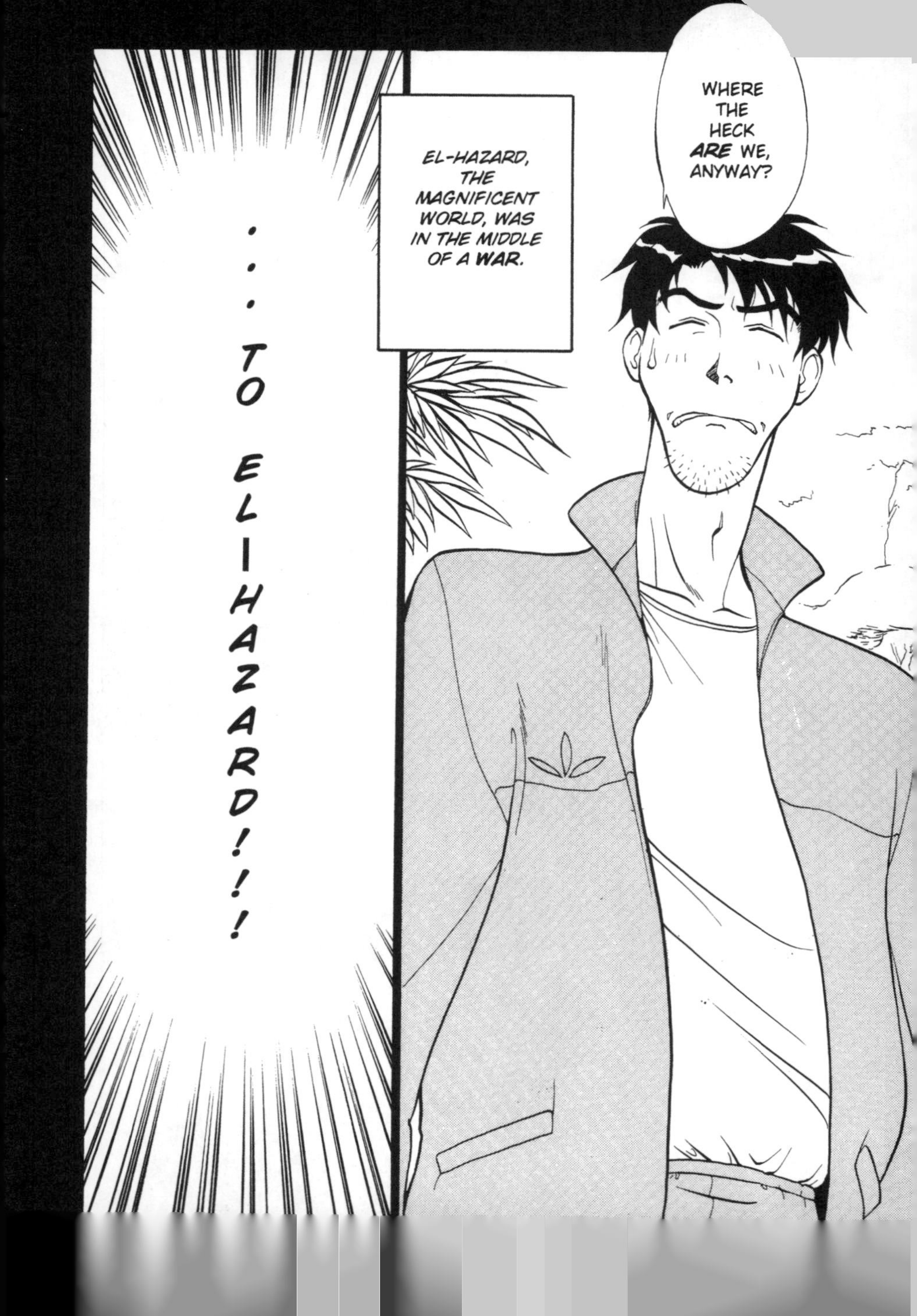
...TO EL-HAZARD!!!
EL-HAZARD, THE MAGNIFICENT WORLD, WAS IN THE MIDDLE OF A WAR.
WHERE THE HECK ARE WE, ANYWAY?

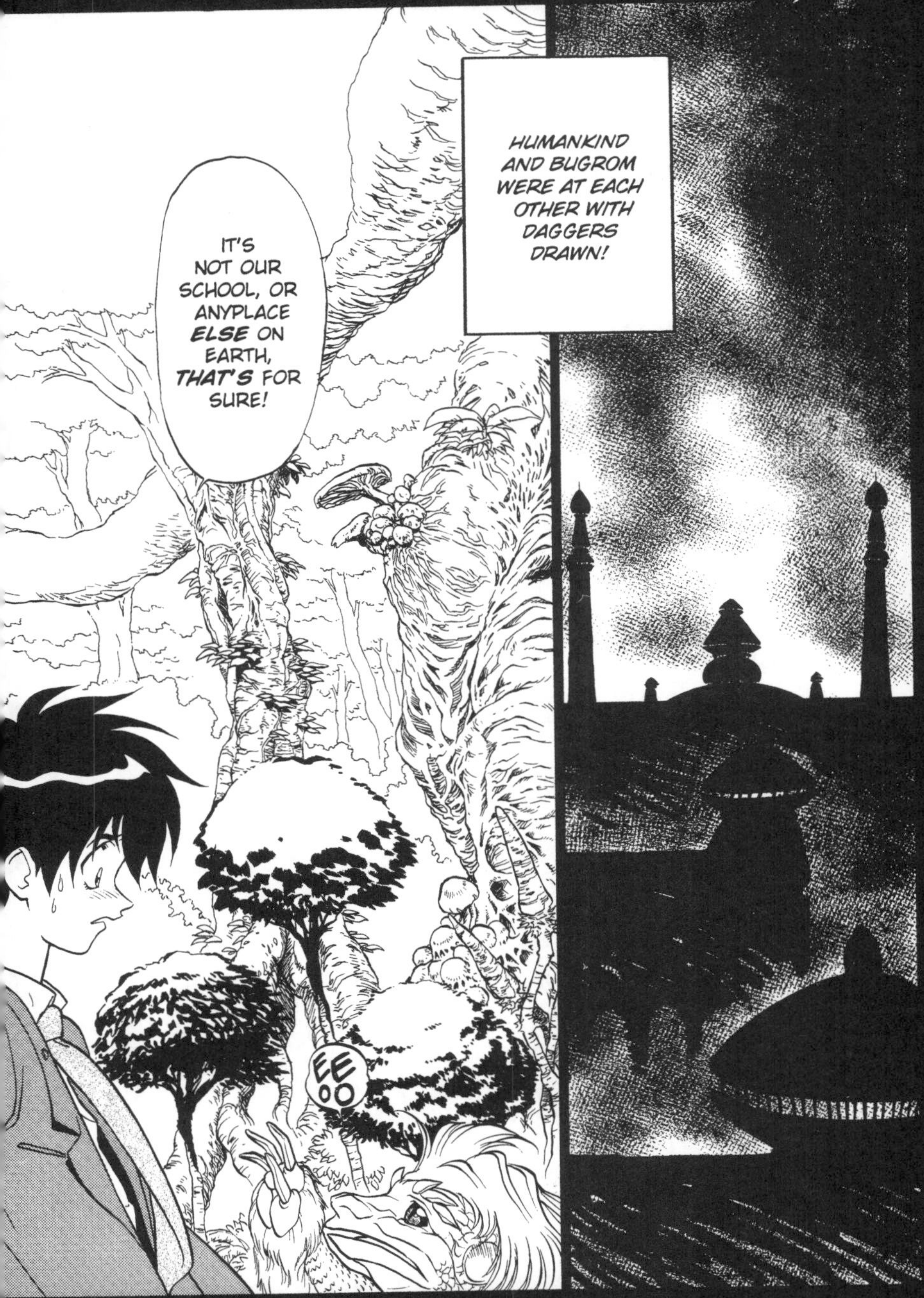
IT'S NOT OUR SCHOOL, OR ANYPLACE ***ELSE*** ON EARTH, ***THAT'S*** FOR SURE!
EEOO
HUMANKIND AND BUGROM WERE AT EACH OTHER WITH DAGGERS DRAWN!

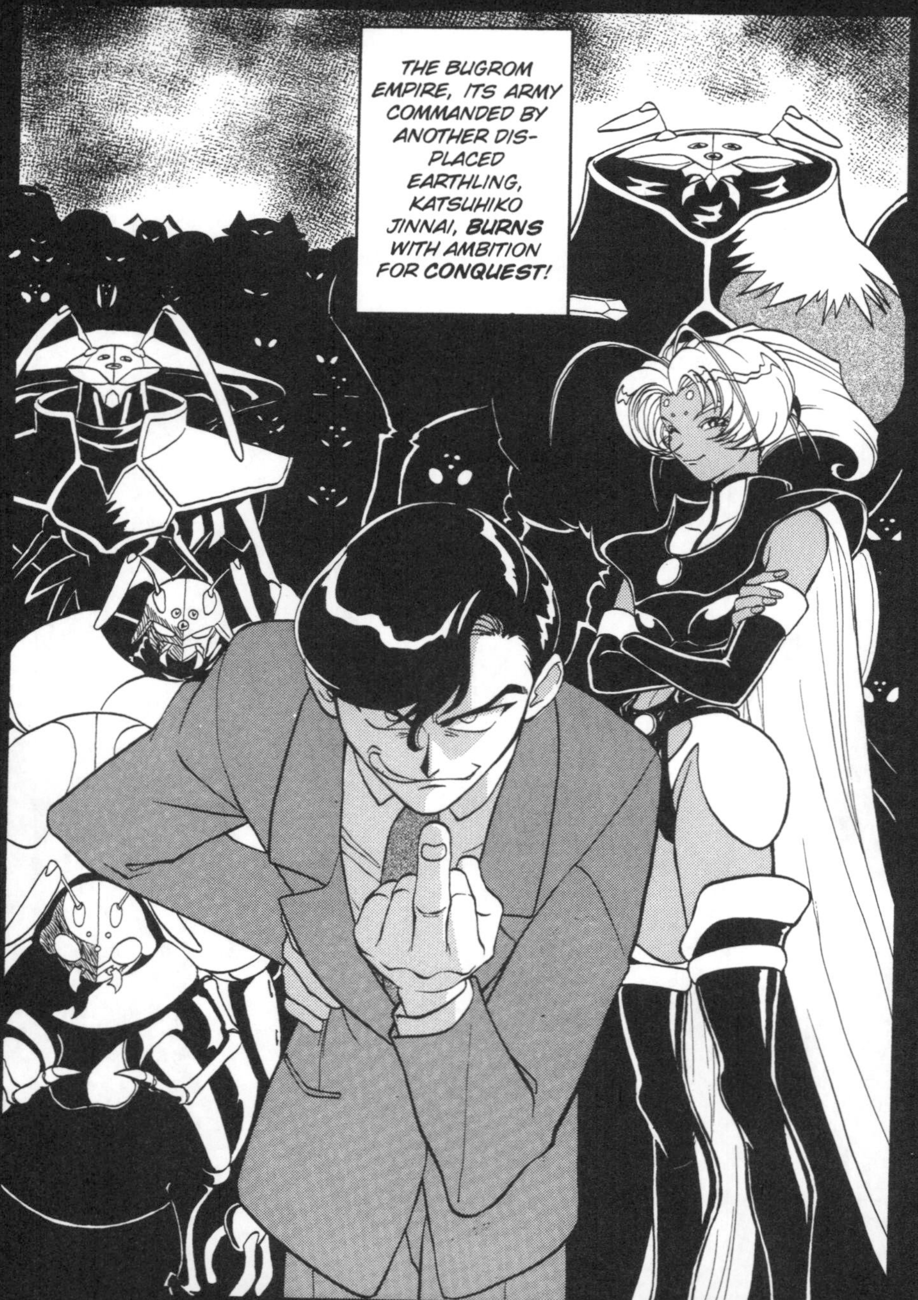
THE BUGROM EMPIRE, ITS ARMY COMMANDED BY ANOTHER DIS-PLACED EARTHLING, KATSUHIKO JINNAI, BURNS WITH AMBITION FOR CONQUEST!

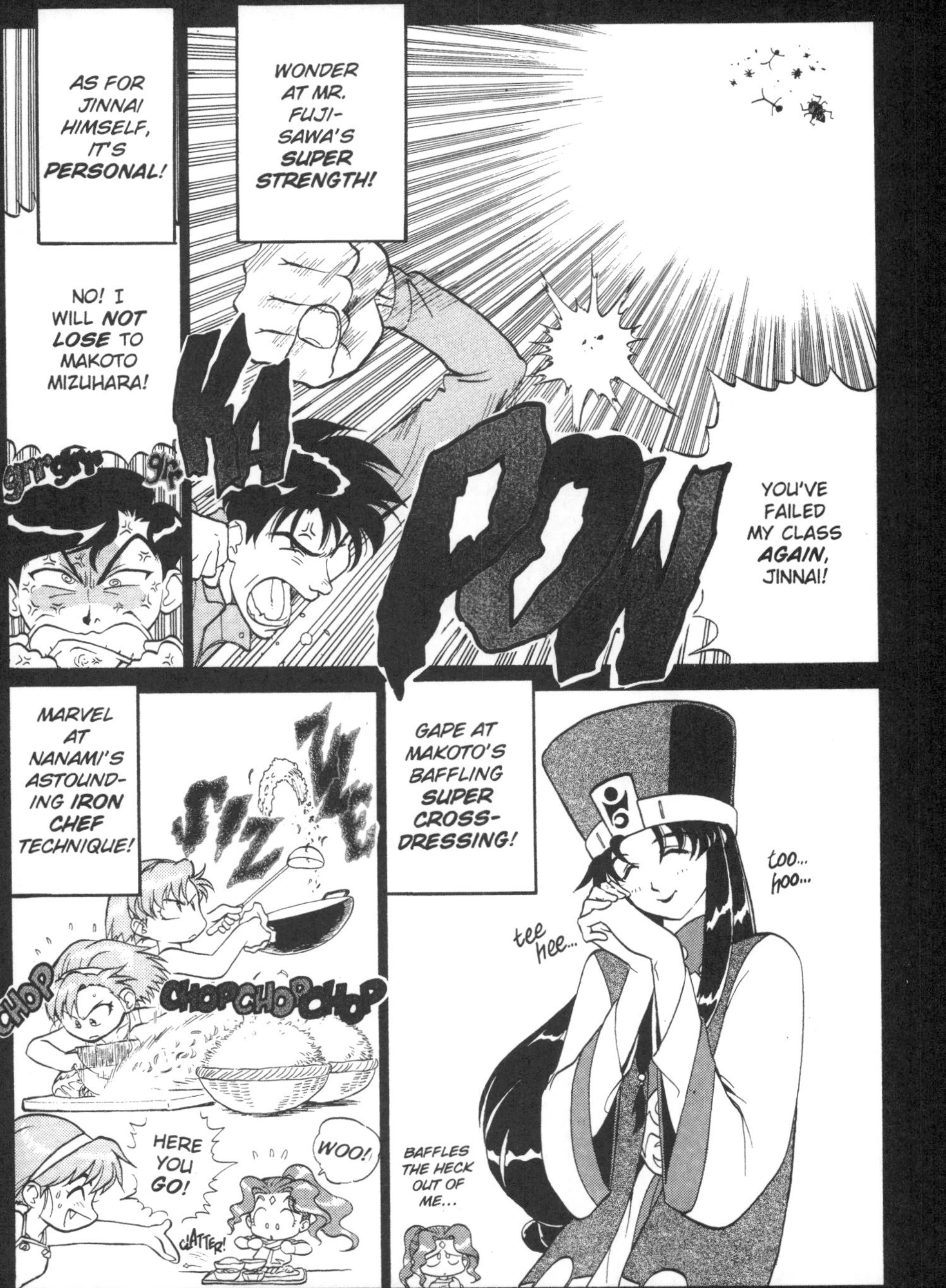

AS FOR JINNAI HIMSELF, IT'S PERSONAL!
NO! I WILL NOT LOSE TO MAKOTO MIZUHARA!
grrr grrr grr
WONDER AT MR. FUJI-SAWA'S SUPER STRENGTH!
WA POW
YOU'VE FAILED MY CLASS AGAIN, JINNAI!
MARVEL AT NANAMI'S ASTOUND-ING IRON CHEF TECHNIQUE!
SIZZLE
CHOP
CHOPCHOPCHOP
HERE YOU GO!
WOO!
CLATTER!
GAPE AT MAKOTO'S BAFFLING SUPER CROSS-DRESSING!
too... hoo...
tee hee...
BAFFLES THE HECK OUT OF ME...

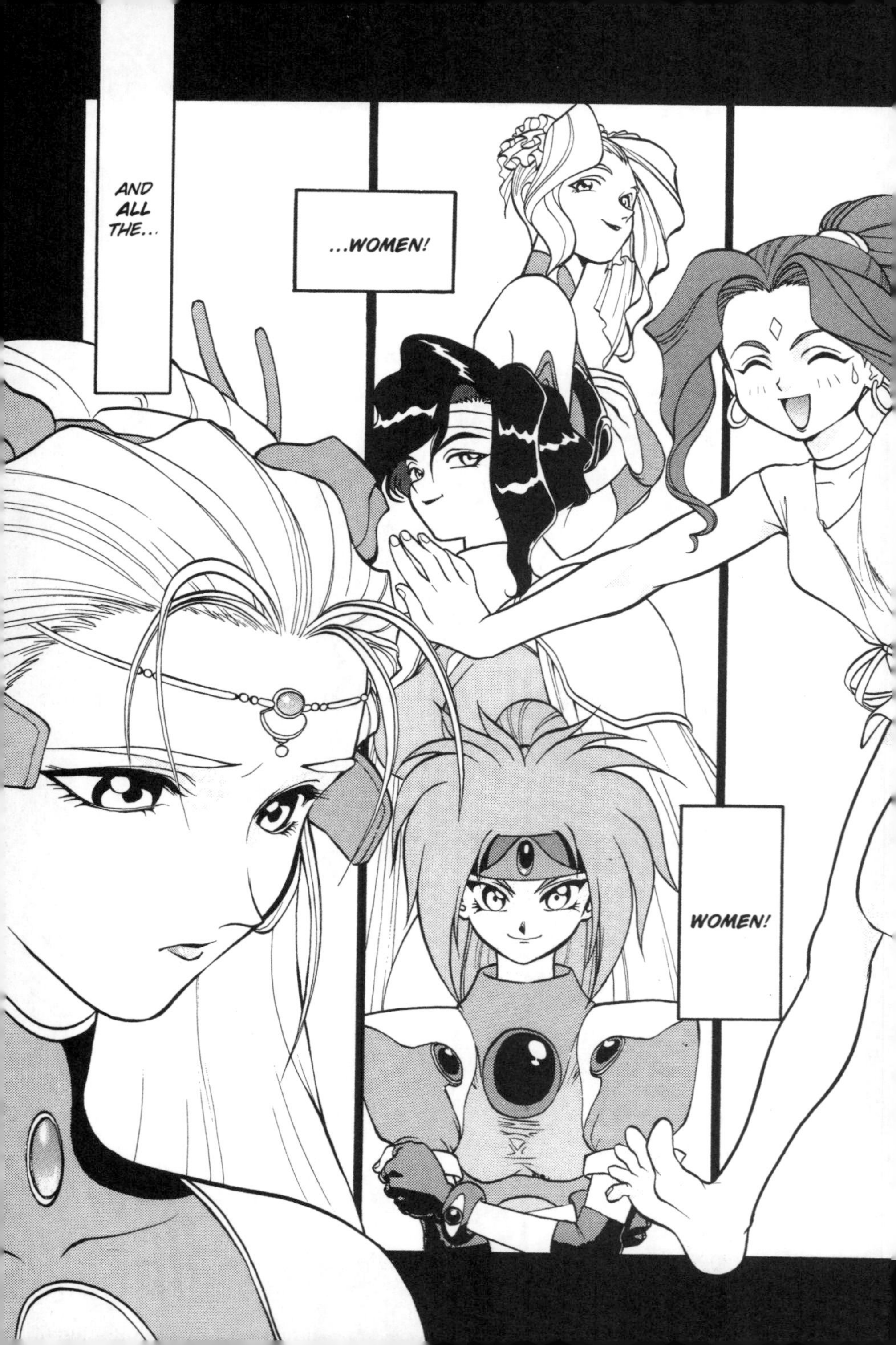
AND ALL THE...
...WOMEN!
WOMEN!

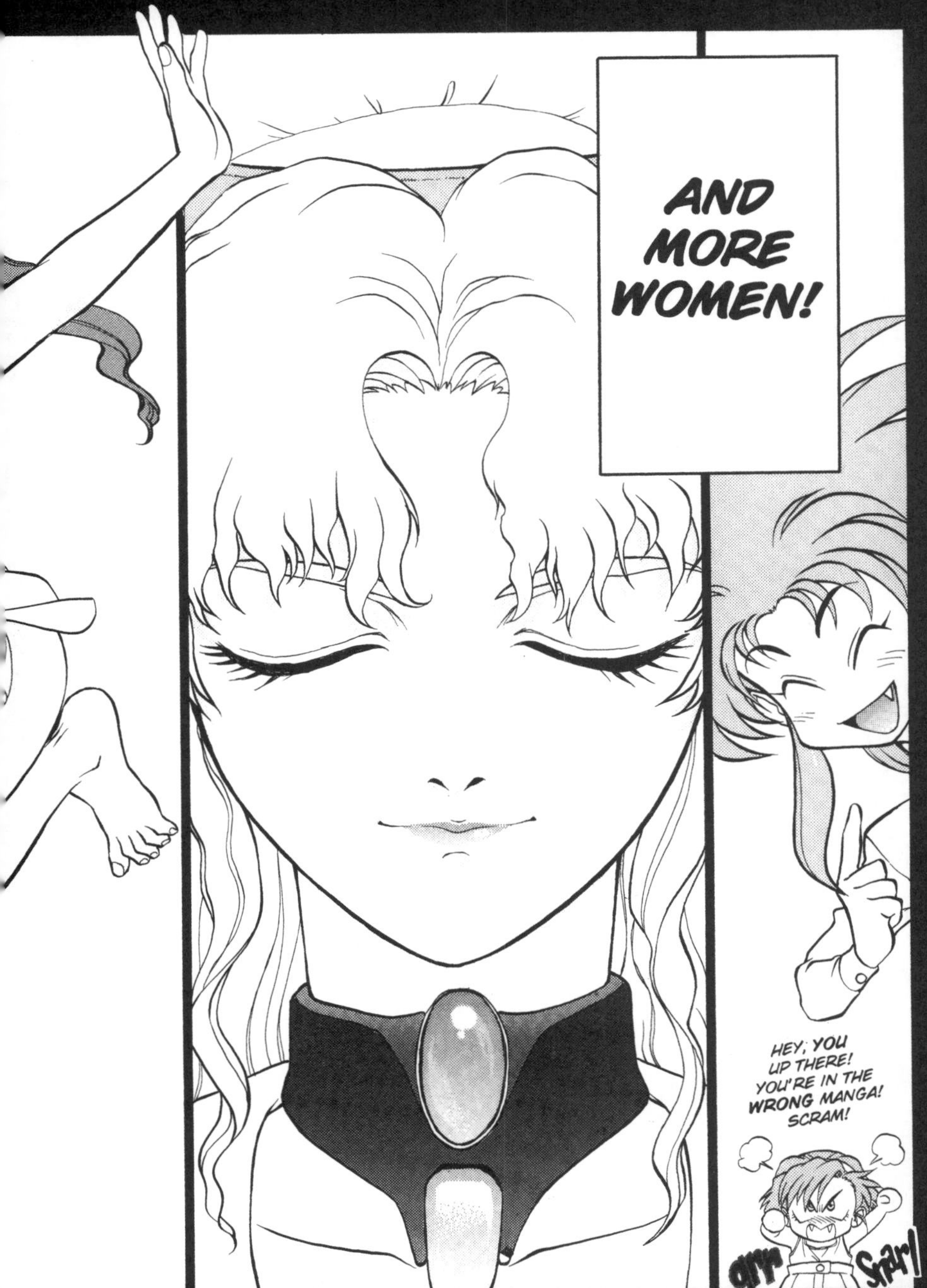
AND MORE WOMEN!
HEY, YOU UP THERE! YOU'RE IN THE WRONG MANGA! SCRAM!
grrr
Snarl

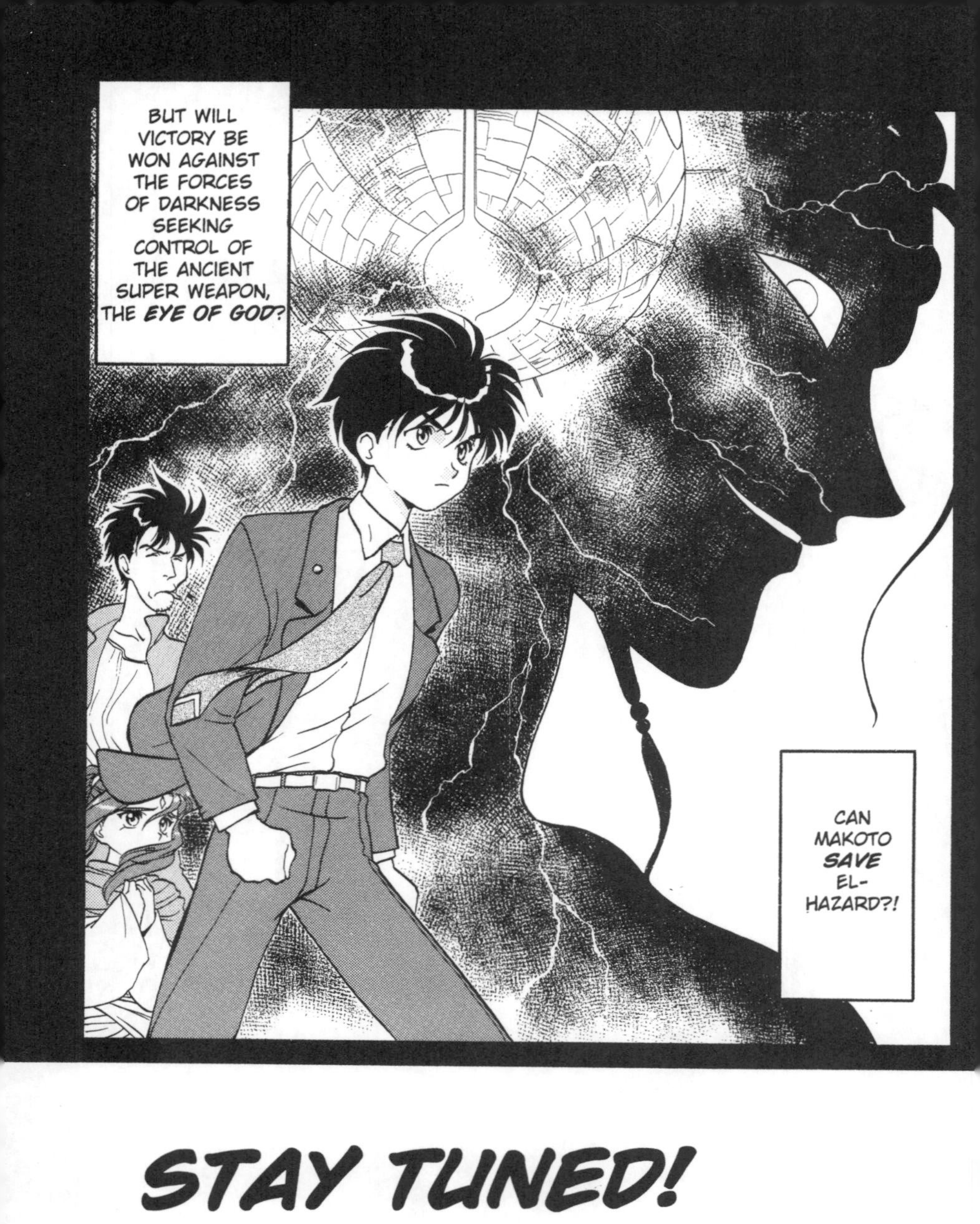
BUT WILL VICTORY BE WON AGAINST THE FORCES OF DARKNESS SEEKING CONTROL OF THE ANCIENT SUPER WEAPON, THE *EYE OF GOD*?
CAN MAKOTO ***SAVE*** EL-HAZARD?!

STAY TUNED!

SERIALIZATION OF EL-HAZARD BEGAN IN DECEMBER '95.

On the following pages, we present the monthly comics covers for *El-Hazard* volume 1 number 1 through volume 2 number 5.

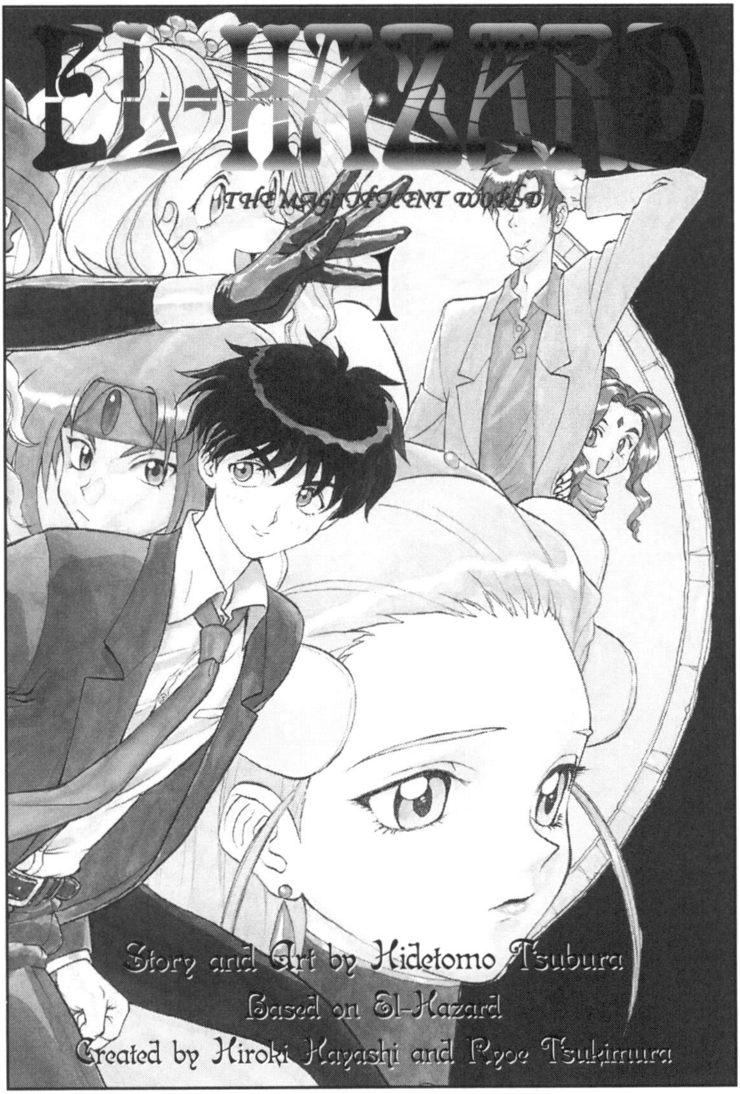
EL-HAZARD
1
Story and Art by Hidetomo Tsubura
Based on El-Hazard
Created by Hiroki Hayashi and Ryoe Tsukimura

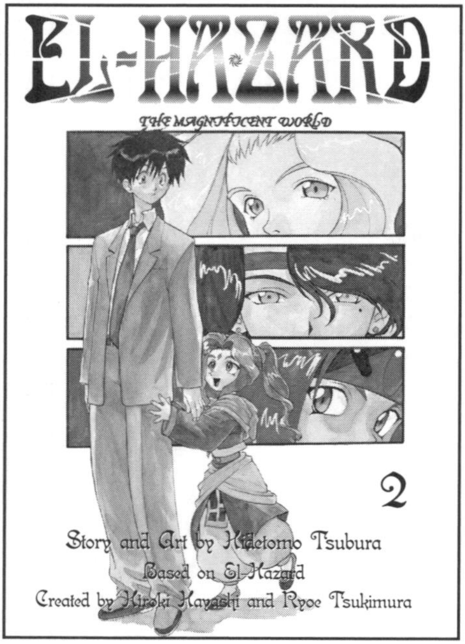
EL-HAZARD
THE MAGNIFICENT WORLD
2
Story and Art by Hidetomo Tsubura
Based on El-Hazard
Created by Hiroki Hayashi and Ryoe Tsukimura

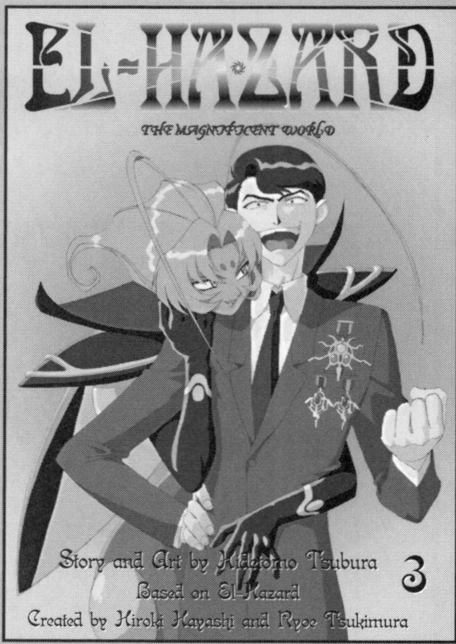
EL-HAZARD
THE MAGNIFICENT WORLD
3
Story and Art by Hidetomo Tsubura
Based on El-Hazard
Created by Hiroki Hayashi and Ryoe Tsukimura

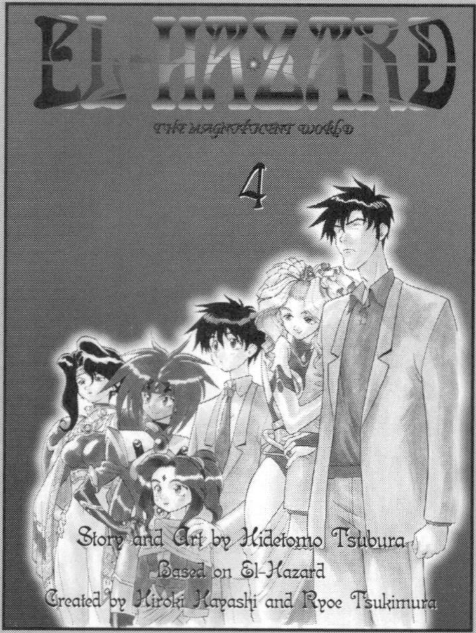
EL-HAZARD
THE MAGNIFICENT WORLD
4
Story and Art by Hidetomo Tsubura
Based on El-Hazard
Created by Hiroki Hayashi and Ryoe Tsukimura

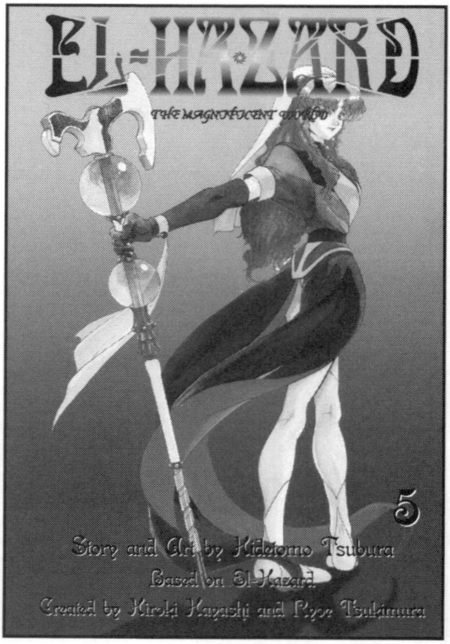
EL-HAZARD
THE MAGNIFICENT WORLD
5
Story and Art by Hidetomo Tsubura
Based on El-Hazard
Created by Hiroki Hayashi and Ryoe Tsukimura

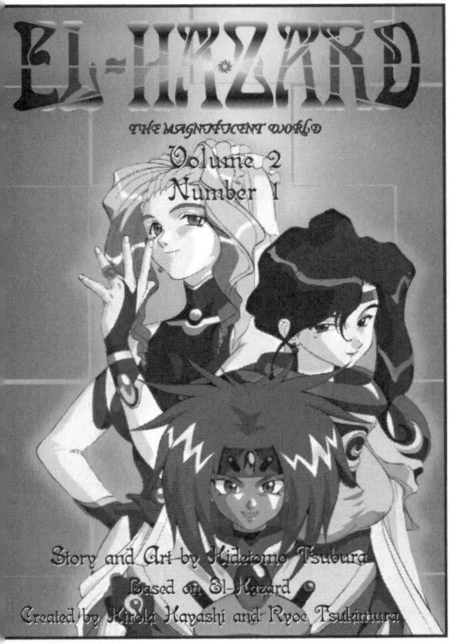
EL-HAZARD
THE MAGNIFICENT WORLD
Volume 2
Number 1
Story and Art by Hidetomo Tsubura
Based on El-Hazard
Created by Hiroki Hayashi and Ryoe Tsukimura
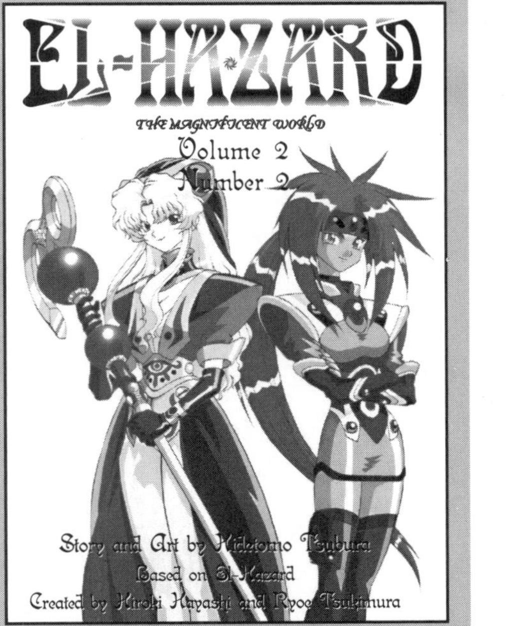
EL-HAZARD
THE MAGNIFICENT WORLD
Volume 2
Number 2
Story and Art by Hidetomo Tsubura
Based on El-Hazard
Created by Hiroki Hayashi and Ryoe Tsukimura
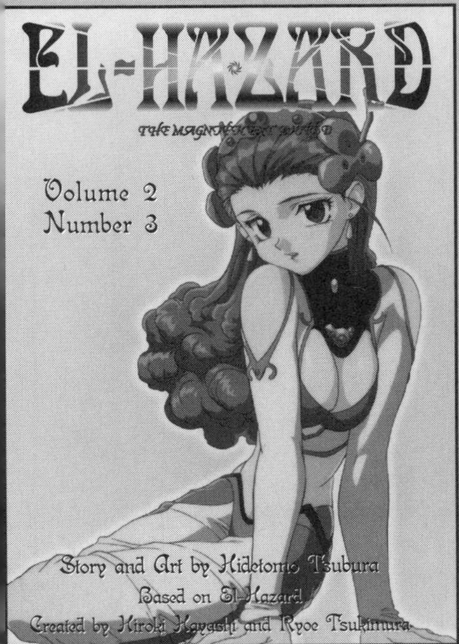
EL-HAZARD
Volume 2
Number 3
Story and Art by Hidetomo Tsubura
Based on El-Hazard
Created by Hiroki Hayashi and Ryoe Tsukimura
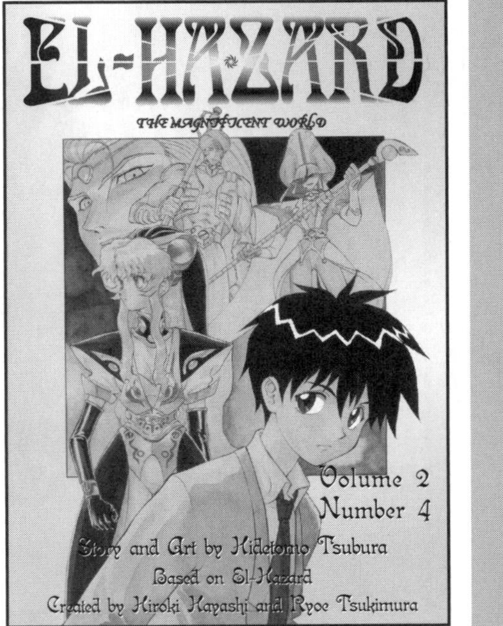
EL-HAZARD
THE MAGNIFICENT WORLD
Volume 2
Number 4
Story and Art by Hidetomo Tsubura
Based on El-Hazard
Created by Hiroki Hayashi and Ryoe Tsukimura

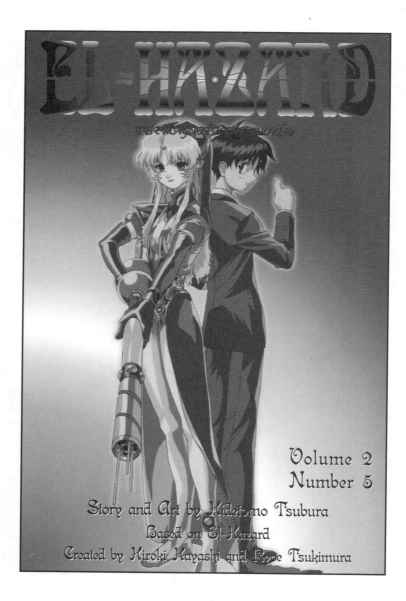

EL-HAZARD

the magnificent world

**Volume 2
Number 5**

Story and Art by Hidetomo Tsubura
Based on El-Hazard
Created by Hiroki Hayashi and Ryoe Tsukimura